HOUSE OF CARDS

HOUSE OF CARDS

Inside the Troubled Empire of American Express

Jon Friedman and John Meehan

G. P. Putnam's Sons

NEW YORK

G. P. Putnam's Sons
Publishers Since 1838
200 Madison Avenue
New York, NY 10016

Library of Congress Cataloging-in-Publication Data

Meehan, John, date.
House of cards : inside the troubled empire of American Express /
Jon Friedman and John Meehan.
p.   cm.
Includes bibliographical references and index.
ISBN 0-399-13654-1 (alk. paper)
1. American Express Company.   2. Financial services industry—
United States.   3. Credit cards—United States.   I. Meehan, John,
date.   II. Title.
HE5903.A55M44 1992   91-42477 CIP
388'.041—dc20

Printed in the United States of America

2   3   4   5   6   7   8   9   10

To my mother and father,
Pat and Phil Friedman—JPF

To my wife, Victoria Meehan,
and to my sons, John, Jeremy and James—JTM

Contents

Contents

Preface

This book can be traced back to the authors' coverage of American Express for *Business Week* in 1989 and 1990. For so long, American Express and its chairman and chief executive officer, James D. Robinson III, had escaped close scrutiny. During the eighties, journalists seemed to rarely look beyond the bottom line when examining financial companies. American Express was no exception. AmEx's stellar earnings, particularly the incredible performance of its card products, masked many of the management mistakes that were made along the way. By 1990, the faults were becoming all too apparent.

We felt strongly that the story of American Express had to be told in as in-depth a manner as possible. In many ways, AmEx's success was a product of the times. No other company seemed to be more emblematic of the excesses of the roaring eighties. And no other company appeared to face the kinds of painful adjustments that AmEx began confronting as it entered the nineties.

American Express and Jim Robinson declined to cooperate with the project. Still, during the course of research, we conducted over one hundred interviews with AmEx executives, both past and present. We also spoke extensively with AmEx's competitors in both the banking community and on Wall Street. Many demanded anonymity.

In setting forth conversations, we tried to interview as many participants as possible. Still, over the course of time, memories may fail. We know that journalists are only as good as their sources and made every attempt to verify dialogue with as many people as possible.

In doing research for the book, several previously published sources proved invaluable. These include *Promises to Pay,* a corporate history commissioned by American Express and published in 1977, and *American Express: The Unofficial History of the People Who Built the Great Financial Empire* by Peter Z. Grossman (Crown Publishers, 1987). Also helpful was *The Year They Sold Wall Street* by Tim Carrington (Houghton Mifflin, 1985).

We would like to thank Andrea Chambers, our editor at G. P. Putnam's Sons, for her skillful editing and advice as well as her encouragement during our first attempt at writing a book; her able assistant, Dolores McMullan; copy editor Katherine Pradt; our photo researcher, Randy Matusow; and our agent, Jane Dystel, who had the foresight to recognize that the story of American Express was a worthwhile subject to explore in a book.

We would also like to acknowledge the help and support of Victoria Meehan. In many instances, she was our first reader, copy editor and often chief critic. Her advice was helpful and invaluable and her suggestions were incorporated throughout this book.

Jon Friedman wishes to offer special thanks to: Larry and

Barbara Friedman, Carla Karen, Michael Dinhofer, Mark Diamond, Jackie Coyne, Philip Bashe, Patty Romanowski, Susan Panisch, Daniel Small, Stuart Cohn, Diane Goldner and Jude McNeela.

HOUSE OF CARDS

ONE

The Evil Empire

Jim Robinson was fuming. He rhythmically ran his hand from his forehead to the nape of his neck, a gesture his subordinates had come to recognize as trouble. He stared at a grainy black and white photograph of a restaurant owner who had impaled an American Express card on the tip of a foot-long butcher knife. The blade had neatly severed the neck of the helmeted centurion, the charge card's ubiquitous emblem. The assailant's face was fixed in a triumphant smirk. The caption on the *Boston Herald* photo read "Pointed Protest."

Normally unflappable, a study in supreme self-discipline, the chairman and chief executive officer of American Express Company was inflamed. Worse than an insult, the photo was an abomination.

Robinson gazed at the clipping on his desk. The image was as hypnotic as it was repugnant.

It was more than just a matter of appearances or corporate sensitivities. To Robinson, image was everything, the cornerstone of American Express. From credit cards to traveler's checks, competitors offered similar products. Some were even better. But none of the rivals had ever matched AmEx for cachet. The company's blue box logo was a badge of prestige, its charge card the hallmark of affluence.

Throughout his fourteen-year tenure as AmEx's CEO, nothing had been as important to Robinson as how he and his company were viewed. Image was a halo that set American Express apart. "It's our most valuable asset," he would lecture his staff.

Not just a catchy slogan, it was a personal conviction. Robinson's vanity was legendary in both his professional and personal life. He attended the correct parties, befriended the right people. Robinson was even fanatical about his own appearance.

From his monogrammed Turnbull and Asser shirts to his slavish dedication to physical fitness, James Dixon Robinson III cultivated the correct look. His daily schedule started every morning with 300 sit-ups. On weekends, he added thirty minutes of weight lifting. Even at fifty-five, he showed no signs of slowing down. Trim and athletic, Robinson sported sculpted biceps and solid pecs. He had a full head of wavy brown hair, streaked with gray, and looked a decade younger.

"Jim is the kind of guy who could win the New York Marathon but would worry that his shirttail is out," recalled a friend, sardonically.

The card attack wasn't an isolated incident. The article in the *Boston Herald* was one of a dozen that Robinson was studying on that chilly April morning in 1991. They all described at length what AmEx's staff had begun to call the "Boston Fee Party." Fed up with exorbitant fees, roughly one hundred restaurants in the Boston area were threatening to stop accepting AmEx plastic. "It's too damn costly," said one protest organizer.

For years, American Express had charged merchants a

commission of 3% to 5% every time a customer used the green or gold card. The "discount fee" had been common throughout the card industry. It had been a key source of revenue to every card issuer. But AmEx's fee was the highest in the business. Visa, the leading bank card brand and AmEx's closest rival, charged only 2%.

AmEx's vaunted image justified the higher charge, company spokesmen asserted. AmEx customers were upscale and well-educated. Better yet, they had expensive tastes. On average, the typical American Express customer would spend twice as much as other card users. "We invented the yuppie," AmEx executives would brag.

During the eighties, merchants accepted AmEx's argument. Times were good; business was booming. American Express could be forgiven some excessiveness. But in the sobering nineties, they blasted AmEx's greediness.

As the recession took hold in late 1990, sales plummeted and merchants howled. The clamor was strongest in New England, the most depressed of any region. With unemployment rising, luxuries were slashed from family budgets. At many households, eating out was the first luxury to go.

By 1991, restaurant owners in the Boston area grew desperate. They had trimmed their staffs to the bone and were fending off bill collectors almost daily. Many received concessions from suppliers. Even insurance companies were willing to lower their premiums.

AmEx had refused to budge. Wholesome, almost charitable, was the way AmEx's marketing team portrayed the company. But when it came to business, American Express was tough, often ruthless. Even with the economy in a slump, the company line was unchanged. "Especially in troubled times, if there's one segment that continues to spend, it's American Express cardholders," Patricia Duffy, an AmEx marketing executive, had told a Boston interviewer, echoing the company's astonishingly smug party line.

Angered and dismayed by AmEx's arrogance, New England restaurateurs were exasperated. Now, they were referring ruefully to American Express as "The Evil Empire." Talk of an AmEx boycott was spreading.

Although the rebellion had been brewing for months, Robinson had paid scant attention. His staff had assured him that the matter would blow over. A little hand-holding was all it would take.

Robinson had seen no reason to question their opinion. As CEOs go, Robinson was more laissez-faire than hands-on, less a leader than a consensus builder. AmEx's chief viewed himself as part strategist, part statesman. Robinson prized advisory committees, memoranda and corporate chains of command. He was the consummate delegator. Only when he felt matters slipping out of control did he become autocratic.

But as he flipped through the clips, Robinson probably regretted his inattention. Over and over, he read disparaging remarks about AmEx. Again and again he saw the word "boycott." Robinson feared that the merchant discontent would spread beyond New England. Something had to be done. By 8:00 A.M., he was on the phone to Aldo Papone.

A Robinson loyalist, Papone had been in charge of the card business until the end of 1990 when heart problems forced him to retire. Still, he remained a member of AmEx's board and a close friend and advisor to Robinson. In his days as head of the card division, Robinson himself had hired Papone.

Milan-born, Papone was warm and gregarious, and downright likable. Some people felt his management skills were not his strongest suit; yet, he was the only one in the company who could make Robinson laugh. But as soon as he answered the phone at his house in Greenwich, he knew better than to make small talk.

"Did you see the paper? Did you see it? Did you see what's happening in Boston?" Robinson thundered. He sounded panicked. "What the hell is this?"

Papone was stunned by the depth of Robinson's anger. He had never heard Robinson sound so frantic. He tried to soothe AmEx's chief.

"Oh, it's only a few restaurants, Jim," Papone said, trying to sound offhanded.

Robinson cut him off. He wouldn't be placated. "What? Only a few restaurants! No way, Aldo! No way!" Robinson said. "This has to stop now."

Within minutes, Robinson scheduled an emergency meeting with the heads of Travel Related Services. One of a half-dozen companies within the American Express family, TRS was the lifeblood of the corporation. It was responsible for the card, from green to platinum, as well as AmEx's lucrative trade in traveler's checks.

TRS was run by two AmEx veterans who acted as co-chairmen. Edwin M. Cooperman, forty-six, was in charge of the U.S. and Canada. G. Richard Thoman, forty-four, was responsible for the rest of the world. Around the card industry, they were perceived by some as lightweights. Visa and MasterCard were coming on strong, and Cooperman and Thoman had not been able to stop the erosion of AmEx's core business.

A Queens-born Jew, Cooperman was a corporate lawyer by training. By AmEx's conservative standards, he was brash and flamboyant. Cooperman chafed at AmEx's rigid, buttoned-down style. Cooperman was lauded by *Forbes* magazine for helping spearhead the corporate campaign to move the Grammy Awards from Hollywood to New York. In his office hung a photograph of him with Kathleen Turner taken just after her opening-night performance in *Cat on a Hot Tin Roof* in 1989.

By contrast, Thoman's office trophy was an autographed photo of Prince Charles. One of a long line of AmEx executives to graduate from McKinsey & Company, Inc., the giant New York management consulting firm, Thoman was cool and cosmopolitan. He spent much of his time in Europe and had a vacation home in the south of France. When in Paris, he conducted press conferences in French.

Two hours after Robinson's call, promptly at 10:00 A.M., Cooperman and Thoman arrived at the CEO's office. Like errant schoolboys about to be scolded by the headmaster, they shuffled in quietly and sat down in front of Robinson's desk.

"Gentlemen, I think it's time for a reality check," Robinson said. His tone was stern, his anger visible.

Shit! Cooperman thought.

The phrase had deep meaning. Robinson was never direct. He disliked arguments and confrontations. He ruled AmEx through innuendo. Catchwords and gestures were integral to his management style. "Reality check" was a favorite. Both men knew it was Robinson's way of saying "I have a problem—you."

"I trust you've already seen these," said Robinson, clutching the stack of newspaper clippings in his fist.

He singled out the photograph of the knife-wielding restaurateur. Again he stared at it, shaking his head slowly from side to side.

"In my entire career, my entire career," began Robinson, nearly lifting himself out of his chair as he thrust his face toward his subordinates, "I have never seen anything as distasteful as this goddamn thing."

As he talked, Robinson lapsed into a deep Southern accent. His Georgia drawl always grew heavier in times of stress.

"How could you let this get so far?" he asked rhetorically. "Do you know how this makes us look?"

Cooperman and Thoman were silent and squirming. This was turning into more of an inquisition than a strategy session.

"What I want to know right now is what we're doing," demanded Robinson.

"We can't have our SE relationships paraded around in the goddamn papers," continued Robinson, using the card company's shorthand for "Service Establishment," or merchant. "My patience is wearing thin."

Sensing an opening, Cooperman tried to respond. As head of domestic operations, Cooperman knew Robinson's anger was more directed at him than Thoman.

"We're going to stop this rebellion," he vowed. "We're stepping up our advertising. We'll show the community we care."

Robinson was unmoved.

"If that will help so much, Ed, why didn't you do that before this bullshit got started?" Robinson asked. "Why? Tell me."

Cooperman began to clear his throat as if to respond. But then he fell silent.

With Cooperman vanquished, Robinson moved on to Thoman.

"How do we stand in Europe?" AmEx's CEO asked.

It was an appropriate question. Although merchant rebellions were a relatively new phenomenon in the U.S., American Express had for years been fighting a guerrilla war against revolts overseas.

Throughout the 1980s, some hotels in Asia had periodically surcharged AmEx card users to compensate for the lofty fees. In France, restaurant owners had asked American tourists to use Visa instead of AmEx. And in Britain, merchants had been skirmishing with AmEx for years. Dixon Group PLC, a consumer electronics retail chain, had even canceled its AmEx participation in 1989.

"We'll make sure everyone's happy," Thoman said. "We don't think this thing is likely to spread beyond our control."

Thoman sounded confident. Robinson wasn't that sure.

"Listen, I don't want to read in the goddamn *Economist* about anything like this happening in Europe. Or anywhere else," Robinson growled. "You got that?

"If you guys can't do it," Robinson continued, "I'll find someone who can."

Later that morning, a colleague phoned Thoman to find out how the meeting went. "It was fine," Thoman answered nonchalantly. "No problem." Cooperman had a different reaction. He would tell a friend, "Today, Robinson put me on notice."

The battle with Boston restaurant owners was only one of a succession of increasingly severe problems besetting American Express. Six months later, AmEx would again be embarrassed by unexpected losses in its Optima credit card program. Amazingly high customer defaults would force TRS to post its first quarterly loss in history. Furthermore, to pay for the defaults, AmEx would have to do major restructuring and lay off about 1,700 workers. If that weren't enough, Moody's downgraded about $7 billion worth of AmEx debt. This, too, was a historic first for the company. The company would look bad. The boss would look worse.

For much of Robinson's reign over American Express, his talents and wisdom had gone unchallenged. Revenues were buoyant, earnings stellar. More importantly, he had presided over a tireless corporate expansion in the 1980s that transformed AmEx into a financial empire. American Express was a household word. When it came to name recognition, its only rivals were Coca-Cola and McDonald's.

At the height of his glory, Robinson had been hailed as the Secretary of State of Corporate America. He was ranked among the best and the brightest. Robinson was once even considered for a cabinet post in Washington. It was an ambition that was shared by Robinson and his wife, Linda Gosden Robinson, a former Reagan aide and a powerful business figure in her own right. Few corporate wives have been as visible or as influential when it came to their husbands' careers. Linda was regarded as the Nancy Reagan of American Express.

But by 1990, the pristine image of American Express and that of its leader was battered and scarred. Fireman's Fund Insurance Companies and Trade Development Bank, onetime corporate trophies of AmEx's rapid growth, had been sold off. AmEx's brokerage house, Shearson Lehman Brothers, the once mighty symbol of the company's bold foray into Wall Street, was teetering.

Worse, Robinson was dogged by scandals. In 1988, Robinson's close friend and advisor, Salim B. Lewis, pleaded guilty to propping up the price of Fireman's Fund stock, as AmEx tried to sell off its shares in its former insurance subsidiary. The following year, Robinson's corporate ethics came into question again when he had to apologize to Lebanese financier Edmond J. Safra for a global smear campaign instigated by American Express.

As part of an unusual public penance, Safra, a onetime AmEx official turned competitor, demanded that Robinson pay $8 million to his favorite charities. The apology was painful, the payment humiliating.

After that, Robinson was under siege. Shareholders were angry. The press began questioning his strategy. On Wall Street, he was being derisively referred to as the "Teflon Executive," a barbed description of Robinson's ability to avoid blame for AmEx's problems.

Robinson's biggest fear was being labeled a failure. With AmEx's image blemished and the pressure from competition mounting, it was doubtful that American Express would recapture its former glory. The only other alternative, Robinson believed, was to sell the company. Some other CEO could worry about AmEx. Robinson could step down graciously, his reputation mostly intact.

He approached the board early in 1989. The topic of a merger wasn't new. In the past, the board had discussed the possibility of selling when AmEx's stock price was high, and its shareholders hungry. But nothing had ever come of it.

This time, matters were different. Robinson was anxious. The future was in doubt. AmEx's normally compliant board members agreed. It was time to shop for a buyer.

Secrecy was paramount. Selling the company was one thing, putting it in play another. Throughout the roaring eighties, Robinson had seen other CEOs destroyed by the turbulence of takeover battles. They were often overwhelmed by market forces. Many were abruptly retired or fired outright. He winced at the thought of an unseemly bidding war if word got out that American Express was for sale.

To guard against leaks, Robinson bypassed his own investment banking team at Shearson. Discretion wasn't their strong point. Robinson also questioned their capabilities. He still blamed Shearson's CEO, Peter Cohen, for bungling the leveraged buyout of RJR Nabisco.

Instead, Robinson turned to his longtime friend and advisor Felix Rohatyn, the legendary and statesmanlike investment banker from Lazard Frères & Co. When it came to deals, Rohatyn was unflinching. He was also trustworthy.

Robinson then began a selling campaign that amazingly

escaped the press. General Electric Company headed his list of potential buyers. Jack Welch, GE's tough-talking CEO, was a friend. And his financial services unit offered everything from car loans to credit cards. AmEx would be a natural fit. Welch, however, wasn't interested. He was still digesting his previous acquisitions, Kidder Peabody and NBC.

In the spring of 1989, Robinson quietly contacted Robert Allen, chairman of American Telephone & Telegraph. At the time, AT&T was seriously considering launching its own card venture. AT&T and American Express had even talked briefly about developing a long-distance calling enhancement for its card. When those talks faltered, Robinson himself suggested another alternative to Allen.

"Why don't we do business together?" he proposed.

Allen was astonished but intrigued by the prospect. It would have been one of the largest acquisitions in history. For three weeks, Morgan Stanley and Company Inc., AT&T's investment banker, faced off against Rohatyn.

Promising at first, the talks went nowhere. Robinson stood firm at $25 billion, or $60 a share, twice what AmEx's sluggish stock was trading at. Rohatyn argued repeatedly that American Express was worth a high premium.

"The stock doesn't tell the whole story," Rohatyn contended. "Remember, the card!"

Allen and his advisors at Morgan Stanley soon tired of Rohatyn's stubborn intransigence. They accused Robinson of being unrealistic. Morgan Stanley's patrician CEO, S. Parker Gilbert, grew especially impatient. "That windbag," he called Robinson at a strategy session. The most Morgan Stanley would recommend Allen paying was $55 a share, or $23 billion. To AT&T, American Express wasn't worth the money Robinson wanted.

Though both attempts failed, Robinson hadn't given up

on the notion of selling American Express. He had always felt that he could try again when the economy improved. For the moment, however, he felt he had to squelch the card revolt in Boston to improve AmEx's image.

As the centerpiece of American Express, the charge card was one of the most successful consumer products ever invented. Once a symbol of privilege in the 1970s, the card had become the currency of the eighties. "Charge it!" was the battle cry of a new generation of conspicuous consumers.

It was the card that had paid for much of Robinson's haphazard expansion plan in the eighties. And it was the card's prolonged prosperity that camouflaged Robinson's corporate blunders. By the end of the eighties, there were some thirty-six million American Express cardholders who charged upwards of $100 billion a year.

Yet, inside AmEx, executives privately feared the bank card business had hit its stride. Visa and MasterCard were no longer the cut-rate brands. There were some 400 million bank cards in circulation around the globe. While the credit card business remained fragmented, a handful of banks were coming on strong. Citicorp, for example, boasted as many card customers as American Express. Its card profits, over $500 million a year, rivaled those of American Express.

Other competitors were also on the march. Sears, Roebuck and Co. had launched its Discover Card in 1985. JCB International, a consortium of Japanese banks, was even trying to establish a beachhead with its own card brand.

Far more threatening was AT&T. In March 1990, the telecommunications giant finally began issuing its own Visa and MasterCard. It was dubbed the Universal Card. Worse for Robinson, the AT&T Universal Card was free. Even the banks were alarmed and had tried to block AT&T's card venture.

In the face of all this competition, AmEx was particularly vulnerable. With a $55 annual membership fee for the basic green card, AmEx was the priciest plastic around. By spring of 1991, nine million consumers held Universal Cards, making AT&T the fourth-largest issuer of Visa and Master-Card. The following June, American Express would report the loss of 100,000 cardmembers in the third quarter, its first decline ever.

Even American Express's powerful marketing machine couldn't help. In an industry known for its bulging advertising budgets and slick slogans, American Express was known as the best in the business. With an advertising budget that averaged $217 million a year, AmEx boasted some of the most memorable campaigns ever manufactured by Madison Avenue.

"Do You Know Me?" and "Don't Leave Home Without It" had been the top draws in the eighties. But Ogilvy & Mather, AmEx's ad agency for twenty-seven years, hadn't come up with anything new since "Membership Has Its Privileges" in 1987. And Robinson was threatening to pull AmEx's account.

"We want new ideas. We want big ideas," Robinson lectured Martin Sorrell, the head of WPP Group, the parent company of O&M. "We've had a long relationship, but nothing is written in concrete."

In-house, AmEx's own marketing experts grew envious of the competition. No longer innovators, they became imitators. Following Visa's coup of sponsoring ex-Beatle Paul McCartney's triumphant World Tour in 1989, Cooperman had suggested a similar strategy using Paul Simon. AmEx shelled out $1.5 million for Simon's "Born at the Right Time" tour in 1991. The Gold Card was the official sponsor.

The tour, however, turned into a public relations nightmare. Furious fans accused Simon of being elitist because of his apparent endorsement of AmEx's most visible status symbol. Simon was stunned by the outburst.

At one tour stop, in Hartford, Simon tried to defend his image. He told reporters that he regretted the arrangement. He had been unaware that the Gold Card alone was the sponsor. "I wasn't paying attention," Simon was quoted by the *Hartford Courant*. Several other newspapers across the country reprinted the article.

"We pay him all this money and he pisses all over us," griped one AmEx executive.

Later, matters worsened. To repair any damage to his image, Simon suggested that Warner Brothers, his record company, and AmEx join him in a donation to various charities. Each would contribute as much as $50,000. But ultimately the arrangement fell apart. Simon's spokesman claimed AmEx backed out. Around AmEx, executives said Simon reneged.

Within months, American Express suffered yet another PR blow when actress Meryl Streep made disparaging remarks about the company to *The New York Times*. AmEx had paid $3 million to the two-time Oscar winner to do a single commercial that aired during the Grammy Awards telecast in February. The one-minute spot showed Streep talking casually about life to a group of schoolchildren. At the end appeared a single sentence saying that Streep had been a cardmember since 1980.

A month later, Streep confessed to a reporter for the *Times'* Sunday Arts & Leisure Section that the appearance on behalf of AmEx was strictly business. She was quoted saying, "I don't believe in the company." A week later, Streep claimed she was misquoted.

In November, AmEx would fire its longtime ad agency, Ogilvy & Mather, and hand its account over to Chiat/Day/ Mojo Advertising Inc. But the resulting campaign did little to help, according to Madison Avenue executives. Indeed, the new series of ads that emphasized frivolous spending, such as purchasing a baseball glove for a dog, ended up on a list of "dubious" campaigns for 1991 compiled by the *Times*.

Of all the public embarrassments, none matched the visible and voluble merchant ire, which had been slowly building for years. In the past, AmEx had been swift in crushing merchant revolts around the globe. Its tactics were sometimes magnanimous, sometimes merciless, depending upon circumstances.

When merchants in Sweden and Norway threatened a card boycott in 1985, American Express counterattacked with a classic PR offensive. AmEx latched on to a popular local cause to save the puffin, a small black and white bird that was endangered. AmEx poured $250,000 into its own "Save the Puffin" ad campaign. After two weeks, American Express was one of the most popular corporations in Scandinavia. The merchant protest collapsed under the wave of consumer goodwill that AmEx had generated.

Four years later, American Express took a harder line when Carnival Cruise Lines demanded a cut in its discount fee. American Express at first negotiated. For two weeks, both sides squabbled. AmEx offered a slight reduction from 3.1% to 2.9%. But it never came close to the 1.15% rate that Visa gave Carnival. In March of 1990, Carnival dropped the AmEx card.

Almost immediately, AmEx retaliated with a boycott of its own. The company ordered its network of 1,600 owned or affiliated travel agencies to stop selling Carnival cruises. And AmEx's vendetta didn't stop there. At a subsequent managers meeting for AmEx's travel agents, the company presented a slide show in which a Carnival Cruise brochure was burned. According to Carnival, in May 1991, AmEx ordered its travel staff to boycott the inaugural tour for the cruise line's newest ship, *Ecstasy*. There was nothing illegal in AmEx's actions, but the message to the rest of the travel industry was clear.

Despite its past triumphs, AmEx's response to the Boston revolt had been scattered and largely ineffectual. The company had offered the restaurateurs minimal concessions, including more joint advertising. A change in the fee, however, was out of the question. Unlike bank credit cards, which draw most of their profits from interest payments, the American Express Card was a standard charge card. There was no interest income. Customers were expected to pay in full upon receipt of the bill. Membership and merchant fees were the sole source of card revenue.

"We can't do anything," said one TRS executive arrogantly. "The rate is nonnegotiable. Only the chairman can change it."

But the tactic wasn't working. Steve DiFillippo, the owner of Davio's Restaurant in Boston and one of the ringleaders of the revolt, reckoned that he could have saved $40,000 a year by eliminating AmEx.

"Jesus, you guys just don't get it," he told AmEx executives. "This isn't the eighties anymore. Times have changed."

Within days, AmEx's merchant rebellion was spreading. Upwards of 400 restaurants were threatening to drop the card. They were coming in waves, from the heartland and beyond: thirty in Indianapolis, forty in Toronto. Restaurants as far away as Vail, Colorado, and Sarasota, Florida, began organizing boycotts.

The national media were homing in on AmEx's New England woes. *The Wall Street Journal, The New York Times, USA Today* and the networks were pestering AmEx for comment.

Larry Kurlander, the head of public relations at TRS,

wasn't very skilled at spin control. A prosecutor turned PR man, Kurlander was viewed around AmEx as a political appointee. A former Rochester district attorney, Kurlander was a close political ally of New York governor Mario Cuomo. He wasn't known for subtlety. Kurlander once called the police and had his office dusted for fingerprints when a jar filled with money turned up missing.

Kurlander displayed the same insensitivity in Boston.

"You know this is a publicity stunt for these restaurant owners," Kurlander would tell Boston reporters. "They just want to see their names in the paper."

By late April, the competition was taking advantage. Visa offered to pay for any legal expenses rebellious Boston restaurants incurred. Even Discover, the king of the low-end market, was attempting to exploit the situation. The company had dispatched a marketing team to Boston armed with a 1.5% discount fee, a fraction under Visa's, and fully two points lower than that of AmEx.

His job on the line, Cooperman assembled his staff to devise a new strategy.

"This bullshit had better stop. Right now!" bellowed Cooperman, still stinging from his earlier meeting with Robinson.

"That picture!" Cooperman continued. "That picture of the guy with the butcher's knife just killed Robinson. I want ideas."

Kenneth I. Chenault, the head of the card division, was the first to respond. Smooth, articulate, with rugged good looks, Chenault, thirty-nine, was the only black ever to have risen to a top management position in AmEx's WASPish hierarchy. He was known around TRS as "The Diplomat." He constantly strove to defuse the intramural warfare that raged at American Express.

31

"We have to take action! Show the restaurateurs we're on their side," Chenault said.

In the end, the decision was to capitulate. American Express promised to renegotiate discount fees individually. This marked the first change in the discount fee in thirteen years and the first reduction ever.

Speaking to a group of securities analysts that summer, Robinson assured them the worst was over. A week before, AmEx had reported an earnings drop of 20%, to $256 million. "The problem is not as severe as it appears," he said. "We see growth to be in line with the past."

The groans in the room were audible. The analysts weren't buying it. The next day, Dean Witter Reynolds Inc.'s Michael Lewis, a respected AmEx observer, advised his clients: "There will be no quick fix."

By the end of the summer the rebellion in Boston was waning. But a revolution was in the making elsewhere. By May, catalogue companies such as Lands' End and Joan Cook Inc. were demanding similar fee concessions. So was U-Haul. In fact, Tom Standish, treasurer of the rental outfit, was threatening to band together with Ryder Trucks and car rental agencies "to do what they did in Boston."

For the first time in his career at American Express, Robinson had nowhere to hide. There were no record profits. There was no brilliant PR to conceal his errors. There were no excuses. AmEx's lifeblood was threatened, Robinson's standing as a modern-day captain of industry endangered. Robinson, the control freak, was losing control.

TWO

"Little Jimmy"

Until the late eighties, Jim Robinson's career had advanced with astonishing speed. Moving from one assignment to the next, Robinson glided effortlessly through the corporate maze. His appetite for work was voracious. Fourteen-hour days and all day Saturday, his colleagues would joke. His addiction to detail was legendary. Robinson relished paperwork.

Still, few of his peers would ever describe Robinson as a model CEO. Outside of a shared ambition, he had little in common with such legendary contemporaries as Lee Iacocca of Chrysler or Citicorp's Walter Wriston. Throughout his career, Robinson was less a leader than an overseer, his flashes of brilliance overshadowed by his propensity for bureaucracy.

Even when he was selected to head American Express, his notable accomplishments were spotty. A November 1978 article in *Fortune* magazine described AmEx's new chairman as "a boyish-looking forty-two-year-old Georgian who advanced rapidly on a mixture of long, long hours and excellent family connections."

To understand Robinson's swift rise, one has to go back

to his tradition-bound roots in Atlanta, where family heritage and drive were what mattered. The Robinson name may have lacked the nationwide prominence of the Rockefellers or the Astors. But by Atlanta standards, they were at the top of the social hierarchy. The Robinsons had money. Even more important, they had a treasured ancestry that dated all the way back to the Civil War and James Warren English, Jim's great-grandfather.

English was a furniture shipper who distinguished himself in the Confederate Army. His bravery caught the attention of General Robert E. Lee, at whose side he fought at Appomattox. By 1865, English was a captain. Quick and resourceful, he was determined to succeed in peacetime, too. Settling in Atlanta after the war, he swiftly foresaw the need for a new bank to help the city's reconstruction efforts. Armed with little more than an idea and a splendid war record, English persuaded a group of prominent Atlantans to back the Fourth National Bank of Georgia, which he opened in 1871. As its president, English became one of the city's top financiers and civic leaders. He even served as mayor of Atlanta from 1881 to 1882.

At the height of his influence, English's daughter, Emily, married the first James D. Robinson, the son of an Atlanta manufacturer. Robinson quickly gauged the opportunities at his father-in-law's bank, and went to work for the family business. Showing an aptitude for banking, he skillfully engineered a few mergers that transformed English's institution into a regional banking power. The company was rechristened the First National Bank.

Gradually, English turned the management of the company over to his son-in-law, who in turn would groom his own son for the job. James D. Robinson Jr., born in 1905, was widely known as "Big Jim."

Indeed, there was something almost make-believe about

Big Jim. From his nickname to his imposing frame—six feet four inches, 225 pounds—Big Jim seemed more an invention of Central Casting than the product of a conservative Southern upbringing. He was all charisma and charm, topped off with just a pinch of proper Southern formality. A graduate of Emory University and Harvard Business School, he was friendly and talkative, never glib. Big Jim knew everyone at the bank by their first names, frequently inquiring about the well-being of spouses and offspring. Yet there was no mistaking who was in charge. Big Jim preferred absolute rule, and played the role of patriarch accordingly.

He had a fondness for stiff, detachable collars that seemed to give some definition to his round, cheeky face. And when it came to clothes, dark gray suits were a favorite. Big Jim made it a rule never to work in his shirt sleeves, an almost patrician response to the blistering heat and thicket of heavy humidity that settled over the city every summer. Consequently, he wore each suit fewer than a dozen times, periodically doling out the castoffs to less wealthy associates.

Big Jim was all business. Bold and aggressive, he was always on the prowl for a deal, first as an executive at Trust Company of Georgia and then as chairman of First National. And Atlanta proved bountiful.

Unlike other Southern towns which owed their origins to a rich agrarian past, Atlanta had no such allegiances. Ambitious and entrepreneurial, irreverent and boastful, Atlantans cared mostly about business. They stood in the vanguard of the New South. Southerners themselves had long noted the cultural distinction. In Savannah, Atlanta's closest Georgia rival, it was said that if Atlanta could suck as hard as it blew, it would be a seaport.

When World War II ended, Atlanta experienced an un-precedented boom that transformed the city into the commercial Mecca of the South. The pocket parks and single-story shops along Peachtree Street were swept away. Skyscrapers sprouted at a record pace, and Atlanta's modest skyline began reaching higher.

It was during this tumultuous building period that Big Jim reached the pinnacle of wealth and prominence. By 1951, First National Bank was one of the biggest financial institutions in the city. The big money-center bankers in New York still looked on Atlanta as a provincial outpost. It was Big Jim and a handful of other local bankers who provided the capital to fuel the city's economic engine.

Whether it was over drinks at the Capital City Club on Harris Street, or at intimate suppers at the Robinson home, Big Jim wielded influence like few others in Atlanta.

"He knew regional capitals were emerging," recalled developer John Portman. "He wanted to make sure that Atlanta was ahead of the pack."

Big Jim was widely known for his impatience. On one occasion, he had scheduled a ground-breaking ceremony for First National's new headquarters in 1952 only to find the building site flooded and muddy following a severe rainstorm. Rather than reschedule the event, Robinson trucked in a mound of topsoil from his country club to carve out a dry patch of ground for the invited dignitaries.

As Big Jim's financial power grew, so did his political clout. A big campaign contributor and powerful lobbyist for the city's business leaders, he was a frequent guest at City Hall and the state capitol building. Mayors, aldermen and congressmen were among his closest friends. Indeed, Big Jim was in the vanguard of civic leaders who helped the city adapt to its new urban awareness. He was one of a handful of businessmen who purchased the Atlanta transit system in 1950 and vastly improved its service.

As a member of the municipal housing authority, Big Jim displayed a surprising liberal streak. Robinson was credited with introducing low-income housing for minority groups at a time when racial prejudice still reigned throughout the South. In the 1960s, Big Jim was also instrumental in attracting professional sports teams, such as the Braves, the Falcons and the Hawks.

Still, he didn't abandon his banker-like ways. In 1958 he helped force the city council to adopt a measure limiting Atlanta's budget to the previous year's tax receipts. It was a strict fiscal limit that prohibited deficit spending.

Josephine Crawford Robinson, Big Jim's wife, was similarly tough and determined. At the age of four she had been adopted by a wealthy aunt and uncle after her parents could no longer afford to raise her and her two sisters. "I used to visit my aunt and uncle a lot, and one day I never went home," Josephine would say, half jokingly.

Josephine's adoptive family were well-known merchants and owners of Atlanta's biggest furniture store, Rhodes, a landmark downtown. They treated Josephine as if she were their own daughter. Still, the memories of the adoption always bothered her.

In later years, Josephine would be very protective of her own children. And even though she was smooth and refined, every inch the Southern lady, Josephine had a hard edge. Her voice may have been smooth and melodic, but Josephine was noted for her acerbic tongue. One acquaintance called her a "chocolate-covered spider."

James Dixon Robinson III was born on November 19, 1935. He was the oldest of the Robinsons' three children, and around the house he was known as "Little Jimmy."

Little Jimmy's early years were marked by all the advantages of wealth—servants, private schools, and a governess, Kate Watson, who cared for Robinson and his younger sisters, Frances and Josephine. Kate, who was hired two weeks after Little Jimmy's birth, was the Robinson children's second mother. She was the one who handled scraped knees and nightmares. Robinson grew so attached to Kate that years later he would make a point of visiting her every time he passed through Atlanta.

The Robinson home was an opulent, ten-room Italianstyle villa in Buckhead, Atlanta's answer to Beverly Hills. A two-story expanse on a fourteen-acre spread, the Robinson residence was unique among the mansions along West Paces Ferry.

Nicknamed the Pink Castle by neighbors, it was painted in a kind of muted pink, Josephine Robinson's favorite color. Adding to the pastel display was a long driveway framed by dozens of dogwood trees whose pink blossoms arrived like clockwork every spring.

In keeping with family tradition, Big Jim had hoped that Little Jimmy would one day replace him at the bank, while also assuming his role as civic leader. It would have been unthinkable not to have a Robinson among Atlanta's decisionmakers. The younger Robinson's training was informal at first. Big Jim made it a point of introducing his son to all of Atlanta's business and civic leaders.

By the time he was eight, Little Jimmy was even making public appearances, representing the family at social and civic events, such as presenting the Most Valuable Player award to the Georgia Tech football team.

At thirteen, Little Jimmy was packed off to boarding school. Big Jim was a strong believer in self-reliance, an attribute best instilled, he felt, during a person's youth. The choice was Woodberry Forest School, near Orange, Virginia. Big Jim himself had attended Woodberry, a leading prep school for the offspring of the South's rising families, and had become quite a golfer during his days there. Little Jimmy would go on to master the links as well. In later years, he would become a scratch golfer.

Big Jim and his son were close, seeking each other's company on weekends and school breaks. The golf course was their common playground, and they were fiercely competitive.

"Jimmy would lose his temper and glare and curse if he wasn't putting well," recalled Frances Robinson Huber, Robinson's sister. "My father didn't like to hear bad language on the golf course. He would chastise Jimmy when he swore."

The closeness, however, didn't conceal the uneasiness that others glimpsed when Little Jimmy was around his father. The younger Robinson was no match for his father's gregariousness. He wasn't given to quick friendships and easy conversation. And the younger Robinson's modest physical stature did little to help his confidence. With a slight, thin build, Jimmy favored his mother's side of the family. Even as he entered manhood, he stood only five feet eight inches and was constantly gazing upward at his towering father.

In later years, colleagues would often contrast Big Jim and his son in trying to explain Robinson's drive. There was a perception that Robinson wanted to outdo his father. Too often, he had observed how sons would inherit their fathers' wealth and never make their own mark.

"Jimmy wanted to prove to Daddy that he could make it on his own," said Huber. "Jim didn't want anybody else to think that he wasn't as good as his father."

By the time he entered Georgia Tech in 1953, Robinson was well on his way to being the next CEO of First National

Bank of Atlanta. Majoring in engineering, Robinson was an above-average student. He raced through college in only three years.

The speed with which he completed his studies had little to do with any driving ambition. Robinson never spoke of his career aspirations, and his extracurricular activities gave little hint of his goals.

The only campus activity that seemed to pique his interest was intramural football, which he played enthusiastically if not skillfully. His short, skinny build earned him the nickname "The Razor's Edge."

Throughout his entire college career, Robinson dated only one girl. He had met Bettye Bradley when he was home on summer vacation before his senior year at Woodberry. Both seventeen, they met at a neighborhood party given by a mutual friend. Robinson had dated numerous other Atlanta girls during previous vacations, but they were simply teenage romances, lasting until the start of the next school year.

Bettye was different. The daughter of a distribution executive for Paramount Pictures, she was soft-spoken, with a small-town shyness, and downright pretty. About five feet five inches and shapely, she had deep brown eyes and long black hair. Her school chums compared her to Elizabeth Taylor. In fact, Bettye was so stunning that she eventually went on to win the Miss Georgia Peach contest of 1955 and worked briefly as a fashion model.

Barely one month after his graduation, Jim, then twenty-one, married Bettye at St. Philip's Episcopal Church in Atlanta, with his father as best man and his sister, Frances, serving as maid of honor. Within a week, the newlyweds headed off to the U.S. naval base at Athens, Georgia. A member of the Reserve Officers' Training Corps during college, Robinson was commissioned an ensign. He then went on to serve as a supply officer at Pearl Harbor in Hawaii.

Robinson returned briefly to Atlanta, working as a securities analyst at Trust Company. But it was only a diversion. He was uncomfortable in Atlanta. Big Jim was the reigning Robinson and there was little room for another. In Atlanta's financial circles the comparisons had begun. Too short, too quiet and too tame, Robinson was not his father's son.

When Jimmy told his father of his desire to leave Atlanta, Big Jim was hurt. Robinsons had always run the bank. Still, he understood his son's need to establish his independence.

Within a year, Robinson took his wife and newborn daughter, Emily, north in search of new opportunities. The first stop was Harvard Business School. When he enrolled in the fall of 1959, Harvard was a passport to the executive suite. No other institution even came close to its track record for churning out business leaders. At the time, at least one-third of the nation's business-school graduates came from Harvard.

Robinson blossomed at Harvard. He seemed to thrive on the harsh competitive atmosphere, graduating in the top third of his class. And he was instilled with a keen ambition that had so long eluded him.

"He had a lot of drive," says Joel Schiavone, a Harvard classmate. "It wasn't that he had an enormous ego. He wanted to make it on his own."

If one trait came to the fore, it was Robinson's talent for consensus-building. Friendly and nonconfrontational, Robinson was adept at developing a rapport with friends and foes alike. It was a talent he would find useful in his later career and one that was admired by his fellow classmates.

"Everyone trusted him. He was good at massaging big

egos," said Morris Showet, a Toronto real estate developer and one of Robinson's classmates.

By the time he graduated in 1961, young Robinson was finally on his way. Armed with an MBA, determination, and family connections, Robinson wasn't especially eager to return to Atlanta.

"I think he was afraid that if he came back to Atlanta, he would go through the rest of his life wondering if he had really become all he could be," said Robinson's sister Frances. The decision proved a big disappointment to Big Jim. But he accepted it.

Morgan Guaranty Trust was the first stop on Robinson's corporate climb. The venerable Morgan had a patrician atmosphere. While other big banks, such as Chase Manhattan and First National City, a forerunner to Citicorp, were courting middle-class consumers, Morgan continued to cater to a rich, selective group of corporations and individuals.

Morgan preferred their young executives to be pinstriped and Protestant. The Harvard finish helped. Robinson fit right in.

What's more, Big Jim was well known at Morgan. As one of the gatekeepers when it came to doing business in the New South, he was on a first-name basis with the heads of every New York bank and many of the city's top businessmen. He even maintained an apartment at the Carlton Towers on East 64th Street for his frequent business trips. Big Jim's New York friends included such notables as Chase Manhattan CEO David Rockefeller and publishing magnate John Hay "Jock" Whitney, owner of the *New York Herald Tribune*.

Morgan CEO Thomas Gates was especially eager to cement his ties with Big Jim. Gates himself was hired because of his connections. He had been a senior executive at General

Electric before serving as Secretary of Defense under President Dwight Eisenhower. At the time, Morgan wanted to broaden its franchise. The bank no longer wanted to be seen as Eastern Establishment. It wanted a nationwide business. Hiring Big Jim's son furthered the cause.

Robinson entered Morgan's management training program right out of Harvard. After serving two weeks in the mailroom, Morgan's traditional rite of passage, Robinson moved on to stints at the bank's trust department and investment division. But he never stayed long at any one assignment. Gates wanted to expose Robinson to as much as he could. He had plans for his young recruit. "Teach him what you can and then send him on," he would tell Morgan's department heads.

Robinson shone during his time at the bank's bond department. There, he was surprisingly aggressive and innovative. Though only a trainee, he reorganized the trading desk. Robinson wrote an instructional manual on how to trade money market instruments, such as Treasury bills and certificates of deposit. He also had a computer installed to track trading flows and help pinpoint buying and selling opportunities. Years later, computers would be a common trading tool. But in the 1960s, they were rare.

Robinson was only twenty-seven, but he impressed his superiors with his dedication and zeal, not to mention his impeccable manners that so well fit in with the Morgan image. Indeed, he seemed to go out of his way to portray himself as the perfect Morgan Man. He even came to resent his years at Georgia Tech. He would never even mention his alma mater when small talk with his fellow trainees turned to their college days. Most trainees at Morgan had done their undergraduate work at Princeton, Yale or Harvard.

To his superiors at Morgan, Robinson's strongest attribute was his work ethic. "Jim works so hard, he'll be dead by the time he's forty," Gates would tell his staff. A tireless employee, Robinson worked up to sixteen hours a day.

At home, a three-bedroom apartment on East 86th Street, there were now two little Robinsons; James Dixon Robinson IV had been born in June 1961. But Robinson left the parenting largely to Bettye and made it clear that his first obligation was to his work.

"He didn't spend any time with his family and I was struck by how little he spoke of them," a fellow Morgan trainee would later recall.

Gates was fond of Robinson. Morgan's CEO even nick-named his young star "Jimmy-Three-Sticks," a good-natured jab at the Roman numerals after Robinson's name. In 1965, Gates named Robinson his executive assistant. It was a newly-created position, a kind of chief of staff to the CEO. And Robinson attacked the job with his usual fervor. He supervised Gates's schedule, arranged his meetings and even handled routine matters that the chairman had little time for.

Robinson was dazzled by Gates. Morgan's CEO was self-confident, a hard drinker and a womanizer. And few could match his connections. He vacationed with the Rockefellers at Bar Harbor and with the Kennedys at Hyannis Port. He golfed with everyone from Eisenhower to Lyndon Johnson. It was often whispered around Morgan that the second phone on Gates's desk was a hotline to the White House.

Gates also was a member of the "study group" that was founded by Stephen Bechtel Sr., the chairman of the San Francisco-based construction firm. The group, which included such business notables as Pan American founder Juan Trippe and Texaco Chairman Augustus Long, would meet periodically at the Carlyle Hotel in New York to discuss economic and political topics over brandy and cigars.

"Jim was Gates's shadow," Abram Claude, a former senior executive at Morgan Guaranty, would later say. "He did everything Gates did, went everywhere Gates went."

Robinson achieved a wide visibility within the company—and outside. Finally, he wasn't just Big Jim's son. Robinson's astonishing aptitude for work, his smooth manner and ability to soothe powerful egos helped him establish a reputation. Before long, Robinson's name was well known on the Street. Other banks, even investment houses, began making discreet inquiries about Robinson and at least a half a dozen firms openly courted him. White, Weld & Company was the most eager to steal the hot young executive away from Morgan.

Although it was an investment bank, White Weld was cut from a cloth similar to Morgan's. It was an old-line firm, steeped in the same kind of genteel tradition. And the firm's business had for too long been trapped in a New York rut. White Weld's CEO, David Weld, wanted to build a nationwide franchise. Like Gates, Weld saw Robinson as his inroad into the South.

Though he was more than comfortable at Morgan, Robinson was always eager for a new opportunity. White Weld offered the chance to move beyond the staid climate of commercial banking and into the frenzied world of Wall Street. White Weld was deep into venture capital and offered Robinson the chance to handle some big deals. Doing deals sounded like heady stuff for Robinson after his years of conservative corporate banking. He felt he would like the pace and sense of excitement, and quickly accepted White Weld's offer in 1968.

"I thought Jim would be good at developing new business," recalled Paul Hallingby, the former senior partner at

White Weld who recruited Robinson. "Maybe one out of twenty recruits were good at bringing in new business because of their knowledge of markets or their contacts. But I could see that Jim could do it."

Within a year, Robinson was fairly skilled in the venture capital business and had once again established a reputation as a workaholic. The line around the office was: "When you're working with Jimmy, fly west so there will be extra hours in the day."

His connections, too, helped. From San Francisco bankers to Boston money managers, he had little trouble finding sources to raise capital for start-up operations. High-tech companies were a particular favorite. In the late 1960s, he helped come up with some of the seed money to start the company that would later become Digital Electronics.

It was during his tenure at White Weld that Robinson began thinking seriously about running his own company. It was hardly a farfetched idea. Robinson had a solid background in finance. As a venture capitalist, he had also gained experience in assembling management teams for new companies. And then, there were his connections.

Robinson knew he wasn't likely to assume the top job at any company soon. At thirty-four, he was still too young for any board to consider seriously. His immediate goal was to find a company where he could position himself for a run at the CEO's office. He needed a company with a bright future. But he also didn't want to face too much competition.

There had been talk at Morgan that Robinson was on the fast track. Gates, who turned sixty-one in 1968, was nearing retirement. But even with his achievements, Robinson wasn't the only fair-haired boy at Morgan. He faced equally dim prospects at White Weld, which was family-owned-and-operated. Outsiders had little chance.

46

Robinson began scouting around. Eventually, he compiled a short list of companies that he felt were well run, with solid franchises, and could offer him a promising future. These included Coca-Cola, Trust Company of Georgia and Union Pacific. In the middle of the list was the American Express Company.

THREE

From the Pony Express to Platinum

With his deep-seated respect for image and tradition, Robinson would never look twice at a brash corporate newcomer, no matter how impressive the bottom line. The company where he would eventually settle and solidify his career must be tony and rooted in the values he treasured. American Express fit the bill. It was classy and prestigious. AmEx executives were well-bred graduates of the right schools. They wore Brooks Brothers suits and belonged to the right clubs. Most importantly, they presided over a smoothly run company with enormous potential.

By 1970, AmEx had enjoyed twenty-three straight years of record operating profits. Though best known for its traveler's checks and charge cards, it was pushing deeper into the fledgling financial services industry. The company's aspirations seemed global. Robinson desperately wanted to succeed in a very large pond. AmEx was it.

The company Robinson would eventually run was founded in the nineteenth century by a feisty entrepreneur named

Henry Wells. Livingston, Wells & Co., as Wells and his chief investor, Crawford Livingston, called the company, was set up in 1841 on a dusty road in downtown Albany. It was one of a handful of struggling "express" companies.

They were the nineteenth-century version of United Parcel Service. While the railroad shipped heavy freight and the U.S. Postal Service delivered the mail, express companies delivered pretty much everything else. And though they charged a higher rate than the railroad, they guaranteed a safe and speedy delivery. Express "messengers" traveled by horse, stagecoach, steamship or railroad, whatever it took to reach their destinations swiftly. That was a powerful sales incentive for customers who had grown tired of the Post Office's slow delivery and the limits of the railroad.

Wells was a bit of an odd character, even by nineteenth-century standards. Tall and broad-shouldered, he preferred ruffled shirts. In winter he wore a green velvet Basque cap, topped with a gold tassel. And though he had a deep resonant voice that could captivate listeners, he was afflicted with a lifelong stutter that improved only modestly during his lifetime.

Wells was one of the first to recognize the potential of the express business. A native of Utica in upstate New York, he had worked as a freight forwarder and ticket agent on the Erie Canal, then the focal point of commercial transport in the Northeast. Wells was amazed at the stream of settlers who abandoned the crowded Atlantic coast for fresh opportunities out west, especially Ohio. As commerce and industry followed, Wells envisioned a network of express routes linking emerging business centers.

Before long, Livingston, Wells & Co. began serving all the big cities in the state, from Buffalo to New York. Profits began swelling and so did the payroll. One of his new employees was a twenty-five-year-old freight agent named William George Fargo. Brash and ambitious, Fargo soon operated his own route to Chicago.

Wells's success soon caught the attention of a tough Utica businessman named John Butterfield. Butterfield owned most of the stagecoach routes in western New York State. An express business seemed a logical addition. In 1849, he and a partner, James Wasson, founded Butterfield, Wasson & Co., which became Wells's chief competitor.

A brutal rate war raged for months until someone suggested a cease-fire. It isn't quite clear whether it was Wells or Butterfield who emerged the peacemaker. The two sides began talking about combining their efforts. After a few weeks of negotiations, Wells and Butterfield met in Buffalo in March 1850 to sign the Articles of Association of the American Express.

Disagreements were common from the start. When Fargo suggested in 1852 that American Express begin a California express to serve the booming Gold Rush, Butterfield objected strenuously. He knew such a route would be profitable. But, always suspicious of Fargo's ambitions, he feared such an enterprise would expand Fargo's power base. Undeterred by Butterfield's veto, Fargo teamed up with Wells and founded Wells, Fargo & Company in San Francisco. It soon became California's largest express company and later one of its biggest banks.

American Express prospered over the next twenty years. The company purchased freight cars, called express cars, and handled a growing list of cargo, including fresh fruits and vegetables. In 1883, AmEx even began an express train service that sped nonstop from New York to Buffalo, arriving five hours ahead of the fastest passenger train.

After the Civil War, the express business faced a vigorous challenge from the U.S. Post Office. This competition came in the form of the postal money order. Designed to halt the theft of cash from letters by postal workers, money orders grew steadily in popularity as the American frontier expanded west and individuals sought a cheap and safe method to send money back east.

Recognizing the value of the money order business, American Express decided to develop a competitive version. The task of creating an MO, as the company called it, fell to Marcellus Flemming Berry. Short, balding, and with thin, wire-rimmed spectacles, Berry looked every inch the accountant. But he would end up as one of the heroes of the AmEx story.

Thanks to his inventive mind, Berry soon came up with a money order scheme that was practical and convenient. Initially, it was offered and redeemed only by American Express offices. The company eventually licensed hotels, drugstores and stationers to handle MOs. To prevent fraud, Berry devised a system that was brilliant in its simplicity. The possible face value of the order was printed in nickel denominations from $1 to $10 along the left-hand margin. Sales agents merely tore the margin down to the appropriate value, making it impossible to ask for a higher amount.

American Express sold $1 million worth of money orders during 1882, the first year the MO was on sale. Charging a nickel on orders of $5 or less and 8 cents on orders up to $10, the company grossed $11,000 that year.

Despite refinements in the MO, the money transfer business still had a lot of development to undergo. MOs weren't considered the equivalent of cash. Acceptance was limited. What was needed was some device or product that would be universally honored, yet safe enough to carry without worrying about theft. Before the end of the century, American Express had an answer, the Travelers Cheque, the only original product the company ever invented.

Not surprisingly, the man behind the Travelers Cheque was once again Berry. The instrument that Berry devised incorporated many of the principles behind the money order. But it was tailored to the needs of travelers abroad. Using the British spelling of the word "check," the Travelers Cheque was relatively safe, requiring that each check be signed by the customer when it was issued and then when cashed.

In 1891, AmEx sold $9,000 worth of checks. By 1905, the total reached $13 million. What's more, there was an unanticipated bonus. Because of lost checks and delays in check-cashing, AmEx discovered that it sold more orders than it redeemed each month, leaving it with a positive balance.

Unintentionally, AmEx had invented the "float," doubling its returns and giving future rivals an economic ticket to success. A mere $750 at the beginning, the float would eventually top $4 billion by 1990, generating some $200 million in revenue. The company had virtually created a new international currency.

It also launched AmEx on a global expansion. William Swift Dalliba, a loyal company man, was soon dispatched to Europe to expand AmEx's express business. Dalliba established the first American Express office in Paris on Rue Halévy in November 1895. Later he moved it to its better-known address, 11 Rue Scribe. In the decades ahead, the flatiron building diagonally across from the Place de l'Opéra would become a legendary rendezvous for American tourists.

Although the express business was growing, Dalliba was fascinated by the potential offered by the tourist trade. The AmEx offices were constantly jammed by American travelers and expatriates looking to cash their traveler's checks, or asking for train and steamship schedules. The volume of pedestrian traffic grew so large that by 1899, Dalliba was convinced that

AmEx's business fortunes were tied to tourism, not the old express business.

He even set aside areas in AmEx's offices to allow clients to read their mail and write letters home. Throughout Europe, American Express offices became a refuge for often bewildered tourists. In 1902, Dalliba opened "ticket departments" in AmEx offices to sell berths on steamships. Soon, however, Dalliba began using the ticket windows to sell European train tickets and sightseeing tours. By 1907, AmEx offices were offering their own tours and itineraries.

The express business was losing its allure by the early twentieth century. Regulators were clamping down on rates. Then, in 1913, Congress authorized the Post Office to begin a parcel-post system. Profits at American Express soon tumbled 50% and the company had little choice but to focus its energies on its fledgling tourist trade and its financial-related business.

Still, it wasn't until after World War II that AmEx's travel division really took off, thanks to Ralph Thomas Reed, who became president in 1944. Reed heavily promoted tourism, but his biggest claim to corporate immortality was his decision to get into the card business.

The product that would ultimately define American Express was the brainchild of a New York businessman. Frank McNamara's concept was born out of desperation in 1949 when he discovered that he didn't have enough money to pay his bill at a New York restaurant.

McNamara figured he could have avoided the subsequent embarrassment if he had an easy-to-use payment device. For years, department stores had issued their own charge cards. But there was no so-called universal card that could be used at different establishments.

McNamara soon teamed up with a lawyer, Ralph Schneider, and tried to market the card idea to several New York restaurants. At first, restaurants dismissed the notion. McNamara and Schneider were asking restaurateurs to pay them up to 10% of the tab when customers used their card. That seemed a bit too steep.

Still, the pair persisted, and a few curious restaurants eventually signed on. In March of 1950, McNamara and Schneider founded the Diners Club. The bylaws were straightforward. Cardholders would receive interest-free credit as long as they paid their bill in full each month.

The company had a rocky start. As it celebrated its second anniversary, the new card company was losing $60,000 a year. Restaurants were howling about slow payments. And the Diners Club, buried under an avalanche of paper, was falling further and further behind in its billing schedule.

The only success it had was in membership. The 1950s marked the dawn of the corporate expense account, and business executives were tired of stuffing their wallets with cash and checks every time they ventured away from home for a day or two. The card became a convenient device. Indeed, Diners Club would go down in history as the first travel and entertainment, or T&E, card.

To expand card usage, Diners Club enlarged the list of merchants who would accept the card. Hotels, florists, even Hertz Rent-a-Car signed up. By the fourth year, the company imposed a $5 annual membership fee and Diners finally turned a profit. In its eighth year, charge volume topped the magical $100 million mark.

By 1955, the buy-now-pay-later era had arrived. *Gourmet* and *Esquire* magazines sponsored restaurant cards. The American Hotel Association came out with its own product. Even the

American Automobile Association studied the feasibility of a charge card. American Express also became intrigued by the card business. It was a natural extension from money orders and traveler's checks.

In 1956, Reed and other AmEx board members learned through investment bankers that Schneider and Alfred Bloomingdale, one of Diners' biggest shareholders, wanted to sell their interest in the card concern. Although there had been a public offering of Diners Club the year before, the two men still controlled two-thirds of the company's stock.

At the urging of board members, Reed contacted Schneider and Bloomingdale. The owners of Diners Club said they would be willing to swap their stock for shares in AmEx. They would even support a tender offer by AmEx for the remaining public shares. That would give American Express virtually 100% ownership.

The deal was seductive to some AmEx executives. At the time, Diners Club had 250,000 cardholders, and there was talk of the company grossing $60 million the following year. But Reed was down on the deal. He was reluctant to let Schneider and Bloomingdale acquire a big chunk of AmEx stock. Publicly, he never explained why. But many executives within American Express speculated that Reed was uncomfortable with the notion that two Jews would control a substantial stake in American Express.

Around the time the Diners Club deal emerged, American Express had been under fire for closing its Tel Aviv office. Jewish leaders accused the company of complying with the Arab boycott of Israel. Reed vehemently denied the charges. He maintained the office was losing money. In fact, the company reopened its Israeli operations in 1958.

Over the next several months, Diners Club prospered.

Other card companies sprang up. Younger executives at AmEx began to barrage Reed with memos on the card business. Many felt it was time for the company to launch its own card.

By the end of 1957, Reed finally yielded: AmEx would enter the business. The product they came up with was similar to the card offered by Diners Club. Cardholders would receive a single monthly bill that included a duplicate copy of the sales receipt.

In May, 1958, AmEx received an unexpected boost when the American Hotel Association decided to join the AmEx card program. The AHA had been a reluctant participant in the card business. The sole purpose of its card was to avoid sharing hotel profits with card companies. The AHA had 150,000 cardholders and 4,500 hotels willing to accept their card. But they decided it would be less costly to strike a deal with AmEx than continue on their own.

By the card's launch date on October 1, 1958, American Express had 17,500 merchant locations and 250,000 cardholders. The first cards were made of a lightweight cardboard with a purple border surrounding a field of purple tint. To the left was the head of the well-known centurion. AmEx had first printed the centurion on its traveler's checks to reduce counterfeiting.

AmEx's first card had an annual fee of $6, $1 more than Diners Club. Although calculations showed that the card would be profitable with a $5 fee, American Express decided to charge more than Diners to give the impression that the AmEx card was more prestigious. Merchants would pay roughly 3% of their card charges to American Express.

Although it was a clear hit with the public, American Express had trouble coping with its immediate success. Inexperienced and ill-equipped, the company executives were overwhelmed by the volume of business. The paperwork piled up.

Queries on everything from overbilling to lost applications went unanswered.

Worse, American Express grew increasingly tardy in paying its merchants. AmEx had promised to reimburse merchants within ten days, but the company itself was having trouble collecting. Instead of paying off their bills every thirty days, many cardholders were waiting three to six months to pay. A newcomer to the consumer credit business, AmEx wasn't very effective in dealing with deadbeats. Reed himself didn't like the idea of dunning customers for fear it would damage AmEx's image.

American Express lost $4 million from its card operations in the first two years and a total of $14 million by 1962. Despite the red ink, Reed had remained committed to the card because he felt the company's reputation, as well as his own, was at stake.

His successor, Howard L. Clark, was more interested in the bottom line than in image. Smart and ambitious, Clark had joined AmEx after the war, boasting impeccable credentials. A graduate of Stanford, Harvard Law and Columbia Business School, he worked briefly as an attorney in the prestigious Wall Street law firm of Sullivan & Cromwell. Clark was also a certified public accountant.

Shortly after he took over control of the company, Clark began a sweeping study of its various businesses to judge each one's profitability. When he came to the card business, questions abounded. *Why are we doing this? Why should I care? Will we ever make money?* After a year as CEO, Clark made his first big call: *Dump the card.*

His bailout strategy was hardly unique: a merger with AmEx's old nemesis, Diners Club. AmEx's chief competitor was far more efficient. Billings and collections were well-managed. Clark believed a combination of the card operations

57

would produce a single lucrative venture. But AmEx's attorneys killed the proposed merger after receiving indications that the U.S. Justice Department would oppose it.

In the midst of his attempts to rid himself of the card, Clark decided he had to do something to stop the hemorrhaging at the card division. A management shake-up was in order and Clark began searching outside AmEx for an executive who could end the prevailing chaos in the card business. In 1961, he hired George W. Waters, who in later years would be called the "Father of the Card."

Waters, forty-five, seemed an unlikely candidate to save the business. Blunt and plain-talking, he was the product of a solid Midwestern upbringing. Waters knew nothing about the credit business or the travel industry. Indeed, Waters's father, a South Bend, Indiana, grocer, would often lecture his son about the evils of credit. "A person has no right to own anything, except a home, if he can't pay for it with cash," he would tell his son. Waters himself didn't even have an American Express Card. "Forget it," Waters had said when he heard the membership fee was $6.

Still, Clark liked Waters's hard-nosed manner. He also had the kind of background the card business needed. As chief operating officer of Colonial Stores, an Atlanta retail and grocery chain, Waters was experienced in marketing. And he was a whiz at data processing at a time when most companies were treating computers as space-age luxuries. Waters was a graduate of IBM's management training program. He had even served as a colonel in the Air Force's statistical control center during the war.

Unlike other AmEx executives, Waters was not worried about damaging the company's image by dunning delinquent cardholders. Waters quickly attacked the payment problem. Dunning notices were sent to all cardholders when their bills were thirty days overdue, not ninety days, as was the custom. Repeat offenders suffered the ultimate ignominy. Their cards were canceled.

Waters also decided that cardholders and merchants should pay more for the AmEx card service. The membership fee was raised to $8 and then to $10. As for merchants, Waters began increasing the discount rate gradually until it was in line with the 5% to 7% scale of Diners Club.

"If you have the best product, sell it for a premium," Waters told his managers. "People will pay."

Waters began referring to AmEx's customers as cardmembers, instead of cardholders. He had always frowned on the latter term. "To me, a cardholder was a Communist, as in a card-carrying Communist," Waters recalled. The suggestion of membership also gave the card an elite image.

In 1962, Waters began to go after the airline business. Among the incentives Waters offered was cooperative advertising. American Express would pay to advertise the airlines, while suggesting that passengers use AmEx cards to pay for their flights. The program was a big hit. Charge volume shot up 70%.

By the end of 1962, the card was no longer the black sheep of the AmEx family. AmEx's 900,000 cardmembers could use their cards at 82,000 locations, and the card division finally began making money. Before long, the card was so popular that Waters would begin offering an upgraded version that would include a line of bank credit. "The Gold Card," as it was called, would reign as the ultimate symbol of prestige until 1984 and the birth of the platinum card.

With the card business booming, Clark began focusing on his belief that AmEx would best grow through acquisitions. He was fascinated with the notion of building a conglomerate. This was a popular concept in the sixties, and Clark tried his best to make it work, though he never seemed to have a fixed game plan. For a while, AmEx owned 25% of Donaldson, Lufkin & Jenrette, the Wall Street brokerage. In 1968, the company ventured into publishing with the purchase of *U.S. Camera*, a magazine it renamed *Travel and Leisure*. The biggest acquisition was Fireman's Fund Insurance Companies, which AmEx purchased in 1968.

By 1970, Clark had grown weary of the grind. Without any clear-cut heir inside the company, the AmEx board had flatly turned down his previous requests to step aside. But now, after Clark had served as the top executive for seventeen years, the directors finally relented. The one stipulation was that he find a new CEO.

Clark knew American Express needed someone who was young and energetic to revitalize the musty executive suite. A paternalistic company that seemed almost to rebel at the notion of change, AmEx was populated by aging senior executives, many of whom had spent their entire careers at the firm. Innovation was rare. Stodginess prevailed.

After rejecting all of AmEx's home-grown contenders, Clark began looking outside the company for a likely successor. Tapping friends and acquaintances throughout the business community, he began a quiet hunt for talent. It was an informal search. Lunches, dinners and occasional cocktail parties were handy ways to quiz his corporate colleagues. Clark wanted to prepare a short-list of the up-and-comers. As it turned out, he didn't have to look long.

Jim Robinson wasn't unknown to Clark. AmEx had been a client of Morgan Guaranty when Robinson served as Tom Gates's assistant. What's more, AmEx board member Eugene R. Black, the former chairman of the Atlanta Federal Reserve Bank, knew the Robinson family well. Black had been a boyhood friend of Robinson's father and had known young Jim all his life. He spoke glowingly to Clark of Robinson's capabilities. *He's the perfect choice. You can't do better.*

Clark agreed that Robinson was alluring on paper. And after a few interviews, often on the golf course, Clark was impressed. At thirty-four, Robinson was young, ambitious and eager. And he handled himself with an unusual measure of maturity for an executive who had only eight years of experience under his belt.

Clark marveled at Robinson's connections. AmEx's chief was a strict adherent of the "contact theory" of business. The more influential people you knew, the better your business would do. Clark was always keen on expanding his ties to bankers. American Express's health depended on the willingness of banks to sell AmEx Travelers Cheques and provide a line of credit for Gold Cards. AmEx's own board included members who also served as directors for four of the six largest banks in New York—Chase Manhattan, Chemical Bank, Bankers Trust and Manufacturers Hanover.

Thanks to his family's contacts and those he made while at Morgan, Robinson's network of contacts seemed unlimited. He knew the senior executives at every New York money-center bank. Thanks to Morgan's CEO, Gates, Robinson's string of connections also included a number of Washington bureaucrats and politicians. Gates had also introduced Robinson to Juan Trippe, the chief of Pan Am, one of AmEx's biggest clients.

Robinson had never run his own company. But in Clark's eyes, what his young recruit lacked in experience, he more than made up for in breeding. Robinson had the kind of background that AmEx's tradition-bound board would warm to instantly. Clark finally offered Robinson a job. He told him the top job would be his one day. How many years of grooming it took would be up to Robinson.

When he arrived in 1970, it was an open secret that Robinson was destined for the top job. At the time, CEOs were generally unchallenged when it came to the personal task of picking successors. Search committees, headhunters and open debate within the top ranks were uncommon. AmEx's board certainly didn't object. Black advised Robinson that Clark's job could eventually be his.

"Don't mess up," he warned him.

Clark already had a plan of action to assure Robinson's succession. It was a kind of fast-track training program that would give Robinson a deeper understanding of the company while propelling him through the executive ranks.

First came a two-year stint at AmEx's tiny banking division. Clark then pushed Waters aside to make room for Robinson at Travel Related Services. Waters reluctantly agreed to stay on.

From the start, Robinson was tireless. But he wasn't willing to rock the boat. The last thing Robinson wanted was to unnerve the board through drastic changes.

Nevertheless, he believed he had to shake up the marketing department and instill a strong merchandising culture at American Express. Under Clark's tenure, the card had become a household word largely through deed and reputation. But there was very little attempt to sell the card to consumers. When Robinson took over TRS in 1972, the card marketing department had fifteen people and a mere $4 million budget.

In the corporate culture of AmEx, marketing was considered the domain of supermarket chains and packaged goods. Television revolved around cereals and soaps. Clark had never had any use for publicity.

"A whale that surfaces ends up getting harpooned," he would tell his subordinates.

Robinson thought otherwise. Image had always been important to him in his personal life, a legacy of his patrician roots. For a company that was quickly becoming a consumer giant, public perception was critical.

"I want us to think like merchandisers," said Robinson, who had a fondness for slogans. "Let's bring these products to life."

To help, Robinson turned to Aldo Papone. A top merchandiser for R. H. Macy's, Papone was an odd addition to the AmEx staff. He was what one colleague called "totally uncorporatelike." Flamboyant and personable, he preferred loud ties and brightly colored suits, in contrast to AmEx's uniform pinstripes. But he had a talent for selling.

"He could stick his finger in the air and tell you what would sell," recalled one AmEx colleague.

One of his first projects after he came to American Express to head the travel business was to revamp AmEx's overseas offices. Papone persuaded Robinson to hire a designer and an architect. Soon, many of the offices were gutted. Stairs gave way to escalators. Desks were replaced by counters. And AmEx staffers were required to stand and greet customers and to serve them as quickly as possible.

Not all of Papone's ideas were brilliant. An early plan to have the staff of AmEx offices wear uniforms much like airline reservation clerks was scrapped when employees balked. Later, Papone came up with the idea for radio spots using an old Negro spiritual as a theme. The "I Got the Whole World in My Hands" campaign aired only once. It was pulled after civil rights groups protested.

Still, with the aid of Papone, Robinson was gradually able to shift the attitudes at AmEx. Marketing became essential. In 1976, American Express began advertising in earnest on television. Thanks to the creative talents of AmEx's ad agency, Ogilvy & Mather, the "Do You Know Me?" campaign became legendary in the late seventies and early eighties.

The sixty-second spots featured a celebrity with little face recognition, who would explain the virtues of the card, tell how long he or she had been a cardmember, and end up with the tag line "Do You Know Me?" The answer came in the final five seconds as the name was typed out along the bottom of a green AmEx card.

Not only was the campaign a hit with the public, but with celebrities, too. Although they received only $15,000 for appearing on the ad, personalities lined up. Singer Julio Iglesias even sent a letter to American Express asking for a shot. It was, he wrote, to be a key part of his U.S. publicity campaign. AmEx turned him down, believing his name was not well enough known. The most memorable appearance was that of William Miller, Barry Goldwater's vice presidential running mate in the 1964 campaign. Though Miller's name was familiar, he was virtually unrecognizable.

Another early campaign by O&M was "Don't Leave Home Without It," which was hatched in 1975. At the time, Robinson was about to fire O&M. But he decided to give the agency one last chance if it could produce a new campaign that had a "synergy tag line," a slogan that fit all AmEx businesses.

Within two weeks, Ogilvy produced a phrase that would become synonymous with the American Express Card: "Don't Leave Home Without It." Karl Malden, made famous from his role as a detective in the television series "The Streets of San Francisco," would later popularize the traveler's check version, "Don't Leave Home Without Them." Around AmEx they joked that Malden sold anxiety better than anyone else.

Even better for AmEx, the competition was weak. In the late 1950s, banks had introduced credit cards. They differed from the Diners Club and AmEx charge cards by offering the option of an extended payment plan. Yet, these individual programs offered by banks were very localized.

In 1965, Bank of America tried to build a nationwide card by forming licensing and payment agreements with out-of-state banks. The following year, fourteen eastern banks joined together to form Interbank, a payment system for credit cards. The association later acquired Master Charge, a similar program based in California.

By the end of 1969, a total of 1,207 banks offered either BankAmericard, which later was renamed Visa to enhance its brand-name appeal, or Master Charge, later redubbed Master-Card. But growth was slow through the 1970s. Interstate-banking regulations placed severe restrictions on banks. And few banks had any national recognition among consumers.

In 1977, Citibank began its first national campaign, mailing solicitations to twenty million households. But it soon became apparent that new cardholders had few qualms about ignoring bills from a bank hardly known outside the New York environs. The bank ended up losing more than $500 million over the next three years. Eventually, Citibank would develop a sophisticated marketing technique, enabling it to turn the card business around. Citibank would later purchase Carte Blanche as well as Diners Club.

Robinson occupied the chairman's office at American Express Plaza in lower Manhattan in 1977. Because Robinson had been waiting in the wings for years, the succession had occurred with little fanfare. The company that he inherited was in fairly good shape. The American Express Card was established as the premier travel and entertainment card. Cardmembers numbered 8 million. The card was accepted by more than a million merchants worldwide. And profits from the card were rising at an annual rate of 15%. Net card earnings stood at a record $70 million in 1977.

The big question remaining for board members was whether their new CEO, fresh-faced and only forty-one, could keep up Clark's impressive momentum. Indeed, at Clark's retirement party, Robinson was given a pair of oversized shoes, supposedly belonging to his old boss, as a gag gift.

From the start, Robinson knew he needed a thriving card business to convince any skeptics on the board. To maintain the card's growth, Robinson turned to Louis V. Gerstner Jr. Stocky and square-jawed, Gerstner had all the charm of a drill sergeant. Outside the office, he was a devoted family man, a devout Catholic. During the week he was tough and abrupt. He barked orders only once.

A graduate of Dartmouth and Harvard Business School, Gerstner had spent twelve years at McKinsey & Company, a management consulting firm. Robinson had first met Gerstner when he came to American Express in 1975 to work on a marketing campaign. Like Robinson, Gerstner was a big believer in merchandising. But he leavened his marketing zeal with flow charts and demographics.

For the most part Robinson was pleased with his new hire, but he had nagging doubts about the card's future. The product had been around almost twenty years. Around American Express, top executives even began referring to the plastic phenomenon as a mature business. Robinson's concerns only deepened as the years went by.

The bank card associations were becoming bolder. After years of signing up middle-income customers, they began eyeing AmEx's elite client base. "We are taking dead aim at American Express's market," Dee Hock, Visa's feisty president, told an interviewer in 1978.

The outlook for traveler's checks wasn't much better.

Citicorp and BankAmerica were coming on strong with their own versions. Master Charge and Visa were also planning their own check products. If the bank card associations succeeded, TRS executives feared that member banks might not want to sell American Express Travelers Cheques.

Robinson, however, had a strategy to keep American Express out front: growth through acquisition.

FOUR

Expansion Fever

For years, AmEx executives had been preaching about the need for another income stream besides the card, traveler's checks and insurance. Around American Express they referred to it as the "fourth leg." Not only would a new business enhance AmEx's bottom line, it would also protect the company during rough times by diversifying its earnings.

Everyone supported the strategy. Even Howard Clark spoke of the need for another leg. How to accomplish that goal, however, was often debated in the upper echelons of American Express. One faction believed in an evolutionary approach, gradually adding new products to AmEx's established stable. Others who recalled the heavy start-up costs for the card wanted to purchase a business outright.

From his days as a venture capitalist at White Weld, Robinson knew firsthand of the expense and dangers of start-up operations. But he was impatient to grow. Ever since he replaced Clark in 1977, he wanted to transfrom American Express into a giant, a global company on a par with Ford Motor Company or General Electric. "I want a worldwide company," he would tell his staff.

Just as important, AmEx's young CEO was eager to put his own imprint on the company. The Clark Years were over. The Era of Robinson had arrived. "Robinson wanted to make everyone forget about Howard Clark," one of Robinson's aides recalled.

Clark's previous attempts to transform AmEx into a conglomerate were feeble and ill-planned. But it was still difficult to find substantial fault in his management. Clark was a legend around American Express. During his seventeen-year tenure, AmEx's profits grew geometrically from $7.1 million in 1960 to $194 million. Assets increased almost elevenfold to $10.4 billion in 1977. It would be difficult for Robinson to match that kind of performance.

To Robinson, buying companies was the easiest and cheapest method to continue and even surpass Clark's record. By the late 1970s, long before it became fashionable on Wall Street, Robinson pushed AmEx onto the acquisition trail.

Shortly after he became CEO, Robinson established the Strategies and Acquisitions Department at American Express. He put Roger H. Morley in charge, and directed him to compile a list of possible takeover candidates.

Morley had been recruited by Clark in 1974. A former executive vice president of finance and accounting at Gould Inc., Morley was brought in when the board complained that it wanted a longer list of candidates to consider for Clark's job. From the start, however, Morley had little chance of competing with Robinson. He was inarticulate, often visibly nervous. He was a chain-smoker and often when he spoke to the board, Morley would fidget in his chair.

Even Morley recognized that he was a dark horse. After Robinson's arrival, Morley became his chief supporter. He would often side with Robinson at strategy meetings. As a reward for his loyalty, Robinson later picked Morley to replace him as AmEx president.

"Synergy" was a favorite Robinson buzzword. Any acquisition that was made should enhance AmEx's basic card franchise by opening up new marketing avenues or attracting new customers. As it turned out, Robinson was more an opportunist than a strategist. He considered any and all targets, making an art of finding synergy in the oddest places. And the bigger the target, the better.

"Size is not a deterrent," he told an interviewer in 1977. "Each merger requires a lot of work. So if you're thinking of a new stream of income, you might as well make it big."

In 1975, when he was head of TRS, Robinson even pushed a plan to acquire his hometown favorite, Coca-Cola. He assembled a top-secret staff to crunch the numbers. Coke was codenamed Red. AmEx was Blue. Ultimately, he was forced to drop the idea when Clark intervened. AmEx's boss was far less ambitious than Robinson when it came to acquisitions.

When he became CEO, Robinson pursued the same kind of eclectic takeover strategy. In his first nine months as CEO, Robinson made runs at Book-of-the-Month Club, Philadelphia Life Insurance Co. and Walt Disney Productions. All failed.

Robinson bid too low on the first two. Disney was another story, however, and particularly disappointing to Robinson. He had longed for some kind of an alliance with Disney ever since he headed TRS in 1974.

Disney had an upscale wholesome image, and its theme parks in California and later Florida made the Disney name a top tourist draw. At one point, Robinson wanted to build an American Express pavilion at Disney's Epcot Center. Other big companies such as IBM and General Motors had plans for their own exhibits. He pressed Clark. *We have to get closer to Disney. Its image is compatible with ours.*

Clark turned Robinson down. He wasn't as preoccupied with image building. Still, Robinson never gave up on his plans for Disney. No sooner had he been named CEO than Robinson once again pursued his strategy. He talked openly of acquiring Disney. In 1977 Robinson, Morley and Clark, who by then had dropped his opposition, met with Disney chairman Donn Tatum in Los Angeles. Within the first half hour, Tatum made it clear that he wasn't interested in having his company acquired, or even doing business with American Express. At the time, the business press speculated that the sixty-one-year-old Tatum was outraged at the thought of working for the youthful and inexperienced Robinson, then only forty-one.

By December of 1977, Robinson was nine months into his tenure as AmEx CEO, but he had little to show for his acquisition strategy. Embarrassed, he began publicly backing away from his stated strategy. "This might be a good time to stay at home," Robinson mused. Morley quickly supported his boss. "We have no compelling reason to acquire," Morley told an interviewer.

Less than six months later, however, Robinson and Morley found another target: McGraw-Hill, Inc. The New York publishing company was a giant in the field of information services. Its empire included four television stations, the Standard and Poor's credit rating agency and F.W. Dodge, which provided data on the construction industry. And when it came to publishing, McGraw-Hill had sixty trade magazines and newsletters and *Business Week,* the company's flagship publication.

Robinson would argue that McGraw-Hill would be a natural fit with AmEx's own expanding information technology business. By 1978, American Express had one of the most elabo-rate and sophisticated technology networks in the world in order to handle card transactions. Others saw Robinson's ex-planation as a reach at best. Many executives within AmEx and analysts on Wall Street chalked it up to Robinson's desperation for an acquisition.

The deal was to be quick and painless, a sure thing. Mor-ley sat on the McGraw-Hill board. And Robinson's opponent, McGraw-Hill CEO Harold McGraw Jr., was perceived by many on Wall Street as slow-moving. And if it came to a proxy fight, Robinson felt he had an edge given the disharmony within the McGraw family. In 1977, Harold, who owned over 3% of the company's shares, had ousted his cousin Donald, who owned 2%. In 1978, another cousin, John, quit. He, too, owned around 2% of the company's shares. The word on the Street was that family members wanted to sell.

Robinson phoned Harold in the summer of 1978 to suggest a friendly merger. What was said, however, remains unclear. McGraw would claim later that he told Robinson he would consider the offer provided AmEx's CEO would not move for-ward with a takeover plan if the answer was no. Robinson agreed to this condition, McGraw later insisted. A few days afterward, McGraw-Hill's chief turned the offer down. Robin-son, however, denied that he ever offered any such assurances. Moreover, he would later insist that McGraw indicated that he would welcome a public offer.

Whatever was said, it didn't dissuade Robinson. By the following October, he had put together a takeover team that included himself, Morley, several board members and two in-vestment bankers. Felix Rohatyn, the star of Lazard Frères, was one. The other was Howard Clark Jr. of Blythe Eastman Dillon. Robinson had hoped that involving Clark's son would limit any meddling from AmEx's former CEO.

Robinson was so confident this acquisition would succeed that he even eschewed the formality of attorneys when he made his offer. On January 8, 1979, he and Morley personally waited outside McGraw's forty-ninth-floor office at the McGraw-Hill Building at Rockefeller Center to give the publisher notice. They ambushed McGraw as he was returning from a company party to celebrate McGraw-Hill's record profits in 1978.

"We have something here for you, Harold," said Morley, as Robinson pressed a small white envelope into his palm.

A few minutes later in his office, McGraw read the proposal closely. American Express was offering $830 million, or $34 a share, for his company. At the time the stock was trading at $25.75. Robinson was even willing to pay cash for up to 49% of McGraw-Hill's common stock. The balance would be paid with AmEx stock.

Once again, both sides disputed what occurred. Robinson said McGraw wanted to talk and they stayed for forty-five minutes. At no time did he voice any real opposition, they would later insist. McGraw disagreed. He said he was in shock and warned the pair they would face a fight if they pursued the takeover.

Regardless of what transpired, the next day McGraw marched across town to the Park Avenue offices of Wachtell, Lipton, Rosen & Katz. There, he hired Martin Lipton, a pioneer in takeover defenses. He, in turn, hired Morgan Stanley and Company Inc. and the public relations firm of Kekst and Company to handle the publicity. McGraw's defensive line was awesome and aggressive.

Within a week, McGraw's team had readied a vicious campaign. Lipton asked the Federal Communications Commission to postpone the merger until they could rule whether AmEx was entitled to own television stations. He even filed a suit in the New York Supreme Court alleging that Morley, who by then had been labeled as AmEx's Trojan Horse, had violated insider trading laws by having served on McGraw-Hill's board. Lipton even persuaded the House Banking Committee to investigate mergers that could affect the public interest. It was no secret that American Express would be the chief target.

Worse for Robinson, McGraw-Hill took direct aim at AmEx's image. Before long, in full-page ads in the nation's leading newspapers, McGraw-Hill claimed that Morley had violated a public trust by serving on McGraw-Hill's board. The ad even questioned the morality of the traveler's check because AmEx paid no interest on funds to customers. The campaign rekindled the debate over whether American Express had cooperated with the Arab boycott of Israel when it closed its Tel Aviv office in 1956.

Finally, the publishing company raised ethical questions about whether AmEx should control *Business Week*. How could a company that could be the subject of *Business Week* articles objectively run the magazine? Other media figures had similar reservations and joined in a kind of nationwide AmEx bashing. Publications from *The Christian Science Monitor* to *Advertising Age* published editorials opposing AmEx's takeover.

Robinson was stunned by McGraw's venomous assault. Around AmEx, they referred to it as Harold's "scorched earth policy." Still, Robinson felt compelled to respond. There already was talk circulating around Wall Street that Robinson didn't have the talent or toughness to pull off an acquisition. An immediate surrender would be too humiliating.

AmEx's CEO soon counterattacked. He promised to insulate *Business Week* and McGraw-Hill's other publications from any interference. AmEx also sued McGraw-Hill for libel, but by then the damage was done. AmEx's integrity had been tarnished.

As a final act, Robinson decided to sweeten his offer to $40 a share. McGraw-Hill's board had thirty days to respond. If they rejected it, Robinson pledged to end the battle. Many on Wall Street viewed the move as an outright capitulation. The $40 offer was still considered low. Indeed, McGraw-Hill's board quickly rejected it.

With his company's image under attack, Robinson quickly retreated. But the McGraw-Hill episode was far from over for AmEx's young CEO. AmEx board members were openly questioning Robinson's abilities. Word even spread through AmEx that Robinson's days were numbered.

Board members Ted Etherington, the former head of the American Stock Exchange, and Rawleigh Warner Jr., the CEO of the Mobil Corporation, were enraged. Their cacophony of criticism was relentless. *We looked foolish. You made us look ridiculous. This never happened before.*

The most disappointed board member was Howard Clark. He had hand-picked Robinson for his maturity and background. But here was his young successor, fouling the company's image with an ill-prepared and poorly planned scheme. Within days of the offer's withdrawal, he visited with Robinson privately.

"Jim, you should have known better," Clark lectured Robinson. "We looked like amateurs. Where was the preparation?"

Still, Clark wasn't willing to force Robinson to step down. There were no ready replacements. He had spent seven years grooming Robinson for the top job and he himself was in no mood to return. The board agreed. A resignation would have only attracted even more negative publicity.

As head of the acquisitions department and Robinson's point man in the takeover attempt, Morley was in a very awkward position.

Eventually, Morley chose to resign. Any hope of finding a comparable job elsewhere was shattered.

Humbled, but ever eager to add to AmEx's girth, Robinson tried a new tactic several months later in the summer of 1979. He decided on a partnership with Warner Communications. Warner was trying to build a nationwide cable television franchise. It was desperate for cash as much as Robinson was desperate for an acquisition.

According to those familiar with the deal, Felix Rohatyn suggested the alliance. He knew Warner needed capital to build its cable empire. He also knew Robinson was eager for a friendly deal to help erase the bitter memories left from McGraw-Hill.

Although Rohatyn had served as an advisor to Robinson during the McGraw-Hill fiasco, AmEx's CEO still respected Lazard Frères' most public partner, the hero who helped rescue New York City from bankruptcy.

Robinson knew little about Warner Communications or its flamboyant CEO, Steven J. Ross.

"Isn't he some kind of rock and roll guy?" Robinson asked Rohatyn, facetiously.

"Get to know him, Jim," Rohatyn advised. "He has a lot of interesting marketing ideas. He might even have some ideas for the card."

When Robinson finally met Ross two weeks later over lunch at the 21 Club, he was indeed fascinated by Ross's concepts. Although many of Robinson's subordinates questioned the strategic wisdom of linking up with a cable TV outfit, Ross convinced Robinson that cable was just the first step in an information-technology revolution.

Robinson was especially keen on Qube, Warner's two-way cable system which would someday allow subscribers to shop, make travel arrangements, and even bank from their homes. The system was tailor-made for AmEx's card business, because customers would be unable to pay by check or cash. Robinson could barely contain his enthusiasm.

"It's the future, Jim," Ross told Robinson. "Together, we can be on the cutting edge of technology."

After his first meeting with Ross, Robinson couldn't stop talking about Ross's view of the future, his "Electronic Cottage." "We're going to be on the cutting edge," Robinson would tell his staff, repeating Ross's upbeat prediction.

Many AmEx executives were less enthusiastic. They were unsure whether Robinson was seduced by Ross's well-reasoned logic or merely charmed by the Warner CEO's showmanship. Fashionable and flamboyant, Ross was something of a corporate hybrid, part businessman, part movie mogul. His lifestyle was pure Hollywood. Ross's friends included Clint Eastwood, Carly Simon, Barbra Streisand and Robert Redford.

His corporate life was just as flashy. When it came time to sign the final contracts with Robinson to create Warner-AmEx Cable Communications Inc. in November, 1979, Ross flew by helicopter from midtown to Wall Street. A cab would have made the three-mile trip in half the time.

Some AmEx board members were uncomfortable with Ross. At the time, Warner had a share in Westchester Premier Theater, a suburban dinner theater, which was being investigated for alleged links to organized crime. American Express's board found any kind of notoriety unwelcome.

Ross, however, was delighted with the partnership. AmEx's financing and prestigious name proved invaluable assets in the bloody franchise wars of the early 1980s.

"The thought of combining finance with entertainment would have made it hard for any city or state to turn us down,"

77

recalled Ross. "AmEx gave us a fantastic name and immediate credibility. We won the battle for cable contracts in Queens, Brooklyn, Houston, Dallas—all over the country."

Moreover, Ross remained in control. Robinson rarely interfered. Knowing little about cable or entertainment, he deferred to Ross in most major decisions. "Ross knew how to handle the American Express people. Every time they'd show up, he would have lots of celebrities on hand," a Warner-AmEx executive recalled later.

AmEx shelled out $175 million for a 50% stake in the new company, Warner-AmEx. For years to come, it would be seen by many AmEx insiders as a foolish investment. But their boss thought otherwise. He believed in Ross and his theories. It was a solution to his quandaries about the card. Even better, it helped erase the bitter memories left over from the ill-fated attack on McGraw-Hill. Cable TV could mark a new era for American Express.

"Miss Piggy, move over," Robinson declared at the new company's first board meeting. "We're in show business."

Despite his enthusiasm, Robinson wasn't about to stop with Warner-AmEx. The cable TV company was just the beginning on his road to rehabilitation in the eyes of the board. Two months later, Robinson purchased First Data Resources for $50 million. The company was the leading processor of bank credit-card transactions.

But those were hardly big enough deals to bury the painful memories of the McGraw-Hill fiasco. Robinson craved other acquisitions. He wanted bigger ones, more important ones. Before long, he would turn to his old friend Sandy Lewis to help him finally realize his ambitions.

FIVE

The Buying Binge

It was a muggy July morning in 1980, barely 6:30 A.M., as Salim B. Lewis's car turned into the concrete driveway leading to the River House. The sun had just begun to climb above the grimy Queens skyline directly across the East River from the posh twenty-seven-story co-op. But Lewis was already in high gear, fidgeting in his seat, barraging his driver, Willie, with nonstop patter.

Lewis wasn't much for conversation. He was a virtuoso at the art of monologue. He raced through topics like a stand-up at a comedy club. Lewis was in unusual form that day. During the forty-five-minute drive from his Short Hills, New Jersey, home to Jim Robinson's River House apartment, Lewis touched on everything from an approaching Canadian cold front to the hostages held at the American Embassy in Iran. Mayor Edward Koch's political ambitions also came in for some armchair kibitzing.

A friend of AmEx's CEO since the two shared adjoining offices at White Weld in the sixties, Lewis was Robinson's chief advisor outside American Express. He guided the novice chairman through the treacherous shoals of boardroom politics. Lewis also provided Robinson with key intelligence about Wall Street and the competition.

A large, portly man with a thick mound of dark red hair, "Sandy" Lewis was an odd concoction, even by Wall Street's liberal standards.

Lewis was a risk-arbitrageur. Near the bottom of Wall Street's social order, arbs were the parasites of trading desks, feeding on rumor and speculation. They would bet millions by buying stock in potential takeover candidates. Guessing right, they would make a bundle. A couple of mistakes, and they were ruined. It was life on the edge.

Nevertheless, Lewis was better known on Wall Street as a benign eccentric. He was always cooking up deals. Some were logical, most were fanciful. Still, Lewis saw himself as innovative and radical. Others perceived him as a full-time nuisance.

A quiet, polite figure when off-duty, Lewis was a holy terror on the trading floor. To psyche himself before a big trade, he would grit his teeth and let go with a primordial scream. It became known as Sandy's war cry.

And if Lewis became frustrated, clerks and secretaries would run for cover. Blunt, often nasty, he exploded into fearsome rages. Epithets and stationery, even an occasional phone proved handy ammunition when Lewis lost his temper.

His colleagues would plead with Lewis to calm down. *Take it easy. Relax. Sandy, enough,* they would say. Lewis, however, rarely took such advice. "You worry about your own damned trades," he would respond.

Tales of Lewis's antics reverberated throughout the Street. One afternoon at White Weld, Lewis was in the middle of a large "block" trade, involving shares in a defense contractor. But he wasn't sure how much stock to buy until he had more information on the company's business.

"Get me the White House on the phone—now!" Lewis screamed at his secretary. "Look up the goddamn number if you don't know it."

"Wait, Sandy," said a nearby trader.

"No, damn it. Let's go to the top. Let's find out what the hell is going on."

Lewis tried in vain to get information from the White House. No one in authority answered. But Lewis's bluster made a deep impression on colleagues. Richard O'Grady, a young trader, nudged the fellow sitting next to him.

"This guy has balls," said O'Grady, nodding deferentially toward Lewis.

He always would. Later, when Lewis worked for Merrill Lynch, he smuggled a *Wall Street Journal* reporter onto the trading floor. It was a blatant violation of company policy.

"Sandy, who the hell is this guy?" challenged fellow trader John Mulheren. (Mulheren would be indicted for insider trading in 1987. He was cleared in 1991.)

"Don't you know?" Lewis shot back. "This is Leonid Brezhnev's nephew," he explained. "He wants to learn about Wall Street."

Lewis seemed to be born a misfit. The son of Cy Lewis, the tyrannical master of Bear Sterns, Sandy was a rebellious and wild youth. His behavior was so unpredictable and unmanageable that his parents packed him off to an exclusive treatment center in Chicago. The Sonia Sankman Orthogenic School, affiliated with the University of Chicago, was founded and run by Bruno Bettleheim, the legendary Viennese psychiatrist who believed in creating a therapeutic environment for children with behavioral problems.

Lewis stayed at the school for six years before he returned to live full-time with his parents in New York. But he remained devoted to Bettleheim and his experimental program. Later, after he had briefly dropped out of college at twenty, he enrolled at the University of Chicago and joined Bettleheim as a full-time counselor.

What followed was a series of jobs on Wall Street as Lewis struggled to assemble a career that was independent of his father's well-known achievements. From White Weld to Merrill, Dean Witter and then on to Salomon Brothers, Lewis never quite found a comfortable home. He ended up starting his own firm, S. B. Lewis. Thanks to Robinson, American Express invested $4.5 million in Lewis's venture.

It was because of his eccentricities rather than in spite of them that Lewis became one of Robinson's close friends when the two met at White Weld in 1968. Low-key and reserved, Robinson was fascinated with the kinds of personality traits that he himself lacked or considered taboo. Time and time again he was drawn to daredevils and swashbucklers. A little tough talk and salty language made friendship turn into hero-worship.

Around AmEx headquarters, they attributed Robinson's periodic infatuations to his upbringing in Atlanta. Though his family was well-off, Robinson's childhood was bland and sheltered. Friends and acquaintances were mere cookie-cutter versions of himself.

So taken was Robinson with Lewis that he rushed to console him in 1969 when he learned that Lewis's career at White Weld had suddenly ended. He made the long drive to Lewis's home in rush hour traffic to express his sympathy. Lewis was so touched by the display that he would remain devoted to Robinson for years to come.

Always edgy, Lewis was even more hyperactive than usual that morning in 1980. It was to be a routine breakfast with Robinson, a helping of business and a smattering of gossip to go along with the poached eggs and rolls. But this time Lewis had a specific subject. He wanted to talk merger.

Robinson had frequently told Lewis of his plans to transform American Express into a global empire. Lewis knew Robinson wanted to go a lot further than just Warner-AmEx, his cable TV partnership.

Lewis also had his *own* agenda. Not only could a deal help his buddy Robinson, but it could further his own career. Lewis had wandered from firm to firm, never quite finding a home on Wall Street. Now, he was determined to strike out on his own, to begin his own company. *The bigger the deal, the better,* Lewis thought.

For more than a year he had been playing a mental game, weighing candidates to see which would fit neatly with American Express. Lewis believed he had finally found one.

By the time he reached the Robinsons' eighth-floor apartment, Lewis was anxious to share his news. He was whisked through the front door, past the butler, and greeted his friend warmly. The pair then headed toward the dining room, with Lewis leading the way. Lewis had been a frequent visitor to Robinson's River House apartment since AmEx's chief moved there in 1976.

One of the most exclusive addresses in the city, the River House, at the eastern tip of 52nd Street, was quiet and private. Henry Kissinger and his wife Nancy owned the duplex directly below the Robinsons. A few floors up were John Gutfreund, then chairman of Salomon Brothers, and his wife, Susan.

Robinson preferred his apartment for breakfast meetings rather than noisy restaurants or one of the private dining rooms at AmEx, where office wags made a habit of publicizing the boss's guests.

"Beautiful morning," said Robinson, peering out the window in the direction of the 59th Street Bridge. Just half a mile north, the bridge's rush hour traffic was beginning to slow to a crawl.

Lewis agreed. But he wasn't in the mood to admire the view. Small talk was the last thing on his mind. *Let's talk about mergers.*

"What do you want to do with this company?" Lewis asked Robinson.

Taken slightly aback as Lewis abruptly switched from pleasantries to strategies, Robinson looked at his friend with a puzzled glance. But he quickly recovered. Lewis was known for being abrupt.

"I want to help the card," AmEx's CEO responded. It was Robinson's pat answer. "Whatever merger we consider, it has to benefit the card."

Lewis had a solution. He told Robinson he had a possible merger in mind that could help the card. A brokerage, Lewis said. Big, upscale and aggressive, he thought it would be a clean fit. It would also open up another retail avenue to market the card.

Merrill Lynch or E. F. Hutton was the name Robinson expected to hear next. Merrill was enormous, Hutton white shoe. Both had images that were akin to that of American Express. Robinson himself had wondered at various times what would evolve if AmEx merged with Merrill or Hutton.

Lewis had a different idea.

"Shearson, Jim. American Express should buy Shearson."

Robinson just stared at him. Shearson Loeb Rhoades was the last firm Robinson would ever have considered as a likely match. Far from being compatible, they weren't even in the same class. American Express was mahogany desks, silk screen partitions and lunch at 21. Lean and scrappy, Shearson was ash-stained carpets and empty cups of Nathan's french fries. Above all, Shearson was nouveau-riche and

Jewish, where American Express was Old World and Protestant.

It was precisely because of those cultural differences that Lewis picked Shearson. He was a great believer in invigorating corporations with cross-pollination. *Opposites not only attract,* he thought, *they breed innovative ideas.*

"They are totally different, Jim. A totally new culture," Lewis acknowledged. "But what you have is inbred. You need new blood to take it to a new level."

Robinson had serious doubts. *Would the cultures mix? Would it help the card? What about AmEx's image?* What's more, Robinson knew it would be a tough sell to the board. Ever since his aborted takeover of McGraw-Hill, the board had made a habit of closely cross-examining Robinson on anything related to acquisitions. The Warner-AmEx deal, even the purchase of First Data Resources, came under intense inspection. *Are you sure, Jim? Have you thoroughly studied this? We don't want another McGraw-Hill on our hands.*

Still, to Robinson, Lewis's Shearson suggestion that summer morning was intriguing. A good, solid purchase would reestablish his credibility with the board, as well as satisfy his own ambitions for AmEx.

Although the securities industry prospered and floundered in tandem with the stock market, Shearson was a solid company. The second-largest publicly traded retail broker after Merrill Lynch, Shearson had 325 offices around the country. That was far less than Merrill's network of five hundred. But Shearson had the best record when it came to efficiency and productivity. Even better, demographics indicated that Shearson's typical client was a lot better off than Merrill's. That would be a plus for the card.

Shearson's earnings were hardly of colossal proportions, but they stacked up well against the competition. The bull market was still two years away and Mike Milken had yet to spread his junk bond gospel. Multimillion-dollar deals were rare. Wall Street was in its adolescence. A firm's worth was based on the skill of its trading desk and the output of its brokers. Shearson scored well on both counts.

"Can we pull it off without embarrassing ourselves?" questioned Robinson. "I'm not getting into a fight."

"Sandy Weill is smart and ambitious," Lewis said of Shearson's chief. "He definitely would talk."

Robinson gave the go-ahead. Find out what Weill wants, he said. It was tentative approval, hardly a roaring endorsement, but Lewis was pleased.

As he headed down the elevator of the River House and into his car, Lewis was even feeling a bit smug. The AmEx-Shearson merger may not have been the biggest deal he ever conceived, but it packed the most promise. It was easily a billion-dollar deal.

A couple of weeks passed. Lewis put some feelers out to size up Weill and his operation. He also kept in touch with AmEx's CEO. Robinson required a lot of hand-holding. *Keep it quiet,* Robinson would tell Lewis during their frequent phone conversations. *Let's be sure.* Lewis repeatedly reassured him. *Don't worry, Jim* became Lewis's daily motto.

Despite the confidence he displayed to Robinson, Lewis wasn't quite certain whether Weill was willing to sell. Sandy Weill and Shearson seemed inseparable. They had grown up together on Wall Street. Shearson was Weill's creation, the capstone to his career.

It all started back in 1960 when Sanford I. Weill and three friends founded Carter, Berlind, Potoma & Weill. It was a small brokerage that catered to a middle-class clientele. "The butcher, the baker and the candlestick maker" is the way rivals described Weill's customers. Over the years the firm went through a series of name changes as it acquired and merged with other firms. By 1973, Weill was CEO of Hayden Stone Inc. The following years the firm doubled in size when it acquired Shearson Hammill and doubled again by gobbling up Loeb Rhoades in 1979.

Shearson was big but Weill maintained his mom and pop management ways. He prowled the halls of Shearson's offices at the World Trade Center. Almost daily, he poked his head into every office and corridor, pestering employees with questions. He watched the bottom line with the tenacity of a bulldog. Bonuses and perks were earned, never automatic.

Unlike Robinson's proper and controlled demeanor, Weill was expansive and warm. A Brooklyn-born Jew, with swarthy Mediterranean looks and a paunch that challenged his belt size for most of his adult years, Weill had an Old World notion of friendship. His loyalties ran deep. Even after graduating from Cornell University and climbing to the pinnacle of power on Wall Street, he never forgot his Bay Street roots. His accent was heavy Bensonhurst, his speech peppered with "you know."

He especially delighted in playing the role of patriarch. Weill saw himself as the Vince Lombardi of Wall Street. He demanded loyalty and fraternity. Disharmony of any kind disrupted his team.

Once when Shearson's marketing chief, Hardwick Simmons, was embroiled in a bitter dispute over budget costs with Peter Cohen, the chief operating officer, Weill imposed a truce. He ordered his top executives to a meeting at the Greenbrier Hotel in West Virginia, far away from prying eyes. Weill instructed both executives to drop the matter and shake hands. He then demanded one more display of friendship. The six executives present were to prick their fingers and share their blood in a kind of childhood ritual of becoming blood brothers.

By the beginning of August, Lewis knew enough about Weill and Shearson to hazard a call. He wouldn't tell Weill why he wanted to meet. Lewis said he only wanted to talk a little business. Weill agreed. He suggested a breakfast meeting at the New York Stock Exchange at the end of the month, the Friday before Labor Day weekend.

The message was clear. Weill had never met the Street's other Sandy. But he knew he was an arb, and arbs were always talking deals. Serious business was never discussed on the last working day of summer, just ahead of a long holiday weekend. Weill wasn't interested, or at least that's what he wanted Lewis to believe.

It was cloudy and cool on that last Friday in August. Everyone on the Street, from secretaries to brokers, was wondering about the weather for the upcoming weekend.

Inside the New York Stock Exchange's Luncheon Club, it was hot and humid. Dark, musty and always smoke-filled, the stock exchange restaurant was famous for its mediocre food and snarling waiters. But it was the favorite hangout, a kind of clubhouse for Wall Street's great and near-great. It was often said that exchange members transacted more business over a cup of the commissary's weak and lukewarm coffee than on the trading floor itself.

Lewis was already waiting at a corner table near a window overlooking Wall Street when Weill arrived. After inquiring about the health of shared acquaintances, the previous day's lackluster market showing, and their respective plans for the weekend, Lewis turned to business.

"You have the best, cleanest operation on the Street," he told Weill, who grinned and nodded his assent.

"But that's today," Lewis continued. "The Street's changing. If you want to keep growing, Sandy, you're going to need money, lots of it."

Again, Weill nodded. It was no secret that half the firms on the Street were looking for partners. Trading volume was rising, costs were growing and brokerages needed capital to keep up.

"Did you ever think about a merger?" Lewis asked.

"I'm always thinking," Weill responded.

Lewis then got to the point. "What about a merger with American Express?"

There was a pause. Five seconds at most, but to Lewis it was interminable. He wasn't quite sure what to expect from Weill. Quick-tempered and volatile, Weill could have easily gone into a rage at the prospect of selling his firm.

Instead, Weill expressed mild amazement.

"Interesting," said Weill, his eyebrows rising for a split second.

What Lewis didn't realize was that the AmEx–Shearson marriage wasn't a new concept to Weill. In 1975, Weill himself had approached Howard Clark about a merger. Clark had just rid himself of AmEx's 25% stake in Donaldson, Lufkin & Jenrette. The institutional broker had been a clumsy fit with American Express. DLJ's banking and insurance company clients had little in common with AmEx's distinctly consumer customer base.

Weill had suggested to Clark that Shearson, with its retail customer base, was already serving the types of individuals that Clark wanted to reach. Clark said he was interested. He told Weill that Morley would contact him. Morley never did.

American Express, however, was never far from Weill's mind. AmEx had success, prestige and very deep pockets. It was the logical partner for any number of Wall Street firms. If

AmEx was seriously shopping, however, Weill wanted Shearson to be first on the list. Not only would it benefit his brokerage, Weill reckoned that a merger with American Express could give him the credibility he sought.

A creature of Wall Street, Weill was less a CEO than a fast-talking deal-maker. For years, Weill himself encouraged the perception. He nurtured the image. He especially enjoyed playing the part of the Brooklyn-born, street-smart entrepreneur, who didn't share the same privileged childhood of his Wall Street contemporaries. Not only did it make for favorable and sympathetic press coverage, it also set Weill apart from his competitors.

The image, however, was only partly correct. While he was born in Bensonhurst, Weill's childhood was hardly one of deprivation. His father was a wealthy clothing merchant. Weill himself was educated at the exclusive Peekskill Academy in Westchester and he had little trouble paying the tuition at Cornell University. Though he started his career as a $65-a-week runner for Bear Stearns, he spent very little time in the trenches. Weill had enough money at age twenty-seven to establish his own firm.

Making it on Wall Street didn't necessarily lead to stardom elsewhere. When it came to corporate America, he was still considered an outsider. It bothered him. He longed for some recognition of his skills as a strategist and manager.

Weill, however, remained poker-faced.

"I can't see this ever happening," he told Lewis. "Jim Robinson isn't looking for a partner, and I'm not interested in working for somebody else."

"You're mistaken," Lewis assured him. He told Weill that Robinson was more flexible than most believed.

"If I do it, I'm not just going to walk away," Weill said. "This isn't just a question of money."

Lewis nodded, then he began probing.

"What's it going to take, Sandy?"

"I'd have to be named president of American Express," Weill answered.

That was a tall order even for the cocksure Lewis. Still, now that he knew which carrot would get Weill's attention, he didn't want to dampen the Shearson chief's unexpected enthusiasm.

"That couldn't be a quid pro quo," he told Weill. But once again he assured Weill that Robinson would be generous.

Weill agreed to meet Robinson two weeks later for lunch at AmEx headquarters. Also present was Alva Way, American Express's number two executive, the man Weill wanted to replace. Constantly at Robinson's elbow, Way earned his job through his allegiance to Robinson, Weill suspected, rather than through any discernible business talent. During the lunch with Weill, he rarely spoke. And when he did, Way's comments seemed innocuous to Shearson's CEO.

The three spoke of the merger in broad terms. No details were discussed. Weill and Robinson were sizing each other up. Concluding a deal with Weill would be tricky. Man-to-man, Robinson was no match for Weill's deal-making prowess. Sandy, as Weill was universally called, was outgoing and jovial. And he was something of a legend in the brokerage business. Self-made, decisive and cocky, he was considered a pioneer of Wall Street. For Weill, there was nothing more satisfying in life than doing a deal. He seemed to relish the pursuit as much as the conquest.

Robinson was at the other extreme. At forty-five, he was an Atlanta-born gentleman, stiff and proper. He tensed up in crowds. He even used to prepare for public appearances by practicing his speech twenty or thirty times in front of a mirror until he had memorized every word, intonation and mannerism.

And where Weill was decisive, Robinson was hesitant. Throughout his three-year tenure as head of American Express, he preferred the committee approach to management. Bureaucracy and paperwork were the most common executive tools. And then there was advice. Lots of it. It was often said there were as many consultants as managers at American Express. A legion of counsels was constantly trooping through the chairman's office.

Robinson was well-prepared for the meetings. His staff had briefed him on Weill's personality and Shearson's prospects. There were no surprises. From Weill's ill-fitting suit to his fondness for ketchup on his steak, AmEx's staff had been thorough. For his part, Weill was blunt.

"Sandy Lewis thinks we can do something together. Are we wasting our time? What do you think?" Weill asked. They were practically the first words out of Weill's mouth.

Weill's questions never stopped. *What will happen to my people? What will happen to me? What does your board say?* Robinson was noncommittal.

The only substantive talks centered on Shearson's Financial Management Account. It was a kind of one-stop bank account that offered everything from brokerage services to money market funds. Modeled after Merrill's successful Cash Management Account, Weill envisioned it as Shearson's hottest retail product. Just the week before, Merrill had signed its one millionth CMA customer.

Two weeks later, the Shearson and AmEx marketing staffs continued talking about the FMA. The idea was to offer an American Express card to each account holder, much like CMA clients received a debit card. Without a banking franchise, Merrill couldn't offer a credit card. Instead, the debit card would be used like a check, with funds immediately deducted from a customer's account.

Despite such initial hopeful signs, the deal stood idle for months. Weill was eager, Robinson preoccupied.

AmEx's CEO still wasn't sure he wanted a brokerage. Given the success of Merrill's CMA, the potential of Shearson's FMA was alluring. But there were big hazards with such a product. Banks had gone into an uproar when Merrill unveiled its product. It was a question of turf. The CMA was too much like a bank account. If AmEx went into a similar business, Robinson could also expect a backlash. In AmEx's case, the threats wouldn't all be hollow. American Express depended heavily on banks to sell their Travelers Cheques and provide credit for Gold Cards.

In late 1980, before his meeting with Weill, Robinson had looked at other possible targets. At the top of the list was the Fidelity Investments Company. The Boston-based mutual fund group, one of the first to offer investors a menu of varied investment products, was growing at a phenomenal rate. The company also had one of the best marketing arms in the nation. Its telephone and direct-mail solicitation campaigns were unparalleled in the financial community.

Robinson saw Fidelity as an easier blend with AmEx, especially when selling the card. The only problem was Fidelity's availability; it was family-owned and fiercely independent. AmEx executives ultimately concluded that Fidelity's CEO Ned Johnson wouldn't be in any mood to sell. With his wounds from the McGraw-Hill battle still vivid in his mind, Robinson decided to pass on Fidelity.

If Robinson was interested in buying a brokerage, it didn't necessarily have to be Shearson. A number of firms were interested in an alliance with American Express.

Merrill Lynch's crusty chairman, Donald Regan, had already suggested a merger to Robinson in late 1979. Like Lewis, Regan believed that financial companies would eventually offer an expanded menu of services. However, Robinson's advisors questioned whether the Justice Department would welcome the deal.

Robinson's second-guessing ceased, however, on March 20, 1981. That's when Bache Halsey Stuart Shields, a proud and tradition-bound firm, a pillar of the Street since the nineteenth century, was acquired by the Prudential Insurance Co. Bache had been skating along on thin capital for years. The sharks had been circling for more than a year.

Canada's predatory Belzberg family was the first to take aim. American Can's Gerald Tsai soon followed. Instead, Bache management shocked the Street by accepting a white-knight rescue from the Pru. The largest financial services firm in the world, with $60 billion in assets, Prudential was suddenly a lot more formidable.

A day after the Pru-Bache announcement, Robinson called his advisors together. The Pru's purchase of Bache Halsey seemed to pave the way for AmEx's acquisition of Shearson. If the Pru could do it, Robinson could, too. Even the board would find it difficult to oppose him. The Pru's purchase of Bache was strong evidence that brokerages were in fashion.

Speed, however, was necessary. Wall Street's herd instinct was legendary. Robinson feared a stampede. Rumors were flying that General Motors, General Electric and IBM were about to pounce on lower Manhattan's financial community. After months of dithering, the Shearson deal was hot.

"If we want to do it," Robinson said, "we'd better move very quickly."

He phoned Lewis.

"It's a whole new ball game," Robinson conceded. "Let's get this going."

Slowly hanging up, Lewis said out loud: "Thank you, Mr. Belzberg."

Weill was in Hong Kong when the Pru-Bache news broke. Along with former president Gerald Ford, then Shearson's trophy board member, Weill was touring the Asian branch offices. Pru-Bache was the lead story on the business page of the *South China Post*. Weill grew agitated.

It was shortly before noon New York time, one A.M. in Hong Kong, by the time Lewis reached Weill at his hotel. Separated as much by geography as terms and conditions, Lewis wasn't about to negotiate by phone. But he did extract a promise from Weill not to entertain any other suitor until he heard from AmEx. It wasn't difficult. Weill was eager for the prestige that a merger with AmEx would bestow.

"I won't even accept a phone call from anyone else," Weill assured him.

Not long after Weill returned to New York, Lewis suggested that he and Robinson meet, far away from Wall Street. Weill invited Robinson and his wife, Bettye, to his home in Greenwich, Connecticut. A one-hour drive from midtown Manhattan, it was the perfect setting for easy conversation.

The Weills' country estate was more comfortable than it was lavish. Home was a ten-room Tudor, framed by Weill's own apple orchard on the one side and a three-car garage on the other. Inside was cozy: stone fireplaces, oak end tables and oversized armchairs. It had been a weekend haven for Weill, his wife Joan and their two children ever since his days at Shearson Hayden Stone.

It was Saturday, a brisk March morning, when the Robinsons arrived by limo. After a cordial lunch, Joan Weill took Bettye on a tour of the garden and the neighboring apple orchard. Weill and Robinson headed for the study for a chat.

Located in the rear of the house with a view of the garden, the study was Weill's lifeline to Wall Street. It echoed the warmth of the rest of the house with dark wood-grained paneling, floor-to-ceiling bookshelves and a white oval rug spread over an oak floor. But it was pure Weill, right down to the stack of discarded *Wall Street Journal*s in the corner.

Weill directed Robinson to a couch in the corner. No sooner had the pair sat down than Weill began interrogating AmEx's chief. They were the same old questions. *What would my role be? Who would report to me? What about my responsibilities?* Weill was showing his worst side: his insecurity.

Robinson was evasive. He thought the gathering would be purely social, a quick hello, an even quicker lunch, then off to nearby Westchester County Airport for a 4 P.M. flight to Atlanta. Robinson wasn't ready to get into a lot of specifics. Details were Lewis's job.

Weill, however, pressed him. Again, he repeated his desire to be AmEx president.

Other than a seat on the board, Robinson would not commit himself. He had only met Weill twice. No one else on the board had even exchanged handshakes with Weill.

"You'll have to prove yourself," Robinson told Weill.

Weill's face reddened. Over the past twenty years, Weill had personally negotiated the acquisitions of a dozen or more firms. He had been a CEO for a decade. And here was Robinson treating him like some corporate virgin straight out of business school. Still, he held his temper.

He had another question for Robinson. Weill and Lewis had worked out a deal in which American Express would pay 1.1 shares for each Shearson share. Owning 456,000 shares, Weill stood to make upward of $25 million from the merger. He often wondered whether he would end up wealthier than Robinson. And if so, how would the AmEx chief react?

"What's your net worth?" Weill asked Robinson.

Flustered, Robinson responded half-jokingly, "Not as much as yours."

But when he saw Weill was serious, he assured him that Weill's personal profit from the deal was not a problem. "It's not a concern," Robinson said.

It was an embarrassing session for Weill. But he felt the deal was too important. Ever since his first meeting with Robinson four months previously, Weill had grown increasingly enthusiastic.

When he had first spoken with Robinson, Weill had hoped to get the number two job. Now, months later, he was setting his sights even higher. For years, he had heard talk that Robinson was too courtly and genteel to survive at the helm of American Express. After AmEx's run at McGraw-Hill, the line on Wall Street was that Robinson was weak. After dealing with Robinson and his operation, Weill agreed. Robinson just wasn't tough enough. To someone like Weill, the temptation was overpowering. *I can take him,* Weill thought. *It's just a matter of time.*

Despite the awkwardness of the encounter, Robinson and Weill reported to Lewis that all went well. The merger was on track. Over the next couple of weeks, Lewis continued to shuttle back and forth between Robinson and Weill, fine-tuning the deal. Both CEOs proved very accommodating. What Lewis hadn't anticipated was the separate rebellions that were brewing at AmEx and Shearson.

AmEx's Ivy League executive corps looked on their rough-hewn counterparts at Shearson with trepidation. The staff at TRS, in particular, was in an uproar. Gerstner and his people wanted American Express to grow internally, with new products. They were already working on a savings account, similar to a certificate of deposit, but with a charge card feature. The Shearson acquisition would refocus the company's energies elsewhere.

Moreover, Gerstner and his crew were feeling vulnerable. TRS was AmEx's flagship, the star performer. Shearson posed a challenge. It could end up undermining TRS's prominent position, as well as Gerstner's corporate aspirations. As AmEx's resident marketing guru, he was especially outraged at the notion of renaming the new brokerage Shearson/American Express.

"Nobody will know who's acquiring who," Gerstner raged at his staff.

Robinson began to worry that the press would get wind of the dissension. He decided to put an end to the mutiny.

"When I pay $1 billion for a company, I call it what I want," Robinson told the balky executives at TRS.

Unfortunately for Robinson, the TRS staff wasn't his only headache. Howard Clark shared their apprehensions. From his retirement home in Hobe Sound, Florida, Robinson's predecessor began sending disturbing signals. He had already passed on the Shearson merger once. Yet here it was again. The brokerage business was just too cyclical, Clark argued. Though his official authority was nil, Clark was an influential voice around American Express. Having appointed nearly every director, his clout with the board was awesome.

Bullying the TRS staff was one thing, but heading off Clark would take more finesse. To reassure his old boss and halt Clark's meddling, Robinson dispatched Howard Clark Jr. to talk to his father.

A former investment banker at Blythe Eastman Dillon, the younger Clark was one of the footsoldiers Robinson had employed in his ill-fated campaign to capture McGraw-Hill. A Wally Cox look-alike, Clark was thin and bookish. Nicknamed "H" to distinguish him from Howard Clark Sr., Howard junior was unlike his father in almost every way. Hardly dynamic or tough, H never quite measured up to his father's legend. It was often said that Robinson had hired him just to keep the elder Clark happy. But over the years, Robinson and H would grow increasingly close. H was a good man with numbers and loyal. In 1981 he would be named chief financial officer.

At Shearson, meanwhile, Weill was grappling with the misgivings of his own lieutenants. They didn't see the need for a merger. Shearson was doing just fine on its own. Some executives even suggested that Weill was more interested in the potential for personal fortune than in the firm's well-being.

"Why do we need them?" Shearson's marketing wizard, Wick Simmons, would ask. "We're doing just fine."

Peter Cohen, Shearson's second-in-command, was particularly skeptical. A merger was bound to diminish his authority and weaken his claim to succeed Weill in the future.

"It's good for the firm," Cohen told Weill privately. "But it's not necessarily good for me."

Cohen's support was critical. He was a whiz at operations, the unsung hero of Shearson's success. While Weill was the front man, the strategist, the dealer, Cohen made the back office hum. Cohen was the bill collector, Weill the schmoozer.

A short, stocky man, with a crop of wiry black hair, Cohen was much like Weill in temperament and background. The son of a clothing manufacturer, he grew up on Long Island and graduated from Ohio State University and Columbia Business School. He was fascinated by Wall Street, always buying and selling stocks in his spare time. Cohen turned down a job offer from his father and headed for the Street. At twenty-five, he was hired by Weill's partner, Marshall Cogan, as a securities analyst.

Young and quick with numbers, Cohen was sharp. He earned money in college by selling cases of Colt 45 to fraternities. But he was also impatient. The word was that Cohen wanted to be made Shearson's president when the time was right, but Weill was reluctant. Too immature, Weill fretted. Maybe after a bit more seasoning.

Frustrated, Cohen quit in 1978 and went to work for Edmond J. Safra at the New York–based Republic National Bank. A Lebanese-born financier, Safra had built an impressive private banking operation in Switzerland. And he was making quite a name for himself in the U.S. Cohen met Safra when he was researching Republic. He admired Safra's brilliance and decisiveness. In turn, Safra, seeing some of the same ambitious qualities he had as a youth, took a liking to Cohen almost immediately.

But Cohen was bored by the slow pace of commercial banking. He especially missed the excitement of doing deals. A year later, he returned to Shearson to help Weill complete his biggest deal of all, the acquisition of Loeb Rhoades, the venerable investment bank. By 1979, Cohen was clearly number two in the Weill organization, but his abrupt departure opened a breach with Weill that would never heal. Weill would always question Cohen's loyalty. For his part, Cohen would come to see Weill as an obstacle to his career.

Before Weill could proceed with Robinson, he had to assuage Cohen. He said he would ask Robinson to give his second-in-command a seat on the board. Cohen was genuinely touched by Weill's display of loyalty. It seemed that Weill was finally recognizing his talents.

In fact, Cohen was a compromise candidate. All along, Weill had insisted that Shearson was entitled to more than the single seat that Weill would hold.

"I want some company," Weill would tell Robinson. "I can't be the only one. It wouldn't look right."

Weill wanted two more seats. He suggested Kenneth Bialkin, Shearson's outside counsel, for one of the spots. A partner at Willkie Farr & Gallagher, a top Wall Street firm, Bialkin had also been Weill's advisor for years. Weill wanted the other board seat to go to Dan Seymour, the head of J. Walter Thompson and Weill's close friend.

Robinson refused. *Who's buying who?* he thought to himself. The last thing he wanted was for Weill to establish a Shearson beachhead on the AmEx board. But Robinson, ever the gentleman, wanted to steer clear of a confrontation with Weill. Instead, he explained to Weill that the board was tired of outside attorneys like Bialkin. As for Seymour, AmEx's longtime agency Ogilvy & Mather would rebel. O&M would also want a board seat.

As a compromise, Weill suggested Cohen. Robinson wasn't happy with that selection either. Cohen was outspoken, sometimes abusive. The last thing Robinson needed on the board was another cigar-chomping adversary from Shearson. Once again he found another reason to say no. Cohen was only thirty-four. He would be the youngest board member in AmEx history. Robinson himself was thirty-nine when he was invited to join the board in 1975.

By Easter weekend, the negotiations were down to short strokes. Both sides got together Friday at AmEx to review some last-minute figures. Cohen strenuously objected to the price. He suggested that a ratio of 1:3 rather than 1:1 was more in line with each company's true worth. Eager to close the deal, Robinson agreed to sweeten the deal. The final price for Shearson would be $932 million.

After the session, Weill, Cohen, and George Sheinberg, Shearson's chief financial officer, piled into a cab. They all lived on the Upper East Side.

"Listen, Peter, there's a problem," Weill said, turning to his protégé. Weill hesitated to collect his thoughts. "Robinson doesn't want you on the board. He only wants me." Only CEOs could be AmEx directors, he told Cohen. Cohen was dazed. He had taken the previous day's discussion to be final. In the past, Weill had bulldozed other CEOs into accepting his terms. To Cohen, Weill suddenly seemed timid.

"I was crazed!" Cohen would say later. "I felt sold out. I could have killed him."

Sheinberg interrupted before Cohen could respond.

"Why not make Peter Shearson's CEO?" he suggested. It was easy enough to do since Weill was probably headed toward AmEx's corporate suite in some capacity.

Before Sheinberg could continue, however, Weill whirled and stared at Sheinberg. *Shearson is mine,* Weill thought.

"Let's drop this, OK?" Weill said.

Still, Weill knew he faced the possibility of a new insurrection. Stubborn and ego-driven, Cohen had allies at Shearson. And they couldn't be ignored. Together, they owned a substantial number of Shearson shares. The following day, Saturday, Weill summoned his top executives to his country home. It was time to put down the uprising before it started.

Weill had suggested an 11 A.M. meeting. Passover would begin at sundown, and most of Shearson's executives had planned to get home early for family gatherings for the traditional seder. Cohen was the first to arrive.

"Listen," Weill said to him, as the pair huddled in the study. "Don't upset this merger. Don't screw it up."

Cohen listened attentively. Weill's tone was less tyrannical than it was beseeching.

"Don't worry about me, Sandy," Cohen replied. "I know it's good for the firm."

Shortly after, Shearson's other top executives began arriving. With some sitting on the floor, others on borrowed dining room chairs, Weill began once again to lecture his team about the rewards of the AmEx merger. Once again, his staff questioned the need for it.

This time, Weill had a ready answer.

"How would you feel if Express bought Hutton?"

A murmur rose through the room. It was just the kind of response Weill was hoping for. Long before its embarrassing bad check scandal and subsequent demise, Hutton was arguably the classiest act on the Street. Weill had picked up some intelligence, mostly hearsay, about how AmEx and Hutton had already been talking. But he spoke as if it would surely occur if Shearson backed out.

"Do you want to go up against AmEx and Hutton?" Weill asked rhetorically. "We'd get beaten for sure."

No one was eager to face that kind of competition.

Weill further pointed out the positive responses from many of Shearson's 5,000 brokers. Weill had been barraged by phone calls from his regional staff who were eager to join the AmEx marketing machine. They especially wanted the master list of AmEx's Gold Card holders.

Slowly, the critics backed off.

With the rebellion quelled, Weill went on to talk about expanded career opportunities. It was a rich topic.

"We sat around trying to figure out who was Jewish at American Express," remembered one executive. "We wondered out loud how real was the possibility of a Jew taking over American Express."

So did Weill.

"Do you think I could do it?" Weill asked.

He said it with a broad grin that suggested he was kidding. Some executives present weren't so sure.

"Sandy, you are naive if you think you can run American Express," said Sherman Lewis, Shearson's investment banking chief.

Cohen agreed.

"No Jew will ever run that company," he said.

By the time the group broke up, Weill had won a victory of sorts. No one at Shearson would oppose the deal. He still wasn't sure about Cohen. At 2 P.M. when the meeting broke up, Weill wished the group a happy Passover. He told Cohen that they would meet early Sunday before heading to the midtown offices of Skadden Arps, AmEx's legal advisor, to review the merger papers.

That evening, Cohen, along with his wife and two children, went to his brother Billy's home to celebrate the Jewish holiday. By the time he arrived home at his Park Avenue apartment, the phone was ringing. It was Robinson.

"I hear you're upset," Robinson said.

Once again, Cohen felt betrayed by Weill. He never intended his conversation with Weill to go beyond Shearson's offices. Now he felt he was about to be strong-armed by AmEx's CEO. Fed up and fuming, Cohen was blunt.

"Jim, don't worry. I'll do the right thing. I'll give you six months—till the end of the year. If I don't like it, I'll move on quietly."

Taken aback by Cohen's biting edge, Robinson wasn't about to be conciliatory. He said good night.

The next day, Easter Sunday, executives from Shearson and American Express gathered at the offices of Skadden Arps. To Cohen's astonishment, he was asked to sign a five-year non-compete clause. He was furious.

"No way," he told AmEx's legal advisors. "I told Robinson I'll give him six months and then I'd wait and see. That's all I agreed to."

The following Monday night, the same executives again gathered, this time at Shearson. When Cohen arrived, Weill was there to meet him.

"You're on the board," Weill said.

To placate Cohen, Robinson had relented. Weill was visibly relieved. But Cohen still doubted his sincerity. From that moment on, Cohen would always believe that Weill was somehow responsible for keeping him off the board in the first place. No matter. Cohen finally had what he wanted. So did Weill. "We're moving in," Weill would tell a friend. "We've got them now."

The Shearson-AmEx agreement was formally announced on April 21, 1981. Three days later, the Robinsons and the Weills gathered at the Four Seasons for a celebration with Sandy Lewis and his wife, Barbara.

"We've made history," said Lewis, smiling. He was genuinely impressed by the size of the deal.

"At times, I had my doubts," acknowledged Robinson, who was ecstatic. He now had the deal he had longed for since becoming CEO in 1977. For two years, Robinson had been paying for his McGraw-Hill sins. Shearson, he felt, would be his absolution.

At the end of the festivities, Lewis presented both Robinson and Weill with a piece of Steuben crystal shaped like the New York skyline. He also presented both men with a copy of a book, *Love Is Not Enough* by Bruno Bettleheim. Inside the cover of both copies, Lewis had inscribed: "Without this fellow, our deal would not have happened."

Two weeks later, Robinson handed Lewis a check for $3.5 million. It was the largest finder's fee Lewis had ever collected. Weill himself had tried to bargain the fee down. He argued with Robinson that the payment was too rich. But Robinson wouldn't hear of it. It seemed a fair price for the largest acquisition Robinson had ever made.

SIX

Expansion Blues

From the moment the Shearson deal was finalized, Wall Street wags were betting whether Robinson could survive Sandy Weill. For months, everyone had been openly debating whether AmEx was acquiring Shearson or vice versa. Weill was cunning and ambitious. Most of all, he was used to being number one. It was doubtful that someone as laid-back and accommodating as Robinson would be able to keep Sandy down for long.

Even within American Express, there was a perception that Jim and Sandy were in competition. Executives were identified as Jim's man or Sandy's man.

Robinson sensed the danger. Board members had cautioned him. *Sandy can't be trusted. Watch your back. Weill wants your job.* The warnings were not prompted out of concern for Robinson so much as outright fear for their own jobs. If Weill dethroned Robinson, he was sure to pack the board with his own loyalists.

To forestall the possibility of a coup, Robinson limited Weill's ability to maneuver. Within a month of the acquisition of Shearson, Robinson handed Weill a letter outlining his responsibilities. It was two pages and to the point. Weill remained in charge of Shearson. But when it came to American Express, he was a minister without portfolio. He was named head of AmEx's executive committee, a kind of corporate purgatory. He provided summations on corporate activities at weekly committee meetings. Later, he would also be put in charge of negotiating the lease of a new corporate headquarters at the World Financial Center.

Three months after the merger, Weill had begun a quiet campaign to be named chief operating officer. That would have firmly established him as Robinson's number two. But Robinson refused. *After a while, maybe,* Robinson would say, or brush him off. *Let's give it some time.*

Even when Robinson named Weill president of American Express in January, 1983, Weill's responsibilities remained unchanged: Shearson and little else. And there was no one to appeal to. Although Weill was an effective lobbyist with the board when it came to budgets and five-year plans, he had no solid supporters. And he doubted he would ever have any. *They're Jim's boys.*

"I'm just Deputy Dog," Weill would complain to Shearson colleagues, referring to the hapless cartoon character. "I have nothing to do around here."

Still, few executives believed Weill would remain down for long. Sandy was too smart and Shearson too strong. Thanks to the bull market that erupted in August, 1982, Shearson's profits were soaring. The Dow Industrial Average had begun a feverish climb. And Weill's influence was growing. Fueled by a speculative press, rumors of a Weill coup d'état abounded.

" 'When will Sandy make his big move?' was the biggest question circulating at American Express," Harry Freeman would later recall.

Gerstner was especially suspicious of Weill. The TRS

chief had come to think of himself as the likely heir apparent to Robinson, thanks to his success with the card business.

By 1983, Robinson's earlier fears that the card was sputtering had proven unfounded. The card had become "The Card." AmEx plastic was tapped into the expense accounts of every *Fortune* 500 company. Non-business use was also on the rise. AmEx had 17.7 million cardholders, who were charging up to $75 billion a year. Earnings at TRS were expected to top $300 million in 1983, up a solid 20% from 1982.

The card's success was partly the product of a carefully sculpted five-year plan that Lou Gerstner had put in place when he took over the card division in 1978. The following year, when he was named head of TRS, Gerstner had set some of the most aggressive goals that AmEx had ever known. The paramount objective was to increase earnings between 15% and 20% a year. It was a dream that Robinson shared as well. TRS was to be the cash cow of the 1980s.

While Robinson was off building an empire, Gerstner had transformed TRS into an unrivaled marketing machine. He staffed the card business with what he called "china-breakers," bright, entrepreneurial types who showed little allegiance to convention. It was quite a change from AmEx's traditional "water walkers," the upwardly mobile Ivy Leaguers. His new team ranged from James Calvano, the CEO of the Avis rental car company, to Jerry Welsh, a former Russian and Slavic languages professor who had remarkable marketing instincts. Challenging convention was one of the legacies of his earlier years at McKinsey. The consulting firm had little hierarchy, but it placed a premium on fresh ideas.

"My job is to keep everybody here humble, hungry and turned on," Gerstner once told an interviewer.

He seemed to relish his job. Tough and relentless, Gerstner never eased up on his staff. "Big Ideas" became the chief quarry of TRS staffers. To Gerstner, every marketing concept had a limited shelf life. Even the ubiquitous Take One boxes which accounted for almost 20% of new cardmembers were vulnerable. "The next thing you know, we'll probably be putting them on the urinals at the Yale Bowl," he once told his staff.

Gerstner was generous to those who delivered, but ruthless to those who stumbled. "TRS was one big happy family as long as you could produce," recalled Calvano. "If you couldn't, you were banished. It was like 'Old Don was a good guy, but maybe we should bring in young Mary Jane.' "

Luckily for Gerstner, his tenure at TRS also coincided with the emergence of the Baby Boomers in the early eighties. They were the progeny of a generation that had known hardship firsthand and had vowed that their children would not be deprived. They were educated and career-oriented and cared how they were perceived. Best of all, they loved to spend.

Gerstner and his TRS staff were among the first to recognize the changing values. AmEx's marketing had always emphasized prestige. Now, the message went even further. *The Card will change your life. The Card will make it better. The Card will make you look important.*

Welsh proved particularly uncanny when it came to this new age of marketing. Once, when he was reviewing several ads prepared by Ogilvy & Mather, Welsh found "American Express is a part of a lot of interesting lives." Discarding most of the ad, Welsh kept the concept of "Interesting Lives" and turned it into one of the most successful campaigns targeted at the rising number of professional women.

The ads featured young professional women at work and play. One showed two female engineers talking about a project over lunch. Another featured a young female executive hauling her scuba diving gear along on a business trip. The name American Express was never mentioned. The card was shown briefly at the end. It was the ultimate in soft sell and an incredible success. Even leaders of the feminist movement hailed the ads. American Express "now makes women feel welcomed and invited," Gloria Steinem said. By 1984, one in every three new cardmembers was a woman.

And then there was "cause-related" marketing. American Express linked its name with some fifty money-raising causes in the 1980s, from the Dallas Ballet to the Lincoln Park Zoo in Chicago. Its most successful effort was launched in October 1983 when AmEx began promoting the restoration of the Statue of Liberty. For three months, AmEx pledged to donate one cent of every card transaction and one dollar for each new card member to the reconstruction effort. AmEx raised $1.7 million for the statue. Even better, in the final quarter of 1983, card usage was up 28% over the same period in 1982. New card applications rose 45%.

The card strategy didn't end there. With bank cards slowly gaining wider acceptance, Gerstner decided that American Express had to enhance the card's appeal if he hoped to reach his growth targets. The American Express card had to be used by more people at more places.

To expand its use, AmEx aggressively pursued new retailers. Such discounters as the Dollar and Budget rent-a-car companies were added along with Neiman-Marcus to AmEx's merchant list. AmEx even went after the medical profession to persuade doctors and dentists to accept the card.

At the same time, AmEx began foraging lower in its demographics data to find new members. AmEx had been so successful at enhancing its upscale image in the late 1970s that many qualified consumers never even applied for the card. "Interesting Lives" was broadened to attract young professionals with lower income levels. It wasn't just judges who had American

Express cards; so did legal aide attorneys. The company even began wooing college seniors to hook them on the AmEx green right out of school.

The most telling examples of Gerstner's desire to control both the high and low ground were TRS's new products. In 1982, Gerstner launched "Operation Blue Card" to develop a new card that could compete with bank credit cards. Five years later, American Express would unveil its ill-fated Optima, a virtual clone of Visa and MasterCard. Optima later would become both a victim of the 1991 recession and a symbol of deep corporate malaise.

American Express also fought aggressively to defend its high ground when banks began issuing their own gold cards. By 1983, TRS witnessed a frightening customer migration from AmEx plastic to Visa and MasterCard gold cards. They offered cash advances like AmEx's version, but they were cheaper. The annual membership fee was $35, versus $50 for AmEx's Gold Card. Worse, the public perceived the bank gold cards to be as prestigious as AmEx's brand.

"We have to raise the high end a notch higher," Gerstner lectured his staff. "We need a product that looks even classier than gold."

Before long, TRS was ready with the platinum card. It was supposed to be special, almost unattainable. And its perks were designed to appeal to those who aspired to the ultimate in recognition. It was only offered to those existing AmEx cardmembers who averaged $10,000 a year or more in charges. The platinum product offered check-cashing privileges of up to $10,000 a week, twenty-four-hour travel services and a year-end accounting of every charge.

The biggest dispute over the platinum product was the annual membership fee. At a pricing strategy session with Robinson and Gerstner, Aldo Papone suggested $1,000. *The price alone would make it appear prestigious,* he figured. Calvano argued for $250. *We want the affluent, not the stinking rich,* he thought to himself.

Robinson was typically in the middle.

"How the hell do we determine the price?" he asked.

In traditional Gerstner fashion, TRS's chief immediately stepped in.

"The debate is over. We charge $250," Gerstner declared. Then he turned to Robinson. "Okay, Jim?"

Robinson nodded.

Such exchanges between Robinson and Gerstner were common. Preoccupied by empire building, Robinson had little time for AmEx's core business. Moreover, he was no match for Gerstner's marketing brilliance when it came to the card industry. "Lou was Mr. Inside, Jim was Mr. Outside. Everybody knew that," recalled Calvano.

Robinson didn't mind. In public, AmEx's chief was hailed as the champion of the card, while at AmEx, Gerstner's ascendancy became a powerful weapon against Weill and his ambitions. Divide and conquer. It was Robinson at his best.

To head off Weill and buttress his own position, Gerstner began leaning on his staff to fatten TRS's bottom line. "Trim costs, make money" became the TRS battle cries. By the end of 1983, Gerstner was nudging up the discount fees charged to merchants, arguing that AmEx cardholders spend more so the company was entitled to a bigger share. The increases would go on throughout the eighties. Gerstner outlined his counterattack to a handful of top TRS executives at a conference at Casa de Campo in the Dominican Republic.

"We have to maximize profits over the next few years instead of going for market share or Sandy and Shearson will end up running the company," Gerstner said. "We have a political fight on our hands!"

Weill, however, was less threatening than frustrated. Even on the deal-making front, he felt underutilized and vulnerable. Robinson had expected Weill, a master deal-maker, to further AmEx's expansion. No one else at AmEx had his acquisitive talents or contacts. But his takeover track record at American Express was spotty at best. In two years he had netted The Boston Company, a small money management firm, and a couple of regional brokers.

Even then, it wasn't without some pain. When Weill negotiated the purchase of Foster & Marshall, a Seattle-based brokerage, F&M brokers rebelled. Fearing their commissions would shrink as they fell under AmEx's rule, hundreds walked out.

It didn't help matters that Cohen was finally enjoying more success than his former mentor. In 1983, American Express acquired Edmond Safra's Trade Development Bank, largely on Cohen's recommendation. Safra's bank was then incorporated into the American Express International Banking Corp. At the time this occurred, Safra was considered the world's leading private banker. His reputation was legendary, his franchise unique. From his discreet Geneva headquarters, protected by Swiss secrecy laws, he catered to the world's wealthiest individuals.

A close friend of Safra's, Cohen personally negotiated all the details. It was Cohen who journeyed back and forth between AmEx and Safra's Paris apartment. It was Cohen who persuaded Safra to sell to American Express. And it was Cohen who secured Safra's commitment to stay on as head of AmEx's bank.

Robinson was jubilant. Not only had Cohen come up with a deal that would enliven AmEx's own sluggish banking franchise, but he also snagged Safra himself. Suddenly Cohen wasn't the whiny malcontent that Robinson had thought he was. Cohen was the golden boy. Private lunches with Robinson and social get-togethers with the wives became the routine. Before long, Cohen's opinions on business matters were treated on a par with Weill's.

"Peter Cohen is a genius," Robinson told board members after acquiring TDB.

Cohen's success only fed Weill's sense of isolation. By 1983, Weill felt he was even losing his grip on Shearson. Shut away in AmEx's executive suite, he rarely walked around the offices at Shearson as he once had. He no longer kibitzed with the traders or the secretaries. Weill had no fiefdom to call his own.

Weill complained openly of the generous Shearson bonus system that Cohen had installed. By 1983, Cohen was earning more than Weill or Robinson himself, thanks to various performance incentives. Cohen's compensation totaled $1.3 million, compared to $902,000 for Robinson and $806,346 for Weill. "This is outrageous," Weill would say. Robinson paid little attention. It was not uncommon for the top executives of brokerages to receive staggering compensation packages. Their pay was tied directly to the volume of business their brokers brought in. What's more, Robinson, accustomed to wealth from childhood, never saw money as an issue.

Weill was desperate for his own deal, one that would resuscitate his reputation as the resident wheeler-dealer, while shoring up his position in the AmEx hierarchy. By the summer of 1983, Weill believed he had the answer. It was called Investors Diversified Services, a folksy Midwestern purveyor of financial products.

Weill had discovered the company in 1979 when he was scouting for a financial property to expand Shearson's menu of consumer products. The Minneapolis-based firm sold mutual funds and insurance products through a network of "financial advisors," who sold door-to-door. IDS salespeople were the Avon ladies of financial services.

And it was a low-cost operation. Its future looked unlimited. The bull market was still roaring. And it wasn't just pension fund managers who wanted to buy in. Everyone from teachers to bus drivers had a favorite stock or bond. By Weill's reckoning, IDS would soon become a money machine.

Robinson was curious. He authorized Weill to determine if IDS was for sale and how much the company was worth. As it turned out, its owner, Alleghany Corporation, was interested. A New York conglomerate which owned a hodgepodge of industrial and financial companies, Alleghany had few emotional ties to IDS. If the price was right, Alleghany would gladly unload it.

Following a few sessions with Fred Kirby, Alleghany's chairman, Weill proposed a $1 billion stock swap, much like the Shearson acquisition. Kirby was pleased. The deal would leave him in control of the largest single block of AmEx stock. There was also talk of a board seat for Kirby.

By mid-July the deal was all but completed. Kirby and Weill got together for lunch at AmEx to finalize the terms. The only stumbling point was Kirby's insistence that AmEx commit formally to a price before he allowed the customary "due diligence." Such reviewing of the books and interviewing top managers to determine the health of a company usually preceded an agreement.

Though at the time he thought the request was odd, Weill readily agreed. Robinson had already agreed to the $1 billion stock swap, and Weill expected few, if any, surprises from IDS's books. More importantly, Weill was eager and impatient. He wanted to conclude the deal quickly. The two men shook hands. Weill strode confidently back to AmEx's executive offices to tell Robinson the good news.

Within days, however, Weill was under siege. Although the IDS deal was well-known throughout American Express, the price wasn't. A billion-dollar price tag seemed too rich for a company that was little-known in New York. Almost overnight, detractors began popping up. IDS's perceived flaws multiplied.

At TRS, they fretted that IDS was too downscale for American Express. Could the IDS crowd even qualify for a green AmEx card? His colleagues at Shearson questioned Weill. They jokingly referred to IDS's clients as "those poor people."

Cohen was particularly outspoken. He found the price appalling. Cohen reminded Robinson that he brought in Safra's world-renowned bank at half what Weill wanted to pay for IDS. Still basking in the glory of his smooth and triumphant takeover of TDB, Cohen was difficult to ignore.

Weill tried to get him to change his mind. In August, he even took Cohen, Sheinberg, Gerstner and Papone to Minneapolis to look at what was behind IDS's balance sheet. Weill was sure they would come around. *When they see this operation up front, they'll be impressed.*

The trip didn't help. Cohen remained critical. He was especially disappointed at IDS's limited back-office capabilities. *How could it handle an inflow of new business?* he thought to himself. AmEx would have to come up with millions in fresh investment to help out. For his part, Sheinberg worried about cash flow.

The two former Weill aides shared their doubts, then they speculated about Weill's reaction. Each wondered what Weill would do.

They didn't have to wait long. After the close of the second day of fact-finding, Weill, Cohen and Sheinberg shared a cab back to their hotel.

"So what do you think?" Weill asked his colleagues.

Oh God, here it comes, Cohen thought to himself.

"Sandy, I'm convinced more than ever that this is a solid company," said Cohen, as he attempted to cushion his next words.

"But it's not worth $1 billion," he continued. "We're getting ripped off."

Sheinberg nodded.

"He's right, Sandy," he said.

Weill was furious. His troops were in rebellion.

"You don't know what the fuck you're talking about," he yelled. "I don't give a shit what you think."

As the cab pulled up to the Marquette Hotel, Weill headed for the bar. Cohen and Sheinberg followed, hoping he would compose himself after a few martinis. He didn't.

"Nobody gives a damn what you think, Peter," Weill shouted.

Cohen stared back in disbelief. Weill had become so verbally abusive that much of the bar had begun to notice, including the brass from American Express.

"Fuck this, George," Cohen said to Sheinberg. "I don't need this. I'm getting out of here."

Cohen made a quick exit, with Sheinberg right on his heels.

Back in New York, the chorus of doubts had already reached the chairman's office. Yet Robinson still wasn't capable of confronting Weill head-on. Robinson rarely lost his temper. He felt such displays were common and ungentlemanly. But he felt a nagging doubt about the way Weill had handled the situation.

How could he agree to such a price? Robinson knew Weill was ambitious. He, too, had heard the rumors of a possible palace coup. Before long, he began to believe them. *What was Weill up to? Was he just trying to expand his authority?* Robinson wanted answers. He turned to his old friend, Sandy Lewis. Robinson instructed Lewis to take an independent look at IDS.

"Weill is getting ahead of himself on this one," Robinson confided to Lewis. "I have to know whether we're paying too much."

By the end of July, Lewis came back with an answer. Armed with a stack of statistics, Lewis chipped away at Weill's deal during an hour-long session in Robinson's office. He pointed out that IDS's results were solid, but not stellar. The previous year, the company's profits had actually slumped by 8% to roughly $63 million. Revenue was off another 2% to 1.4 billion.

"Jim, this is not a $1 billion company," Lewis told Robinson. "It's a good buy at, maybe, $750 million."

The evidence was damaging. Robinson grew nervous. For days, Weill had continued his campaign for IDS. He even found someone to run it. His name was Harvey Golub, a consultant with McKinsey & Company who was working on a card marketing project at TRS.

Robinson wanted to avoid a showdown.

"Sandy loves the deal," Robinson lamented. "What am I going to do?"

"You're just going to have to decide which Sandy you're going to listen to," thundered Lewis, by this time disgusted with Robinson's equivocation.

Seven days passed and AmEx's chief had yet to make a decision. Most of AmEx's executives were advising Robinson to drop the deal. Weill, however, was resolute. Predictably, Robinson remained safely on the fence.

To break the stalemate, Robinson decided to organize a task force. It was a typical Robinson solution. Lots of paper. Lots of committees. A dozen executives in all were assigned specific projects, from calculating cash flow to interviewing

IDS's management team. It was to be a thorough, hands-on study of IDS's strengths and weaknesses.

Robinson wanted their findings in ten days. He scheduled a meeting of AmEx's top executives for August 15. One way or another the fate of the IDS deal would be decided.

The mood in AmEx's executive suite was downright chilly by the time the meeting date arrived. Weill was jittery. Cohen was combative. Robinson buried himself in paperwork.

Weill knew he faced an uphill fight. The week before, *The Wall Street Journal* had run a decidedly negative story on the AmEx-IDS deal. The article predicted that the August 15 meeting would be a "sobering session" because AmEx executives were disappointed by what they found at IDS.

"It isn't as happy a situation as we hoped to find," said the article, quoting an unnamed AmEx executive.

A plant, Weill figured. It was probably the handiwork of Harry Freeman, he thought. By then head of public relations, Freeman was one of Robinson's henchmen. He had extensive contacts in the media. And although he was friendly to Weill, there was no doubting Freeman's allegiance to Jim. Regardless, it suggested that Robinson was already into the face-saving stage. The IDS deal was looking more and more tenuous. So, too, was Weill's position in American Express. By then, the IDS deal had taken on the proportions of a vote of confidence for Weill.

It was 10:05 A.M. by the time all those invited settled into the boardroom. Roughly a dozen executives in all were seated around the long, oval mahogany table. Another dozen or so less senior executives found seats along the walls. The usual chatter that precedes such functions was noticeably absent.

Robinson took his seat at the head of the table. In front of him rested a blue, five-inch-thick binder containing the findings of the task force. Weill was immediately to Robinson's left, fidgeting, openly nervous. It was the first time in more than a decade that Weill had to answer to a boss.

"Okay, now," Robinson said. "Let's get to work."

One by one, executives in charge of the various task force assignments summarized their findings. Most echoed Lewis's private report to Robinson. A solid company, most agreed, but hardly worth $1 billion. The folks from Fireman's Fund even questioned whether there would be much in the way of savings if they combined insurance companies with IDS. Weill kept silent, scribbling notes.

Then Cohen chimed in.

"Shearson brokers will have a problem with this," he said. "We're already selling the same products as IDS."

Indeed, mutual funds were popular and Cohen was looking for Shearson to reap huge rewards. It was part of the treasure chest Cohen wanted to build to finance a foray into investment banking. If American Express acquired IDS, Shearson would have an in-house competitor.

"That will not be a problem," Weill responded. His tone was dismissive as if to show that he, not Cohen, knew more about the brokerage business.

Robinson then turned to Sheinberg, AmEx's treasurer at the time. Sheinberg had journeyed to Chicago the previous week to scrutinize IDS's steel subsidiary, MSL Industries, which had been transferred to IDS to simplify bookkeeping chores. As former CFO of Bulova, the watch manufacturer, Sheinberg was the only AmEx executive who knew his way around a factory.

His report was very negative. MSL wasn't doing well. Sheinberg projected potential losses of as much as $10 million the following year.

Weill was visibly shaken. Sheinberg was a friend and ally.

Now, it looked like he was turning on his former boss, just as Cohen had.

"George, if you felt this way, why the hell didn't you tell me about it?" Weill fumed at Sheinberg.

Sheinberg was silent. Later he would explain that he hadn't had enough time to tell Weill of his findings. Sheinberg had spent the previous Thursday and Friday at MSL. He arrived back in New York late Friday and headed to his summer house in East Hampton to compile his notes.

Weill, however, would remain unforgiving. To him, it looked as if Sheinberg was trying to ambush him. In later months, Weill would repeatedly campaign to have his former friend fired. Sloppy and slow, Weill would say of Sheinberg. By the end of the year, Sheinberg would ultimately resign as AmEx treasurer only to be rehired by Cohen at Shearson.

By the time the meeting adjourned two hours later, Weill's defeat looked complete. Silently, he rose from the table and headed for his office. Right behind him walked Golub and Weill's assistant, James "Jamie" Dimon.

That afternoon, Robinson summoned Weill to his office. Robinson was mellow, but determined. He didn't think IDS was a strategic fit. The price was especially outrageous.

"We're going to exercise our option to walk away from this," Robinson said.

Weill shook his head.

"You're dead wrong, Jim," he said, battling to control his temper. Weill knew if IDS was dead, his days would be numbered as well.

"It's a unique franchise," Weill continued. "We can sell the steel company, that's not a problem."

Robinson wouldn't budge.

Weill then tried a different tack.

"Jim, my word is my bond," he said, reminding Robinson

that he had already agreed on a tentative deal. "I'm embarrassed and ashamed about this."

"Sandy," Robinson replied, "it just didn't come up to snuff."

Weill pressed harder.

"It would be stupid to back away now. Everyone knows how far we've gone," Weill reminded Robinson. "What about our reputation?"

Robinson froze. Weill had purposely hit on one of those magical image words that AmEx's CEO could never ignore. Robinson hadn't thought about such damage, but Weill had a point. To back away after four months of negotiations would make American Express look foolish. Wall Street would be laughing. Once again Robinson would be subject to the harsh public criticism that he experienced after McGraw-Hill. Worse, Robinson worried that word would get around that American Express had reneged on a deal.

Robinson's conviction wavered. *I'm not sure. It doesn't look good.* Robinson repeated, almost point by point, the arguments he heard during the morning. Then he stared at Weill and asked about the price. He could accept the deal if it was cheaper. *A billion is too much.*

Weill agreed to talk down the price. He also agreed to another Robinson condition. Lewis would join him in negotiations. To Weill, it was a humiliation. He neither needed Lewis's talents, nor appreciated his meddling. But Weill had little choice. Only with Lewis's involvement would Robinson go along with the deal.

Within two weeks the negotiations with IDS resumed. Kirby was angry that the first deal fell through, but he was still eager to talk. No other suitor had emerged. AmEx was the only company talking. This time Weill insisted on complete due diligence before talking price. Kirby assented.

By October, it was generally agreed that IDS would be acquired. Not everyone understood Robinson's decision, but Jim wanted it done. That was reason enough to deliver.

The IDS deal now appeared close to completion. Due diligence produced few surprises this time. Cohen remained opposed. But with Kirby more flexible on a final sale price, it didn't much matter. And now with Lewis involved more deeply, Robinson was paying less attention to Cohen's complaints.

It was November and the deal was nearly done when Weill received a phone call from Lewis. The two reviewed the final terms. All was satisfactory. Even Robinson was eager to close the talks, Lewis said.

There was one proviso, however. Lewis said Robinson should be the one to finalize the deal. It was only right. AmEx's CEO was the first to authorize the talks, and he later salvaged the deal.

"Jim has to do the deal," Lewis told Weill. "Jim has to finish it."

Weill wasn't quite sure whether Lewis meant Robinson wanted the ego satisfaction of signing off on the deal or that the deal would only get done if Robinson completed it. No matter. Weill stepped aside.

In December, 1983, Robinson signed a contract to acquire IDS for $773 million in cash and stock. IDS would go on to be the single best performer out of all of AmEx's acquisitions. By the end of the eighties, it was far more profitable than either TDB or Shearson.

But Weill's fight to acquire the company was bruising and costly. After the IDS affair, Robinson viewed Weill even more suspiciously. Indeed, Weill's influence at American Express would begin to ebb. Robinson stopped asking for his advice. Weill was conveniently excluded from key meetings.

In his place, AmEx's chief boosted Gerstner's corporate

profile. Gerstner eventually replaced Weill as head of the executive committee. Gerstner would also be named vice chairman. He became a leading Robinson advisor. Before long, Robinson even suggested that Gerstner would someday take his place.

Robinson, however, remained AmEx's only official star. He was credited with transforming American Express into a financial empire. It made no difference that Lewis had delivered Shearson, Cohen had nabbed Trade Development Bank, and Weill discovered IDS. Robinson was a new *wunderkind*.

SEVEN

Family Matters

By the end of 1983, American Express was one of the best-known brand names in the world, one of the most profitable companies—thirty-six straight years of record operating earnings—and it seemed to be getting bigger every day. Following the acquisition of IDS, American Express was one of the largest financial services companies in the U.S. It ranked up there with Citicorp and Merrill Lynch. Robinson, as CEO, stood first in line for the kudos.

The financial press made a hero of him. The eighties was the era when businessmen became celebrities. Lee Iacocca was king. And Robinson was fast becoming a star in his own right. His name appeared as often in the "Suzy Says" column of the *New York Post* as it did in *The Wall Street Journal*'s "Heard on the Street" column.

Civic and business groups wanted him as a speaker. Politicians courted his favor. He even gained the attention of his fellow CEOs. In 1979, Robinson had been admitted to the Business Roundtable, the exclusive and influential club for modern-day captains of industry. At forty-eight, Robinson was rubbing elbows on the cocktail circuit with the likes of Henry Kissinger, Barbara Walters, and General Electric's blustery chairman, Jack Welch.

He sat on the boards of three corporate giants. His favorite was Coca-Cola. There was something terribly satisfying about joining the board of Atlanta's leading corporation. At one time, Robinson's father, Big Jim, had a close working relationship with Coke, but even he never quite made it to the board.

But while his professional life was blossoming throughout the early eighties, Robinson's family life was increasingly unsettled.

When Robinson first started out, Bettye had all the makings of a good corporate wife. Forsaking family and friends, she dutifully followed her husband into the Navy, on to Harvard, and then to New York. Wherever Robinson went, Bettye followed. She always told herself that Jim's career came first. Bettye was a great advocate of such prefeminist notions and was very much an old-fashioned Southern girl in her beliefs.

Pretty and personable, she always made quite an impression on Robinson's business associates. Warm and friendly, Bettye remembered the names of wives and children, and she kept a list of birthdays and wedding anniversaries. Top executives and their wives could usually count on a card or small gift. She was part Miss Congeniality and part ship's social director.

She also had a brusque and formal side in keeping with her role as the CEO's wife. Once, after a welcoming lunch at the River Café in Brooklyn for the Shearson wives, she scowled at Joan Weill, who was about to share a limousine ride home with Karen Cohen.

"This is unacceptable," said Bettye, ordering Joan out of the car. "You should know better."

Joan was to ride with her, Bettye explained. Cohen's wife

would ride with Robin Gerstner. Protocol demanded it, given their respective husbands' ranks.

Beneath the surface, however, Bettye had become increasingly disenchanted with the corporate lifestyle. She disdained charity work and dinners with total strangers. Living in New York was another burden. Bettye preferred the leisurely Southern pace. New York was apartment living and concrete. She hated both. She grumbled often.

Motherhood was another torment. Bettye would frequently complain of her children's unruly, sometimes wild, behavior, and of her own inability to cope. Even with the help of a full-time maid and nanny, she had difficulty raising Emily and James.

Robinson paid little heed, however. Reserved and proper at the office, he was downright distant at home. Robinson never encouraged intimacy. He wasn't one for using "honey" or "dear." Even a simple "I love you" was rare and never heard in public. "I understand," Robinson would respond to his wife's complaints. "Yes, I see." Then he would bury his face in another report and quickly forget.

Always a workaholic, Robinson devoted himself almost exclusively to his professional life. His sixteen-hour workdays seemed to get even longer after he joined American Express. Weekends were set aside for golf games and business gatherings at Blind Brook, a Westchester country club. And then there were the phone calls. Robinson was always grilling some subordinate, somewhere in the world.

"Jim got on the fast track," Robinson's sister, Frances Huber, would later recall. "Without a balance of family and work, a relationship could be very difficult."

Bettye withdrew to the shadows, becoming more an accessory to Robinson's career than a part of it. Before long, she began drinking to escape her isolation. At first it began with evening cocktails with friends. Then she began drinking by herself at home. Eventually, Bettye turned into what one family friend called a "midnight raider," downing Scotch while everyone else slept.

Bettye often slept during the day and didn't answer the phone when her husband called. "Damn it!" Robinson would yell in his office, his control gone.

Bettye's behavior became more eccentric. A chain-smoker, she would roam continuously from room to room, always clutching the same ashtray. She would visit her children's rooms in the middle of the night, switch on the lights, wake them up and ask where they had put their toys.

Once, when Robinson was headed off for his first foreign business trip for AmEx, Bettye showed up at his office to say good-bye. It was late afternoon, and she was dressed in a long black evening gown ready for a social engagement. Bettye was warm, openly affectionate. Robinson ignored her.

Robinson was embarrassed and bewildered by his wife's behavior. Highly disciplined, Robinson was a big believer in such classic notions as strength of character and self-help. He pointed with pride to his own physical transformation from a bony youth to a physical fitness buff who could bench-press 200 pounds without breaking a sweat.

Robinson repeatedly urged his wife to seek treatment. Bettye ignored his pleas. And Robinson was reluctant to force the issue. He disliked confrontations, business or otherwise. Robinson rarely fought with colleagues and hardly ever with his wife.

Bettye was far more feisty. Once during a business trip to the Netherlands, she railed at Robinson for bossing around his aides.

"You think you're such a big deal, Jimmy. But you're not," she yelled at Robinson in the coffee shop of the Amsterdam Hilton. Robinson was mortified by such a public scene.

Though he and his wife were steadily growing apart, Robinson never considered divorce. Although it would have set a precedent in the Robinson clan, tradition wasn't a key consideration. AmEx's board was.

A somber bunch of conservative churchgoers, the board was as preoccupied by image as by the bottom line. Discreet affairs were one thing, but divorce was considered unseemly. Any hint of domestic strife could have scuttled Robinson's journey to the chairman's office.

Not surprisingly, Robinson's marital miseries were kept confidential. Only a handful of his fellow executives ever suspected there were problems at home. Robinson never missed a beat at work. As for Bettye, she cut back her corporate schedule, and she made a point of not embarrassing Robinson at public events.

Bettye wasn't the only cause for Robinson's distressed home life. Over the years, his absence had also strained his relationship with his children. Never a particularly involved or visibly caring parent, Robinson wasn't one for palling around with his kids. Indeed, Emily and Jimmy had to make appointments with Robinson's secretary to see their father even on weekends.

Christmas and birthday gifts were big and expensive and usually bought by a secretary. Family outings were rare. The only time the Robinsons would gather together was to celebrate Christmas at the family's retreat at Sun Valley, Idaho.

"We didn't do much together," Robinson's son would later recall. "He would take only a couple of days' vacation and he would head back to work."

For years, Robinson had dismissed his wife's complaint that the children were uncontrollable. By the time they were teenagers, they had become a real problem.

Angry and rambunctious, Robinson's son was constantly in trouble. He attended three different boarding schools, including his father's alma mater, Woodberry Forest. Each time he was asked to leave because of disciplinary problems.

"I didn't want to be in a boarding school," the younger Robinson would later explain. "I wanted to be home."

Robinson's daughter was equally obstreperous. At seventeen, she ran away from Foxcroft, an exclusive girls' boarding school in Virginia. She hid out at a girlfriend's house in Germantown, Pennsylvania, until her father tracked her down and returned her to school.

Even in later years, Robinson's relationship with his children would remain strained. After her graduation from Foxcroft, Robinson decided Emily needed more supervision. He sent her to live with his mother in Atlanta. (Robinson's father had died in 1967.) Emily graduated from Emory in 1982, married a local architect and settled down as a housewife and mother.

As for Jimmy, he continued to wander. He even drove a New York cab for a while as part of an experimental "life experience" class at Antioch College. Rather than live at home, the younger Robinson stayed at a hotel for transients in Times Square.

Robinson urged his son to quit and return full-time to school. He pressed the point even harder when his son showed up bloodied and bruised at the family's River House apartment one morning. Jimmy had been beaten and robbed at gunpoint while driving a fare across the 59th Street Bridge.

"Of course, you're not planning to drive any more this morning," Robinson lectured his son.

"The hell I'm not," Jimmy shot back.

Robinson grew angry. His voice became agitated.

"Are you crazy?" he shouted. "You could be killed."

Defiantly, Jimmy stormed out of the apartment and finished his shift.

Robinson's son would go on to graduate from Antioch in 1984. Ironically, he, too, would enter Morgan Guaranty's management trainee program. Later, he would also enroll at Harvard Business School. But the similarities would end there. "I call myself Jim Robinson," he would tell people. "You'll find no Roman numerals after my name."

As the strains at home multiplied, Robinson came to rely more and more on his secretary, Ruth Finley. At first, their relationship was strictly business. But that would change as Robinson and Bettye drifted further apart.

Shapely, blue-eyed and blonde, Finley was pleasant to look at, but she was a terror to deal with. She arranged Robinson's office agenda, scheduled his appointments and kept him abreast of office gossip. Finley was the all-important gatekeeper. And she knew it.

Standing only five feet tall, Finley was feisty and contentious. Around AmEx, they called her "Mighty Mouse." She especially enjoyed berating senior VPs for wasting Robinson's time with trivia.

Finley had gone to work for Robinson in 1969, when he was still at White Weld. She initially had been reluctant to work for Robinson. He had a reputation of being demanding and unforgiving, punctual and picky. Long days and short weekends, Robinson's secretaries would gripe.

By the time Finley was offered the job, Robinson had already chewed up a string of secretaries. Personnel was down to feeding him a diet of agency temps. Still, Finley was ambitious. The word around White Weld was that "Jim is going places."

After a few months, Finley's relationship with Robinson became easier and friendly. She was quick and efficient at the office. And as Bettye's abilities deteriorated, Finley gradually took over many of her motherly functions. Buying the kids' clothes and doling out allowances became part of her unofficial job description. She took Emily and Jimmy on vacation to her parents' home in Pennsylvania.

Rather than being resentful, Bettye was thankful. In fact, it was Bettye who suggested that Robinson take Ruth along when he was recruited by American Express.

"She's so good with the kids," Bettye would say.

At AmEx, Finley's relationship with Robinson warmed considerably. Late-night suppers, weekend rendezvous and business trips together soon followed. There were whispers around AmEx headquarters that the pair were having an affair. Even Howard Clark suspected the two. Once he even refused to sign Robinson's expense account because it included a dinner with Ruth at the 21 Club, according to one former AmEx official. Clark and his wife, Jean, had always been fond of Bettye.

After he became CEO, Robinson was less concerned about appearances. He took Ruth to a variety of highly visible social functions as his date. She was seen at his side for charity events and cocktails. Once, she even accompanied Robinson to a July 4th party on Malcolm Forbes's yacht, *Highlander*. "Everyone knew about the affair. It was an open secret," one AmEx executive recalled.

Finley's career began to accelerate, as well. No longer content to be a secretary, she demanded and received a transfer to TRS as a vice president for customer service in 1979. Three years later, she was regional vice president for commercial sales. Robinson was reluctant to lose such a good secretary, but he realized Finley's ambitions wouldn't evaporate.

By the late seventies, Finley began broaching the subject of marriage. But Robinson carefully sidestepped the issue. He made no promises.

By 1980, Robinson was talking to Bettye about the possibility of divorce. Now, as CEO of American Express, he no longer cared about the board's reaction. But she repeatedly dismissed the notion as if Robinson were joking.

"Oh Jim, you don't want to do that," she would say.

He didn't press the point.

In 1981, Bettye's health deteriorated badly. She had put on a great deal of weight. She was forty-five, but looked much older. In May, she suffered a near-fatal stroke. She spent three months at Memorial Sloan Kettering Hospital, lapsing in and out of a coma. The doctors were grim.

Robinson was genuinely affected by his wife's condition. He wasn't weepy or emotional, but he clearly was distracted. At the office, Robinson spoke of Bettye's illness often. He visited his wife's bedside daily.

Robinson also grew closer to his children. His son in particular sensed a vulnerability in his father. Fearing that his mother might die, Jimmy wrote his father a rambling, seven-page letter. He wanted a reconciliation.

"We have to pull together," the letter read. "What's past is past." Robinson was so touched that he folded the letter in quarters and carried it around for weeks.

After Bettye's condition stabilized, she was transferred to the Burke Rehabilitation Center in White Plains, New York. A rehabilitation center specializing in neurological impairments, Burke offered Bettye an intense therapy program that allowed her to regain full use of her arms and legs. Later, Bettye even entered the Betty Ford Clinic for a few months to overcome her drinking problem.

Still, Bettye's illness and Robinson's newfound tenderness

could do little to salvage the Robinsons' marriage. After her brush with death, Bettye took a more critical view of her own life. She could no longer deny that her marriage was over. With her recovery proceeding at a quick pace, the Robinsons agreed to separate. Jim moved out of their River House apartment and into a smaller two-bedroom place at Olympic Towers. In early 1983, the divorce was final. Bettye ended up with a $1 million cash settlement and the family home in Sun Valley.

For years, Robinson had been wealthy and powerful. Now, he had the added bonus of being single again. Robinson was highly eligible, and women rushed to seek him out.

No longer distracted by his wife's illness or drinking problems, he began dating. The women he asked out, however, were not the usual corporate overachievers that he frequently came in contact with during business hours. Robinson was attracted by celebrities. He liked them young and striking. And before long, his name cropped up in the gossip columns of New York and Los Angeles.

Princess Yasmin, the daughter of actress Rita Hayworth and Aly Khan, was a frequent companion. At one point, Robinson even introduced her to his mother in Atlanta.

Skier-turned-actress Suzy Chaffee and slinky blonde Morgan Fairchild, best known for her role on "Falcon Crest," the prime-time soap opera, also dated AmEx's CEO.

"Morgan is one of the brightest women I know," Robinson would tell his colleagues.

At American Express, Robinson's liaisons became the topic of conversation around the coffee machines and water coolers. By 1982, Robinson's subordinates even began noticing a change in their boss's behavior—less stiff, less formal. Robinson wasn't exactly one of the guys, but he didn't seem so distant.

"Jim seemed more human than he ever was," recalled James Calvano, the former head of TRS marketing and later president of Western Union.

Of course, not everyone was happy with Robinson's easier manner. Old AmEx hands like George Waters, the Father of the Card, were especially enraged after Robinson danced until two-thirty in the morning with AmEx staffers during a TRS meeting in Orlando, Florida.

"Appalling," Waters said.

Toward the end of 1983, Robinson found a steady girl-friend. Her name was Linda Gosden.

Robinson had met Linda in 1982 at a Christmas party at his friend Drew Lewis's Washington, D.C., home. A ranking Republican, Lewis was Secretary of Transportation in the Reagan White House. He and Robinson (a frequent Republican fund-raiser) had become friends in the late 1970s. And in 1982, he was frequently calling on Robinson for advice. Tired of Washington's low pay and long hours, Lewis was ready to return to the private sector.

Linda was Lewis's chief public relations officer at Transportation. She handled everything from press releases to news conferences. Stroking the Washington press corps was one of her particular talents.

Robinson came stag; so did Linda. But after Lewis introduced them, they soon paired off. They remained together for most of the evening, later joining a small group which went dancing in Georgetown after the party. They seemed to have a mutual fascination.

To Gosden, the attraction was obvious. Robinson was courtly, charming and surprisingly youthful. He was also powerful, the leader of one of the best-known corporations in the country. In turn, AmEx's CEO found Linda refreshingly different from the women he had been dating.

Tall, slim, with strawberry-blond hair, Linda was hardly stunning. Indeed, she was rather plain. But Linda was tough, confident and very much at ease with AmEx's CEO. Though seventeen years his junior, she was smart, articulate and comfortable when discussing anything from baseball to the boardroom.

Linda was the opposite of Bettye. She was energetic and independent. Instead of complaining about Robinson's long hours and hard work, Linda was a business junkie. She was fascinated by Wall Street, its deals and personalities. Even better, she wanted to be a participant, not just an observer. She even spoke of heading her own company someday.

Robinson was also impressed with Linda's contacts. She was well-known in Washington and Los Angeles. Her acquaintances included Ronald Reagan and Frank Sinatra.

The daughter of Freeman Gosden, who played Amos in the enormously popular radio show "Amos 'n Andy," Linda was born in Los Angeles in 1952. Gosden was fifty-three years old when his daughter was born, and his career had long since faded. He remained a wealthy and influential personality in both the entertainment business and California politics. He and his wife, Jane, were familiar faces in Ronald Reagan's conservative Republican social set in Orange County.

The Gosdens lived like Hollywood royalty. Linda's family had a house at the luxurious El Dorado Country Club in Indian Wells, California, just south of Los Angeles. Her next door neighbor was Dwight D. Eisenhower. CBS Chairman William S. Paley was a close family friend.

At the time she enrolled at UCLA, Linda didn't seem to have any fixed career goals in mind. Her father had warned her away from show business. Too unpredictable, he would say. Instead, she pursued a liberal arts degree, only to drop out in her junior year to marry Stephen Dart, the son of Justin Dart, the founder and head of Dart Industries. Four years later, they were divorced.

Linda drifted for a while. After working briefly as a secretary at the UCLA acupuncture clinic, she returned to school and finished her degree. Law school followed, but she again dropped out after completing one year.

In 1979, Linda finally latched on to something when Reagan announced his candidacy for the presidency. A veteran of Reagan's gubernatorial campaigns and well-known to both the former governor and his wife, Nancy, Linda had no trouble landing a job. There was an opening in public relations and she took it.

Easygoing and plain-talking, she had a natural talent for dealing with the press. James Lake, the campaign's senior PR coordinator, began making frequent use of her skills when they went on the road. Linda soon began rising in the organization. She even developed a close working relationship with campaign manager John Sears and Charles Black, Reagan's political director.

Then came New Hampshire. The first primary went badly for Reagan. A shake-up followed. Linda's mentors, Sears, Lake and Black, were suddenly out. Their replacements were William Casey, Michael Deaver and Edwin Meese. Linda was also out. It was rumored that she resigned after a loud and boisterous showdown with Nancy Reagan.

Several weeks later, she landed another political job. This time, she worked directly for the Republican Party in Washington. Before long, she became friendly with Lewis, then the party's deputy chairman. Two years later, Lewis hired her as his own PR person.

Six months after their initial meeting, Robinson and Linda crossed paths again. Once more, they had Lewis to thank. Now out of government, Lewis was preparing to take over as CEO of Warner-AmEx. Gus Hauser had been head of the partnership since its inception. Although Hauser had been successful in winning many cable contracts in big cities, he was considered somewhat of a spendthrift. Both Robinson and Ross wanted someone who would be a little more frugal with the cable TV company's budget.

Robinson suggested Lewis. Though Lewis was hardly an expert on cable TV, he was a good administrator with solid Washington contacts. Ross went along.

Lewis was quick to accept. He began assembling his own staff to take along to New York. One of the first he approached was Linda. Lewis offered her the job as Warner-AmEx's top PR person. It packed a six-figure salary and a double-digit bonus.

She was reluctant. Washington was all politics, a kind of small company town. She was a player, a fixture on the Beltway's cocktail circuit. By contrast, New York was hectic and corporate. It was a big pond and she feared she would be a very small fish.

Lewis persisted. Remembering how Linda and Robinson had hit it off so well, he asked Jim to intervene. AmEx's CEO needed little coaxing. After a three-hour lunch with Robinson at the 21 Club, Linda agreed to move north. What followed was a classic courtship, complete with phone hugs, bouquets and intimate dinners at La Reserve.

Before long, they were an item. In the summer of 1983, Linda accompanied Robinson to Peter and Karen Cohen's fifteenth anniversary party. It was a lavish come-as-you-were-in-the-sixties party. The Cohens rented and redecorated the Automat just for the occasion. Linda was increasingly at Robinson's side for official events as well. The most notable was the black-tie dinner to commemorate the refurbishing and reopening of the Statue of Liberty.

So taken was Robinson with Linda that his decade-long

relationship with Ruth Finley finally came to an end. Finley had always known that Robinson dated other women. To her, they were "flings," short-term and casual.

"Do you feel you have to bring a date to every single party?" Finley would ask Robinson, half-jokingly.

Linda was different. Their dates were quiet and intimate. Robinson was never boastful.

"It's serious this time," Robinson would tell Finley.

Ruth was devastated. And, as she became less important to Robinson, she became less important to American Express. As Robinson's relationship with Linda progressed, Finley found herself increasingly isolated. She eventually resigned and moved home to Pennsylvania.

After a nine-month courtship, Robinson would suddenly announce to his staff on July 26, 1984, that he planned to marry Linda the following day. "I guess the pilot will be my best man," Robinson shrugged. Indeed, the only guests present at the wedding in Bretton Woods, New Hampshire, were the bride's and groom's mothers.

From then on, Linda Robinson would be seen differently. As Robinson's girlfriend, Linda was treated with respect, often affection. As his wife, she was feared. Over the next seven years, she would emerge as her husband's chief advisor in every major issue confronting American Express. As Robinson's power increased, Linda's influence spread.

EIGHT

The Fireman's Fund Fiasco

It was early morning when Edwin Cutler arrived at AmEx's fortieth-floor boardroom to give his assessment of 1983 and projections for 1984. Friendly and outgoing, the CEO of Fireman's Fund usually enjoyed his trips to New York. A little business, a little shopping, maybe a Broadway play, and then back to Novato, California, Fireman's home base. This time, he was somber and straight-faced, almost grim.

As Cutler headed toward the end of the table to arrange his notes, he paused by the window. Outside the weather was clear and crisp. The autumn sun was sending streaks of gold across the harbor below. Inside, however, Cutler felt hot and stuffy.

It was the second week of November, budget review season at American Express. Around this time, the heads of each of AmEx's business units would traditionally appear before the executive committee to discuss the outlook for the following year. So far, there had been few surprises. Shearson was going gangbusters. TRS was expecting another banner year. Even the bank was looking pretty good thanks to the acquisition of TDB.

Fireman's Fund was another matter. Throughout the fall, there had been ominous rumblings from the insurance company. Executives had been forecasting tough times ahead. Revenues were slipping. Profits were falling.

Robinson, who was in the midst of the IDS deal, had paid little attention. Weill, however, was alarmed. For much of his career, Weill had never left the office before calculating Shearson's overnight trading position. He didn't like surprises. He also was AmEx's second-largest shareholder.

In September, Weill had dispatched his twenty-seven-year-old assistant, Jamie Dimon, to California. Dimon's forte was number crunching. Around the office, he was known as the "Numbers Rat." He made the same trip several times over the ensuing weeks. What he found was a company out of control. The loss reserves were perilously low. Costs were soaring. Scariest of all, the profit picture looked bleak.

Even the media had gotten wind of the problems. *Fortune* magazine's veteran financial writer, Carol Loomis, began pestering American Express in September with questions about Fireman's Fund. Loomis had already been out to the company's headquarters in California. Before long, she had even interviewed a few AmEx executives, including Robinson. "Carol knows her stuff," Dimon had warned Weill. Her story would surely be hard-hitting and potentially very damaging.

This was Cutler's first appearance as CEO before the budget panel. He had replaced Myron DuBain, who had retired in late 1982. At fifty-six, Cutler had been with Fireman's Fund for almost thirty years. Anything but a golden boy, Cutler's rise was more measured than meteoric. He started out as an assistant bookkeeper in 1954, labored in the finance department and was named CFO in 1978.

Cutler's audience was solemn. Gathered around the conference table were Robinson, Weill, Cohen, Gerstner, Howard

Clark Jr. and Gary Beller, AmEx's chief corporate counsel. They all knew the news would be bad. Just how disappointing was the unanswered question.

"I don't have very good news," began Cutler. He then signaled an assistant to kill the lights and begin a slide show.

For the next fifteen minutes, using bar charts and line graphs, Cutler drew a picture of a company trapped in a slow-down. Premium income was off. Competition was stiff. Costs were rising. Slide after slide told the same sad story. This year was tough, next year tougher.

When the lights came on again, Robinson was visibly upset. He shook his head slowly from side to side.

"What's this mean to the bottom line?" Robinson asked. His tone was sharp and angry.

"We're probably looking at about $240 million," responded Cutler. That was some $50 million shy of previous forecasts. "Jim, you have to understand how bad business is."

Robinson paused. He did some quick mental calculations.

"That's not a 15% return," Robinson scowled. "We're lucky if it's 10%. You can't be serious."

Surprisingly, Robinson was less concerned with the specter of the forthcoming *Fortune* article than with the likelihood that Fireman's Fund would fall far short of its earnings target in 1983. If the insurance company missed its expected 15% profit growth, AmEx's record earnings streak would snap. A stellar profits picture was a legacy handed down from Ralph Reed to Howard Clark, and then to Robinson. It was part of corporate culture at American Express, part of the image of excellence.

What's more, the bad news couldn't have come at a worse time. To celebrate American Express's bounty at the close of 1983, Robinson had decided to take the board, the top executives and their spouses on a European tour. It was a symbolic affirmation of AmEx's global status. About sixty people in all would make the trip, a ten-day whirlwind through Geneva and Paris and then on to London for the final board meeting of 1983. Robinson did not want to put a damper on the trip.

The other AmEx managers, sensing their boss's mood, also voiced similar dismay at the news about Fireman's Fund. Gerstner was especially stinging. As the head of AmEx's flagship, Gerstner was cocky. He almost made it a practice of acting superior and somewhat haughty at business gatherings. This time was no exception.

"Ed, good companies earn 15%," said Gerstner. He couldn't have sounded more patronizing. Gerstner then turned away.

Cutler was exasperated. He knew Robinson wouldn't be happy. But he didn't expect such a dismissive reply. Given the recession throughout the industry, Cutler had thought he was doing a Herculean task. Now he was being treated like the village idiot.

"Compared to our peers, we don't look that bad," said Cutler. "Just look at our peers."

He was trying to sound heroic. Instead, he appeared defensive. Weill, who had his back to the screen during most of Cutler's presentation, pounced.

"Look at your peers! Look at your peers!" Weill shouted. "I've been listening to this bullshit for months. Whatever you did was wrong."

The meeting adjourned.

Ever since Howard Clark acquired Fireman's Fund in 1968, the insurance company had always been treated like a distant cousin. Tucked away in Novato, just outside San Francisco in Marin County, Fireman's Fund was old and established, founded in 1863. It never quite fit the role of an

American Express family member, however. Its basic business, property and casualty insurance, was about as exciting as a librarians' convention. It was all actuarial tables and claims processing.

Clark himself rarely took much interest. Fireman's Fund was nearly three times bigger than AmEx when Clark acquired it for about $500 million. But the takeover had been more a marriage of convenience than a strategic coup.

Mildly intrigued by the consumer possibilities of the insurance game, Clark took a look at a number of companies before settling on Fireman's Fund. The company's fat premiums and sound underwriting were not the decisive factors. What clinched the deal was the rising paranoia at American Express. The company was too profitable and too small, easy prey for an acquisitive suitor. Scooping up Fireman's Fund quadrupled AmEx's size. It also made the company quite indigestible for most M&A specialists.

As it turned out, the purchase proved far more beneficial than Clark had envisioned. By the seventies, the insurance business was booming. Corporations, municipalitics and individuals lined up for policies. Annuities and low-cost term life were big hits with the public.

Fireman's Fund's investment portfolio widened and so did its earnings. From 1975 to 1979, earnings climbed at a vigorous 15% annual rate. Unexpectedly, Fireman's Fund was a huge success. By the time Robinson replaced Clark, the insurance subsidiary accounted for 50% of AmEx's earnings.

Robinson was the first AmEx executive to recognize the strategic value of Fireman's Fund. Every expansion requires a corporate cash cow. American Express's insurance subsidiary was in-house and handy. Before long, DuBain and his staff found themselves under intense pressure from Robinson to fatten their returns. New York grew increasingly voracious and impatient. It was like a disease, the classic what-have-you-done-for-me-lately syndrome.

Once, in 1978, a banner year for Fireman's Fund, AmEx president Morley demanded that the insurance subsidiary kick in $10 million to help TRS overhaul its data processing division. It was to be a secret transfer. That way TRS could keep up the appearances and still meet its earnings target.

Cutler, then CFO, and chief counsel Borrell "Bo" Kirschen objected strenuously, but Morley was insistent.

"There's no way to keep this invisible," Kirschen shouted during a conference call to New York. "We're a regulated company."

"We want this done, so do it," Morley said.

At Fireman's Fund, they complained that AmEx was screwing around with their profit cycle. They even had a name for it: Cyclefuck.

Even when the insurance industry entered a slump in the early eighties, Robinson kept the pressure on. He wasn't a believer in the so-called "S" curve, the insurance industry's notorious boom and bust cycle.

After all, the buying binge was underway and Robinson couldn't afford to let up. Let's keep it coming, he told them after acquiring Shearson. We have to do better, he complained after purchasing TDB. Robinson wanted each business at American Express to have profit gains of 15% a year. He was insatiable.

DuBain had warned Robinson that the breathless earnings pace was bound to slow. Competition was cutting into the company's market share. Fireman's Fund fell from being the nation's sixth-largest insurer to tenth place in 1982. What's more, cutthroat competition had slashed premiums to sparse levels. Many insurers were losing money or just breaking even.

"This can't go on, Jim," DuBain complained.

"That's unacceptable," Robinson responded bluntly. He knew to what extent AmEx's earnings record depended on Fireman's Fund.

"You have to do more than just your share," Robinson lectured.

By 1980, however, executives at Fireman's Fund were running out of maneuvering room. Thanks to ferocious price cuts, premium income was falling. Earnings from the investment portfolio were slipping. But Robinson was relentless. "Managing earnings is your job," he told DuBain.

As revenues declined, executives at Fireman's Fund hatched a plan to shave off a portion of the company's "loss reserves" and use it to buttress sagging profits. Insurance companies are required by law to maintain tangible capital reserves, such as annuities and insurance policies, against liabilities. The practice is designed to protect companies from an unexpected wave of policy claims.

Over the years, executives had played games with the company's reserve levels. Fireman's Fund poured a hefty amount of its profits into its reserve accounts when times were good. But when business was off, the company was downright miserly. The practice wasn't illegal. But it created the false appearance of an earnings momentum.

Before long, the company took the strategy one step further. In 1980, Fireman's Fund negotiated an agreement with Insurance Company of North America to swap liabilities, allowing each company to jigger their respective reserve requirements. The strategy was known in the industry as "reinsurance." It, too, was perfectly legal.

Fireman's Fund ended up transferring all its pension-fund liabilities to INA. Thanks to this financial sleight of hand, AmEx's insurance unit freed up $109 million in reserves between 1981 and 1982. INA was paid $43 million for its efforts.

That left $66 million in pretax profits. It also preserved American Express's string of record profits. If it wasn't for such inventive paperwork, profits at Fireman's Fund would have been down in 1982.

While Robinson continued to marvel at the tenacity of Fireman's Fund, others began to grow suspicious. By 1983, Wall Street was openly skeptical about the company's bookkeeping. Gerry Lewisohn, a respected analyst at Merrill Lynch, went so far as to question the reliability of Fireman's Fund's results. *How could this company keep going in the middle of an industry downturn?* he wondered.

Lewisohn's very public suspicions were unprecedented on the Street. But other analysts joined in the speculation. So did California's Department of Insurance. There were rumors that the state regulator was about to launch a probe into unfair pricing practices at Fireman's Fund.

By 1983, even stealthy bookkeeping couldn't help Fireman's Fund. In July, the company reported a $17 million profit for June. The returns slipped to $6 million in July. Seldom had Fireman's Fund reported less than $20 million in a month.

Still, it wasn't until the long-awaited *Fortune* story on November 10 that the public got wind of Fireman's Fund's accounting practices. Robinson had a messenger standing by at the Time-Life Building to pick up a few early editions after the official release time of 5 P.M. Within thirty minutes, the AmEx brass was flipping through *Fortune*'s pages.

Just as Dimon had warned, Loomis indeed knew her stuff. In a 1,200-word article, titled "How Fireman's Fund Stoked Its Profit," she outlined how AmEx's insurance subsidiary pumped up its profits through reinsurance "treaties."

Robinson was quoted in the article defending the practice. AmEx's CEO had spent three days preparing himself for the interview with Loomis with the help of Harry Freeman,

AmEx's PR chief. Freeman believed that if Robinson could put up a strong defense, American Express could blunt the effects of *Fortune*'s article. It hadn't worked.

In the article, Robinson blamed proposed accounting rule changes for the bizarre bookkeeping at Fireman's Fund. He also admitted that he had urged Fireman's Fund to be more creative, "to stop giving me that ten-company-comparison crap." Weill, however, was quoted as saying the liability swap allowed for competitive pricing. Cutler had still another explanation: generating earnings.

Weill raced to Robinson's office.

"Did you finish it?" Weill asked, anxiously.

Robinson nodded glumly.

"What do you think?" Robinson asked. "It's pretty strong."

Weill agreed. The *Fortune* story was detailed and damaging. Worse, the contradictory statements from AmEx managers made Robinson and his lieutenants look foolish.

"She knows more about the business than we do," said Weill, as he paced nervously in front of Robinson's desk.

"Hunting season is open," he continued. "Every regulator, stockholder, every goddamn person connected to the insurance business will be all over us. And don't forget *The Wall Street Journal.*"

Within days, Weill's prediction proved correct. Every publication from the *Journal* to *Business Week* was dissecting the problems at Fireman's Fund. A group of shareholders promptly filed suit against American Express, alleging a cover-up. And the Securities and Exchange Commission launched a hurried investigation to determine if the earnings at Fireman's Fund had been overstated to bolster AmEx's results.

Even Alleghany CEO Fred Kirby was angered. AmEx had agreed to pay $773 million in cash and AmEx stock for IDS.

Thanks to the Fireman's Fund, AmEx stock fell by 10 points. He held up his board's final approval until Robinson made some adjustments. For Kirby, it was a kind of sweet revenge, dating back to the time Robinson nixed Weill's first offer for IDS. Ultimately, American Express agreed to pay $40 million in addition to the original price.

Robinson scheduled a crisis meeting for the following Monday. AmEx's earnings record was in jeopardy. Everyone was in a sweat, particularly Harry Freeman, whose job would be damage control.

Robinson was already toiling away when Weill, Beller and Freeman showed up at his office that Monday for their 8 A.M. meeting. An early riser, Robinson was usually in the office by six-thirty. Breakfast was typically coffee, a bowl of cornflakes and *The Wall Street Journal.*

One by one they filed in. Weill and Beller headed for the couch in the corner. Freeman sat in one of the two chairs immediately in front of Robinson's desk.

At once, they all began talking. Weill bellowed about the lousy management at Fireman's Fund. Beller worried about the SEC. And Freeman pointed to the damaging press clippings he had brought along.

"Okay, okay," said Robinson, restoring order. "We're getting the shit kicked out of us," he said. "We can't afford this. What will we do?"

Freeman explained how he had spent the weekend on the phone with his counterparts at Fireman's Fund. "Refer all questions to New York," he told them. "Don't say a word." It was the ultimate in spin control.

"We'll be the ones to tell the press what happened," he said confidently. "Don't worry about that, Jim."

Tall, with thinning gray hair and a pair of thick rounded

lips that were set in a perpetual grin, Freeman was more than just AmEx's head flack. A former lawyer and Washington bureaucrat, he had joined American Express in 1975 as its chief lobbyist. As PR chief, he obsessed over every crisis, big or small.

The next step was easy. Cutler was out.

"He's got to go. We need new management," Weill said. "We need somebody who can get the job done."

Robinson quickly agreed. A new management team would make it appear that he was quick and decisive. *Image, gentlemen. Let's not forget the image.* Robinson also felt it was an opportune time to install a friendlier CEO, someone more sympathetic to the needs of the home office, someone who could deliver a 15% profit gain.

"Right after Thanksgiving," he vowed.

Weill argued that Fireman's Fund needed more than just a corporate clean sweep. He believed the company needed a shake-up. And that meant exporting more than just a new face to California. The job needed talent as well—"someone who could kick ass," Weill said.

"Without some major changes, we could get messed up again," he told Robinson.

"Fine," Robinson said. "But who the hell do we have who can do it?"

Both men began making notes. Who was capable of the job was the first qualification. Who was expendable was the next. The pair came up with a short list, three names at most.

George Sheinberg, AmEx's treasurer, was one of Weill's leading candidates. Still smarting from what he believed was Sheinberg's ambush during the IDS acquisition, Weill would have gladly shipped his former friend 3,000 miles away. Robinson objected, however. Not enough management experience, he said.

Then they discussed Bill McCormick. A former McKinsey consultant, McCormick had been regarded as a brilliant strategist at TRS. But he was outspoken. In Gerstner's eyes, he was downright irreverent.

"Not our man," Gerstner said.

Once again, Robinson turned thumbs down.

That left Robert Smith. A bean-counter extraordinaire, Smith had been a finance executive at General Electric before becoming AmEx's treasurer. After the acquisition of Shearson, he was shunted aside to make way for Sheinberg as a way of showing corporate harmony. But Smith was still highly regarded. He was hard-nosed and hungry. Ever since he lost his post to Sheinberg, Smith had been eager for a task that would finally earn him some recognition. Weill in particular was a big fan. A native of Staten Island, Smith had the same rough edges.

"He's the toughest son-of-a-bitch in the company," Weill said. "Nobody can bullshit him."

Robinson smiled.

"Sandy, that's our man," he said.

It was cloudy and cold on the Saturday morning after Thanksgiving. A stinging wind was sweeping across the tarmac at Westchester County Airport as the crowd from AmEx gathered in the company hangar for some last-minute announcements. To handle the crowd, the company had mobilized the entire American Express air force. Two Gulfstream III corporate jets would be fully stocked with caviar and champagne. One Gulfstream was set aside just for the luggage.

Robinson played genial host, greeting every board member and spouse in turn. Also helping out with the reception duties was Robinson's mother, Josephine. At that time, Robinson had been dating Linda for less than six months and felt it wasn't proper to bring her along on such a formal business trip. Instead, he had asked his mother to accompany him. Robinson graciously accepted the ribbing about his "older date."

As AmEx's sleek, gray Gulfstreams lifted off one by one into the clouds, Robinson was surprisingly relaxed. With the decision to send Smith to Fireman's Fund, Robinson finally felt relieved. The past two weeks had been an ordeal. Over the next ten days, Robinson was hoping to unwind.

Throughout the eight-hour flight, Robinson was cheerful. He was even gregarious. On most trips, Robinson would generally sit alone, culling through the contents of twin black briefcases that accompanied him on all out-of-town journeys. This time the satchels remained unopened all the way to Geneva. Instead, he sipped some white wine and made small talk with board members.

High on the European agenda was some hand-holding with Edmond Safra. Ever since AmEx had acquired Safra's Trade Development Bank the previous January, Safra had grown increasingly disenchanted. He felt neglected, out of the loop.

The first oversight in Safra's mind occurred shortly after signing the merger agreement, when he was informed matter-of-factly that AmEx's Bob Smith would be his number two man at the bank. Safra was dumbfounded by the news. He had never been consulted and had hoped to give the job to his second-in-command at TDB, Albert Benezra. A Turkish Jew, Benezra had been a Safra confidant for decades. He was Safra's operations man, who oversaw every detail at TDB, from staffing to client contact.

Still, the worst insult to Safra was Robinson's near-total disregard for him during the acquisition of IDS in the summer of 1983. Safra learned of the $773 million acquisition from the Dow Jones ticker.

Incensed, Safra had phoned Cohen at home. It was 10:00 A.M. in Geneva, 4:00 A.M. New York time, but Safra would not wait for an explanation.

"What is DSI? Or SDI?" he yelled over the phone.

"Edmond, what is it? Oh, you mean IDS," replied a bleary-eyed Cohen. "Didn't Jim tell you?"

"Tell me what?" thundered Safra. His tone turned suddenly hostile. "I'm the company's biggest shareholder and nobody's been telling me anything."

"I'm not happy," he complained frequently to Cohen, his friend and closest ally at AmEx.

Though he was worldly and sophisticated—he spoke five languages fluently—Safra preferred to do business the old-fashioned way. He favored handshakes and eye contact over memos and committees. Throughout his negotiations with Cohen, he kept badgering Shearson's chief about Robinson's character. "Can I trust him?" he asked time and time again. Now, it appeared he couldn't.

The European junket was a chance for Robinson to heal the rift. Safra and his wife, Lily, were designated the official hosts of the tour. It seemed only fitting. As a member of the board and head of AmEx's bank, Safra was the ranking executive in Europe. He also knew the continent better than anyone at American Express. Though he was born in Beirut, Safra divided his time between a house in Geneva and an apartment in Paris. He was continental to the core.

By the time the group landed at Geneva International Airport, it was early evening. Everyone was jet-lagged, tired and achy, eager to get to their hotels. Safra had an advance team ready. With almost military precision, the luggage was unloaded, customs expedited. A dozen Mercedes limousines stood ready to ferry the travelers to their destination.

Safra was waiting at Robinson's hotel when the AmEx

contingent arrived. Warm and effusive, he didn't quite fit the image of a mysterious international financier. Safra was balding and heavyset. He had a round, chubby face with a bulbous nose and deep furry eyebrows.

He was the consummate host. Bouquets of roses, chocolates and gold Piaget watches awaited his guests in each of their rooms. "With the compliments of Lily and Edmond Safra," the attached cards said.

The first night was all social. Albert Benezra, Safra's right-hand man, threw an elaborate dinner at his lavish apartment just outside Geneva. Business was out of bounds that night. The main topic was the upcoming week's itinerary. Dinner with Edward Rothschild, a reception for the Duke of Edinburgh, and a private tour of Notre Dame were some of the highlights. Betty Ford, whose husband was an AmEx board member, was looking forward to shopping at Hermès, a chic Paris boutique.

By Monday morning, Safra was ready for business. His earlier complaints about American Express were now dwarfed by the pressing problems at Fireman's Fund. Not only was he stunned by the setbacks at Fireman's Fund, but it was costing him money as well. Safra was paid $550 million in AmEx stock for TDB. Now, in a matter of days, he had lost millions.

He had scheduled a 9:00 A.M. meeting with Robinson at his suite at the Hotel Des Bergues. True to form, Safra was punctual.

Robinson was already talking over some business with Weill when Safra knocked.

"Edmond, good morning," Robinson said warmly, as he opened the door.

Safra shook his hand briskly. The warmth that had been there in previous days was clearly gone.

"Jim, I am very unhappy," said Safra as he sat down across

from Robinson. His tone was subdued, but purposeful. "I look like a fool because of your company's problems."

"Edmond, I . . ." Robinson began. Safra cut him short.

Rising from his chair, Safra continued, his voice growing increasingly agitated.

"This Fireman's Fund business. It's outrageous, these losses," Safra railed at Robinson.

AmEx's CEO was silent. Robinson knew Safra was upset, but only now did he realize the depth of his anger.

"What is going on here? This is your company, is it not?" asked Safra, leveling his index finger directly at Robinson. "Is American Express out of control?"

As Safra's momentary outburst subsided, Robinson began to respond. Quietly and soothingly, he tried to reassure his newest executive and shareholder.

"Edmond," Robinson said. "We have recognized the problem and we are going to fix it."

"And just how do you intend to perform this miracle?" Safra shot back facetiously. "I really would like to know."

"It's simple," interrupted Weill, who had remained silent during Safra's tirade. "We're going to put new faces in Fireman's Fund. I guarantee you it will be better."

Safra calmed down and reclaimed his seat. But the peace wasn't long-lasting. When he was told that Smith would take over Fireman's Fund, Safra erupted again.

"No. Not him," Safra thundered.

Smith was Safra's point man in New York. He was the bridge between Safra and the rest of American Express, his eyes and ears in New York.

"I need Smith," said Safra. "It's out of the question."

Robinson and Weill were growing impatient. But neither wanted to offend Safra. They explained why Smith was the logical choice. One by one, they ticked off their reasons.

Safra didn't care. Ever since the Fireman's Fund scandal broke, Safra had suspected that Robinson had misled him about the health of American Express. Now he feared that Robinson was trying to further isolate him by taking Smith away.

"If Smith goes to California, then I will leave American Express," Safra said. A quick look at Safra's face showed he wasn't bluffing.

Robinson, the consummate consensus-builder, assured Safra that nothing would occur without his consent.

"We'll work something out that will make everyone happy," said Robinson. He was smiling to defuse the tension.

Safra calmed down.

"Fine, but I want to be consulted from now on," Safra said. He bid Robinson and Weill a polite but curt good-bye.

After Safra left, Robinson and Weill sat speechless. Safra's rage was unexpected. Fireman's Fund had suddenly become a problem again. Smith was out. Robinson needed someone else.

It was midafternoon by the time Robinson came up with a compromise candidate, someone acceptable to Safra and the board. He phoned Weill's suite and asked him to drop by in fifteen minutes. Weill was there in five.

"Look, we have to do something dramatic about Fireman's Fund," Robinson told Weill. "We have to make a statement. We have to show that we truly care."

Weill agreed. But who did Robinson have in mind? The answer was something of a shock.

"I want *you* to go to California, Sandy," Robinson said. "Put this Fireman's Fund problem behind us for good."

Weill stared straight ahead, gripping the arms of his chair. He didn't say a word.

"Take Bill McCormick. You two will make a great team," Robinson continued. "The situation calls for creative problem-solvers. You two fit the bill."

Weill hesitated. He was in no mood to pick up and move to the West Coast. That was 3,000 miles away from home and the home office. He suspected that Robinson was trying to banish him. But he had few defenses left. By the end of 1983, Weill had been encircled, his once freewheeling style dramatically curtailed. At the top, Weill was wedged between AmEx's CEO and Gerstner. From behind, he worried about Cohen. Worse, the board remained Robinson's territory. Weill was outgunned and outmaneuvered.

"Your mind is made up, then?" Weill asked.

"It's the best solution," Robinson responded.

"What about Shearson?" asked Weill. Surely, he thought, he couldn't abandon Shearson.

"Shearson can report to me. Don't worry about that, Sandy," Robinson said. "Yes, I think this will work just fine."

Robinson had every reason to savor the moment. It was a fatal blow to Weill. AmEx's president would be out of New York and out of mind. Even better, Weill would be completely severed from his remaining power base at Shearson. There would be no more talk of Weill unseating Robinson. It was a win-win solution. If Weill solved the problems at Fireman's Fund, so much the better. If he couldn't, Weill would be out. AmEx's chief delighted in his own brilliance. *Now I've got him.*

In later weeks, Weill put on a brave front. He would tell his colleagues that he welcomed the assignment. After all, he still owned some $30 million worth of AmEx stock. He also said he welcomed the challenge of managing a turnaround. But it was obvious to everyone at AmEx that Weill was on his way out.

"I'm being exiled," Weill confided to his friends.

Seven days later at the prescheduled board meeting in London, Robinson outlined his plans. The board approved. Weill was made chairman of Fireman's Fund. McCormick would become the company's CEO. Cohen was named CEO of Shearson.

Weill knew now that he would never topple Robinson. Still, he carried on. He loved challenges. Sorting out the problems at Fireman's Fund was just the kind of task he could enjoy for a while. It was like old times.

By January, Weill was in high gear. A sudden surge in insurance claims in the last months of the year sent Fireman's Fund reeling. Earnings for 1983 tumbled to a paltry $30 million from $244 million the previous year. What's more, AmEx had to shore up the company's loss reserves by pumping in $230 million in fresh capital. AmEx earnings fell 11% in 1983—the first decline in thirty-six years.

Weill and McCormick embarked on a nationwide tour of Fireman's Fund offices, from Chicago to Houston and then to Los Angeles. They spoke with sales agents, office managers and underwriters. It was a crash course in insurance. Fireman's Fund 101, they would joke to each other. Two weeks later, it was off to Novato.

Weill rented a small apartment three miles away from the company's offices. Rather than uproot his family, he would catch the red-eye to New York every Friday and head back again to California on Monday.

Through January and February, Weill labored full-time in California. Then he cut back to one week a month through the rest of the year. At first, there was a bit of culture shock. Weill's office overlooked a cow pasture.

At Novato, Weill went out of his way to repair the damaged morale. Everyone had liked Cutler. He was honest and fair. To them, he was merely a scapegoat, a sacrifice to Robinson's public relations machine. Weill tried hard to win the staff over. He acted more like a cheerleader than a boss. He spoke of "team spirit" and "sticking together."

Cutler sounded the same themes during a farewell party in the company cafeteria. It was fiery and emotional. He ended with: "By God, we'll triumph." Weill walked over, embraced Cutler and kissed him on the cheek.

It wasn't long before Weill had fashioned a recovery strategy. Fireman's Fund was trying to live the good life of the seventies on the diminishing returns of the eighties. It was slash and burn time in Novato.

Borrowing a page from his Shearson management manual, Weill pared the staff by 20%. Nearly 1,500 people received pink slips by the end of 1984. Costs shrank by $65 million. Weill also tried to rid the firm of its tedious bureaucracy.

"They do a lot of memos—Mr. Somebody to Mr. Somebody," he told an interviewer. "I prefer first names."

In New York, Weill's position at American Express was growing more tenuous. Robinson had hoped that by exiling Weill to California he could stop looking over his shoulder. Indeed, for a while, the grapevine was silent. But Weill's success in dealing with the fiasco at Fireman's Fund provided new ammunition for the rumormongers.

Once again, Robinson became defensive. *Why won't Sandy go away?* In March, 1984, Robinson fumed at the Bing Crosby Pro-Am Golf Tournament at Pebble Beach. Weill's foursome included Gerald Ford and Jack Nicklaus. The most notable member of Robinson's group was a Florida surgeon.

And it wasn't just Robinson who was suspicious of Weill. Although their marriage was still four months away, Linda Gosden was slowly emerging as a chief advisor to Robinson on matters ranging from PR to personnel. She had grown especially distrustful of Weill, say AmEx executives. Sandy was shrewd. Jim was a gentleman. She cautioned Robinson: *Sandy wants your job.*

In late March, Robinson and Linda dined with the Weills at the 21 Club. Invigorated by his early success in California, Weill began to outline his other plans for American Express. Tighter budget controls and less red tape were high on Weill's list. Robinson agreed. Linda was quiet. To her, it sounded like Weill was on the move again. Silently, she doodled on her napkin. Over and over again, she wrote one word: *Power.*

Before the end of 1984, Robinson had finally decided to unload Fireman's Fund. It was during that time that AmEx's CEO had decided to rid himself of all corporate stragglers. Indeed, at roughly the same time, Robinson began taking the necessary steps to sell off Warner-AmEx. After investing another $200 million in the cable company, AmEx had still not earned a nickel. The board was anxious and Robinson was nervous. He sold AmEx's 50% interest to Ross for $450 million. In doing so, he walked away from almost a billion dollars' worth of cable franchises, just at a time when the company was beginning to pay off.

To Robinson, Fireman's Fund was more painful. He treated the company as if it were a leper. He paid little attention. Indeed, throughout 1984, McCormick, the CEO of Fireman's Fund, seldom heard from Robinson. In November, Robinson was shocked to learn that he had to inject another $200 million into the company.

Just how bad Robinson wanted out would become quite clear at an AmEx managers' meeting at Boca Raton in early 1985. McCormick made a forty-minute presentation on Fireman's Fund. It was upbeat and hopeful. But when he finished, the room was silent, not a single clap, not even a comment.

"Great job," Weill told him later. "But it's too late. Robinson wants to get rid of the company."

Carefully groomed to be the CEO of American Express, James D. Robinson III has always presented the perfect patrician image.

(AP/Wide World Photos)

Beset by corporate worries on his AmEx jet, Robinson had little time
to contemplate the horizon.

Several weeks later, Weill got wind of a rumor that AmEx was about to dump Fireman's Fund. The report had it that West Germany's giant insurance conglomerate, Allianz, had approached Robinson with an offer. Weill began to think.

He pressed Robinson for details. AmEx's CEO confirmed the report. Yes, there was an offer. Yes, Fireman's Fund was for sale. Weill then made his pitch.

"Look, Jim," he said, "I may not be around the company much longer. Why not sell it to me?"

Weill went on to explain how he was thinking about a leveraged buyout.

At first, Robinson hesitated. It wouldn't look good for one of his senior executives to buy a big piece of the company. But he finally relented.

"All right," Robinson said. "But keep it quiet."

Weill flew into action. Within days, he had located a potential partner. He knew he would need someone with a sterling reputation to sway Robinson and the skeptical American Express board. Weill was sure he had a winner: Warren Buffett, the CEO of the Berkshire Hathaway Group.

Buffett was one of the more unlikely investment gurus, a Midwesterner, plain and simple. He disdained Wall Street, preferring to set up shop in his native Omaha. But his image was squeaky-clean. In later years, Buffett would be tapped to head Salomon Brothers after John Gutfreund resigned amid a government securities trading scandal. And Robinson would call on Buffett himself in 1991 to invest in American Express as a way to boost market confidence in the company.

Conveniently for Weill, Buffett was planning to come to New York the following week on business. He agreed to meet for breakfast at the Plaza.

"Warren," Weill began, "I'm thinking about an LBO of Fireman's Fund."

Buffett looked at him curiously. "Are you sure?"

"I know what you're thinking. But listen to me. I don't bet on losers."

For the next hour, Weill outlined his turnaround strategy. He would cut costs further, restore profits and cash in when the industry rebounded.

"Are you interested?"

"Sandy, I am interested, but I have one problem. I don't like the insurance business," Buffett said. "Too volatile."

"Warren, I agree," said Weill. "But there's one surefire way of minimizing the risks."

"What's that?"

Weill winked at Buffett. "Good management."

Buffett was intrigued enough to invite Weill out to Omaha for a follow-up meeting. Weill was again very persuasive. Buffett had done his homework as well. Within two days, Weill returned from Nebraska with a new partner.

By May they made an offer. The terms Weill and Buffett offered Robinson were simple. American Express would retain 40% of Fireman's Fund. Buffett would receive another 40% and Weill would get the remaining 20%. The deal was worth $1.6 billion.

Robinson studied the offer for almost a month. It was attractive. But the board wasn't very enthusiastic. "Too much debt," Howard Clark Sr. complained.

Image was a far more serious problem. Robinson worried that Weill could resell Fireman's Fund at a higher price. Indeed, AmEx's attorneys warned that the board faced potential shareholder suits if Weill sold it for a handsome profit. Worse, the industry could rebound. Weill would look like a genius, Robinson a patsy.

Not surprisingly, Robinson turned the deal down.

Two weeks later, Weill walked into Robinson's office. He

wanted to discuss his future. Robinson had offered him the chance to run Fireman's Fund full-time for American Express. As an enticement he offered Weill a compensation package potentially worth $80 million over five years. It would have been the biggest paycheck in corporate history.

Weill, however, wanted out.

"Jim, I'm flat-out exhausted, mentally and physically," Weill said. "I just want to leave."

Within days, on June 25, 1985, American Express would announce Weill's resignation. Simultaneously, the company would appoint Gerstner as AmEx's president.

NINE

The Mysterious Edmond Safra

For American Express, Fireman's Fund was a turning point. It was the biggest blow to Robinson's image since McGraw-Hill. Robinson claimed he was taken completely by surprise by the insurance company's troubles. But critics openly challenged the AmEx CEO's veracity as the story unfolded. *How could he not know? Who's in charge?* Edmond Safra would remain among the toughest questioners.

The suddenness of the Fireman's Fund fiasco and the fact that Robinson was caught off guard stunned Safra. And his angry exchange with Robinson in Geneva only reinforced his low opinion of AmEx's CEO. "Are these real businessmen?" he would ask his colleagues.

Especially galling was learning through press reports about the dire condition of Fireman's Fund. It was IDS all over again. Not once had he ever been consulted about AmEx's insurance unit, Safra complained to associates. The Lebanese banker was enraged. To him, Robinson's handling of Fireman's Fund was the latest in a string of tactless affronts and perceived slights.

Long before the news broke about Fireman's Fund, Safra had already been grumbling about his relationship with American Express and its CEO. He complained about the lack of contact with Robinson. He also griped about the messy interiors of AmEx's corporate jets. Safra's headquarters at AmEx was a source of more contention. Instead of an office in the executive suite near Robinson on the fortieth floor at American Express Plaza, Safra found himself on the twenty-third floor with the rest of the banking staff.

AmEx's tangled bureaucracy had been another sore spot. Safra once tried to donate a $500,000 bonus he had received from AmEx to one of his favorite charities, the International Red Cross. But officials of the American Express Foundation blocked the donation. Safra was told that the Red Cross had already received their maximum allotment from American Express. "This is crazy," Safra shouted. "This is *my* money to give away!"

And then there was AmEx's annoying marketing arm. No sooner had the merger of AmEx and TDB been completed than Safra's customers were deluged with junk mail from American Express. AmEx hawked everything from term life insurance to Shearson's real estate partnerships.

AmEx's marketing mavens even came up with a new product, the Black Card. It was supposed to be the most prestigious link in AmEx's color-coded line of plastic. Black Card holders could call AmEx hotline numbers anywhere in the world for a seemingly endless list of services. From sending flowers to hiring a bodyguard, the Black Card program was available to anyone with at least $500,000 on deposit. Once, with only twenty-four hours' notice, AmEx even provided a Black Card holder with 50,000 pounds for a down payment on a house in London's exclusive St. John's Wood.

Safra was horrified by such intrusive marketing techniques. And when his longtime customers began complaining, Safra demanded that Robinson halt the program. "You're up-setting my customers," he repeatedly told AmEx's CEO. "You'll ruin my business." Indeed, AmEx's modern-day theo-ries of product cross-selling and mass marketing were anathema to Safra. They were an invasion of privacy. He was a Swiss-style private banker. To Safra, discretion was the cornerstone of TDB, client anonymity a virtue. Safra was angry that lists of his clients were being widely circulated at American Express.

They were traits that had served Safra and TDB well. Headquartered in Geneva with branches in Paris and London, TDB was one of the classiest banking franchises in the world. It was the centerpiece of the Safra empire that also included Banco Safra in Brazil and Republic National Bank of New York. Founded in 1956, TDB catered to the needs of only the wealthiest of individuals. The minimum deposit was $500,000. Transfers of $10 million were common.

But there never was a dearth of customers. By the time Safra sold the bank to AmEx in January, 1983, TDB had roughly $5 billion in deposits. Many clients were attracted by Safra's low-key approach. They preferred sleeping easy to investing recklessly. There were no junk bond funds and few stock port-folios to speak of. TDB was banking at its blandest: low-yield deposit accounts.

Safra himself was TDB's most valuable asset. Indeed, by 1980, the Safra name was synonymous with private banking. Moreover, people spoke of the Safra mystique.

A Sephardic Jew, Safra was descended from a long line of Syrian bankers, who at one time financed much of the camel caravan trade under the old Ottoman Empire. Gold trading had been another centuries-old family specialty. In fact, "Safra" is the Arabic word for yellow.

Yet, Safra's roots were more international than regional.

He was born in Beirut, carried a Brazilian passport and divided his time between apartments in Geneva and Paris and, later, a castle-like villa on the French Riviera. La Leopolda, as it was called, was once the summer home of the King of Belgium.

Safra was never especially enthusiastic about joining the AmEx empire in 1983. On the eve of the merger agreement, he flew to São Paulo to consult with his brother, Joseph. He even visited his father's grave site, hoping for some guidance. "Every time I do something I talk with him about whether it's right or wrong," Safra told friends.

Even in the midst of negotiations, Safra hesitated. Just three hours prior to signing the final papers, Safra astonished Robinson when he suddenly suspended the talks. It was only after his brother flew to Montreal for last-minute consultations that Safra proceeded with the deal.

Despite his misgivings about the merger, Safra had little choice. His bank was in need of a benefactor with deep pockets. TDB held upwards of $800 million worth of bad loans made to countries like Brazil and Mexico. And the likelihood of a further deterioration in TDB's Third World loan portfolio threatened Safra's other banking interests.

Prior to the merger with American Express, Safra had explored other avenues. One solution was to have Republic acquire TDB. As a U.S. bank, Republic and ultimately TDB would have access to the Federal Reserve, the lender of last resort. But central bank officials balked at the potential liabilities.

Of all AmEx's executives, Cohen was the most sensitive to Safra's unease. The merger with TDB was Cohen's idea. Moreover, the Lebanese banker was a close friend. "He's like my second father," Cohen would say.

Cohen frequently found himself thrust in the uncomfortable and unwanted role of mediator: soothing Safra on one end while nudging Robinson on the other. "He's really steamed," Cohen would tell Robinson. "Talk to him." To Cohen it was a no-win situation. Often, keeping Safra happy meant upsetting Robinson.

Initially, Robinson was responsive. AmEx's chief had long been a great admirer of Safra's reputation and international connections. He felt sure that an alliance with Safra would enhance AmEx's business ambitions abroad, as well as invigorate AmEx's sluggish banking franchise. *You can't put a price tag on the Safra name,* Robinson would tell his staff. He was eager to ease Safra into AmEx's bureaucracy as painlessly as possible. Frequent phone calls and occasional weekend trips to Geneva were common at first. American Express even hired several Sephardic Jews from the New York branch of Israel's Bank Leumi so that Safra wouldn't feel totally alien.

The honeymoon was short-lived, however. Within months of the merger, Robinson began looking at Safra as more eccentric than legendary. Although sophisticated and worldly, Safra had strong Sephardic roots. He tried to avoid signing a contract on a Monday, which he is said to have considered bad luck. Indeed, Safra insisted that the merger agreement be signed on January 18 because the Hebrew word for life is the equivalent of the number 18, which to him implied good fortune.

Worse, Robinson complained increasingly that Safra rarely came to New York. Safra's office at AmEx's headquarters was routinely vacant. He was either in Europe or Brazil and considered hard to reach. "Where is he?" Robinson would ask. Once Harry Freeman recalled that Safra even balked at boarding an AmEx Gulfstream II that was sent to fly him from Geneva to New York. Safra felt slighted because he knew AmEx had a newer Gulfstream III model in its air force. "You had the feeling you were dealing with God," Freeman later would say of Safra.

By the spring of 1984, Safra and Robinson were barely speaking. Safra communicated with Cohen while Robinson dealt mostly with Smith. As TDB's number two man, Smith had also grown tired of Safra. He coveted the top spot at the bank and was eager to ingratiate himself to Robinson. "He's never around," Smith would routinely lament.

Feeling encircled and frustrated, Safra had had enough. "I have to get out of this," he told Cohen.

But rather than ask Cohen to serve in his customary role of intermediary, Safra cautioned Shearson's CEO to be distant. Indeed, Cohen was already looked upon as a Safra ally. Harry Freeman had even accused Cohen of being a double agent. "He's not part of our team," Freeman would counsel Robinson.

"Peter, I don't want you to get hurt in the cross fire," Safra told Cohen. "Jim will mistrust you if things go badly between him and me."

Safra notified Robinson of his decision by phone. He wanted to resign from the bank. The conversation was short and polite. The two agreed the parting should be amicable. It was just a matter of simple negotiations. Robinson, however, was distraught. Without Safra's name, he questioned the value of TDB's franchise. American Express's mighty publicity machine had made quite a splash after the acquisition of TDB. AmEx had trumpeted Safra as the company's point man in Europe.

He also wasn't looking forward to an embarrassing confrontation with the board, so soon after the debacle at Fireman's Fund. AmEx's acquisition of TDB had been controversial all along. Several board members questioned the wisdom of combining such a secretive banking operation with a giant publicity-oriented corporation like American Express. Former AmEx CEO Howard Clark Sr. had led the opposition. "Safra won't fit in. This deal could be trouble," he had advised

Robinson. Robinson did not want to be reminded that Clark had been right.

In September, both sides began discussing the terms of Safra's withdrawal. Jeffrey Keil, a Safra protégé and president of Republic National Bank, handled the negotiations. Keil was leery of AmEx's intentions. A former investment banker at Shearson, Keil was a close friend of Cohen's and was well aware of AmEx's bitterness toward Safra.

"This is a PR-driven company," Keil warned Safra. "Be careful or they'll lower the boom on you."

To counter AmEx's publicity apparatus, Keil decided he needed some PR muscle of his own. He turned to Gershon Kekst. Kekst & Company was one of the best gunslingers on Madison Avenue and its reputation was well-known to Robinson. Kekst had handled McGraw-Hill's PR counterattack during Robinson's aborted takeover attempt years earlier.

Despite the avowed intention of both Robinson and Safra to part friends, the talks dragged on for months. Often tense, sometimes bitter, both sides could find little common ground.

Robinson's biggest concern was that Safra would found a competing bank and siphon away many of AmEx Bank's clients. He demanded that Safra agree to a "non-compete" clause in his severance agreement. The provision prohibited Safra from opening a new bank or hiring away any of his former staff until March, 1988, three years away.

Keil agreed. It would take that long just to put together a new banking operation. Still, he used the clause as a bargaining chip. He wanted to persuade Robinson to sell TDB's Geneva headquarters back to Safra. When it came to Swiss banking, the six-story building overlooking Lake Geneva was nothing short of a landmark.

The next stage proved much tougher. Safra and Robinson

had to agree to the wording of the press release announcing Safra's resignation. AmEx's first version suggested that Safra wasn't up to the job. With all his other commitments, Safra didn't have adequate time to devote to American Express Bank, the release suggested. Keil and senior executives from Kekst objected strenuously. It was a none-too-subtle slight.

"Jim, this is not acceptable," Keil told Robinson. "Edmond is quitting. You make it look like he's being fired."

Ultimately, Robinson agreed to a more benign wording. But that didn't stop executives at American Express from taking potshots in the press. *The Wall Street Journal* quoted Smith as saying, "I think it's awfully difficult to motivate a billionaire. I don't think he wanted to be involved in the day-to-day operations of a complex organization such as this."

After the negotiations ended, Safra believed his dealings with American Express were finally finished. But they had only begun.

To AmEx, Safra had not only backed out of his commitment, but the prospect of a new Safra bank loomed large. Around AmEx headquarters, Safra became Public Enemy Number One.

Freeman was especially unnerved. As one of three executive vice presidents, Freeman's responsibilities included corporate and government relations, as well as advertising. He was the lord protector of AmEx's image.

Freeman was among the strongest advocates for Safra's non-compete clause. "He'll kill us if we give him half a chance," he told Robinson. "We have to think of our image."

Safra was publicity-shy, almost reclusive, a PR man's nightmare. Outside of a few initial requests immediately after the merger, Safra would routinely ignore Freeman's pleadings to be more outgoing and responsive to the press. "He isn't living up to his end," Freeman would complain. "He's making us look foolish." Soon, Freeman grew to loathe Safra.

What's more, he even feared him. Safra's secretive ways fed Freeman's suspicious nature. "He smelled conspiracies everywhere," recalled a former AmEx board member. "That was his whole life: plots and ferreting out conspiracies." In his darkest moments, he even foresaw an alliance of Safra, Cohen and Weill, which could overthrow Robinson.

Freeman continually fed his fears to Robinson. Over the years he had become Robinson's closest advisor, a sounding board on matters ranging from personnel to politics. The two met every morning in Robinson's office promptly at 7:00 A.M. to discuss the chairman's agenda. "Coping with the crisis *du jour*" was the way Freeman described his job.

After one such meeting in late October, Freeman emerged from Robinson's office red-faced and angry. The Safra resignation was beginning to look bad. There was talk of shareholder lawsuits in the wake of Safra's abrupt exit. The press was openly speculating about TDB's viability. So was the board. "Safra could cripple our bank," lamented one board member.

Freeman assembled his staff. Damage control headed the agenda. He wanted to make sure everyone understood the company line. It was all Safra's fault. And he expected to see that same explanation in every publication, from *The Wall Street Journal* to the *Des Moines Register*.

"We better be together on this," he told them. Freeman was manic. Few could remember seeing him so edgy.

"Shit!" Freeman howled. "We played this takeover up as the foundation of our bank. People said it wouldn't work—and it hasn't."

Freeman's strongest ally in the anti-Safra campaign was

Smith. After Safra's departure, Robinson toyed with the notion of finding another buyer for TDB.

"What will we do next?" Robinson asked Smith. "Can we do it on our own? Can we compete with Safra in Europe?"

Smith vehemently opposed selling. With Safra gone, Smith had a clear shot at the bank's top job, but he had to convince Robinson that he was as skilled as his predecessor. He had to be another Safra.

"Even if we run it poorly," Smith told Robinson, "we can make more money."

"I'll commute to Europe and hold customer hands if I have to. I can do it. This is my number one priority."

Smith's arguments were forceful and convincing. Just as persuasive in Robinson's mind was the likelihood of further bad press if AmEx sold TDB. A sudden sale would only raise more questions about AmEx's direction. By the end of 1984, Robinson's vision of a financial services empire was badly tattered. Fireman's Fund was a disaster, and he was just beginning to consider dumping AmEx's share in Warner-AmEx.

Smith was named the new head of AmEx's banking unit. Within days of the Safra announcement, the mighty AmEx PR machine went to work portraying Smith as a top-notch international financier, rivaling Safra.

Despite AmEx's PR pitch, Smith appeared to be no match for Safra. Essentially an accountant, he wasn't noted for charisma. Smith spoke in a low-pitched monotone and short, gruff sentences. His taste in fashion didn't help. Unlike his colleagues, who favored custom-made suits, Smith had a fondness for off-the-rack models, usually blue. Around the office they referred to him as "The Banker from Dubuque."

Safra remained Smith's chief worry. At last, he was in a position to have his talents recognized at American Express.

But Safra could easily sabotage Smith's career. Although there were no mass desertions of depositors after Safra quit, Smith was certain this would not be the case for long. To blunt any possible move by Safra, Smith and his aides began scouting for any information that might harm Safra. If Safra could be made to look disreputable, Smith reckoned his client loyalty would evaporate.

Before long, Smith had hired private detectives and accountants throughout the world to uncover damaging information about Safra. For more than two years after Safra's departure, they explored every possibility. Once AmEx investigated whether Safra used his corporate plane for personal trips. Safra's tax situation in the U.S. also came under scrutiny.

The campaign grew steadily in intensity. Then in 1987 the project became an obsession for Smith when he suspected that Safra was violating his non-compete contract. More than twenty TDB employees had quit and gone to work for Safra's Republic Bank. Smith became even more alarmed when an important computer tape with proprietary customer information turned up missing.

"I felt that he wasn't living up to his contract," Smith would say later in explaining the investigation. "It was part of my responsibility as head of the bank to do something. I was getting paid to defend shareholders against unfair competition."

Safra denied any wrongdoing. Although several former TDB employees went to work for Republic, Safra insisted he did not recruit them. They merely preferred the Safra organization to American Express. Indeed, there was no hard evidence that linked Safra to any unfair practices. AmEx detectives even tailed at least one TDB executive in London to see if he had any dealings with officials at Republic's nearby offices. They never discovered any contact.

Smith persisted, however. And Robinson, still smarting from the dressing-down he received from Safra over Fireman's Fund, urged his new banking chief on. Robinson was bitter. Now the acquisition of TDB looked hasty and ill-planned. Without Safra himself, his bank was weakened. To Robinson, his problems with Safra were more than a personality clash. Before long, he felt he had been deceived. He questioned whether TDB's founder ever had any intentions of remaining with American Express. All he wanted to do was dump a troubled bank. Robinson was the unwitting accomplice.

"Jim and I never had any disagreements about what we were doing," Smith would later recall. "He would tell me that everything was just fine and to pursue it in the courts to the fullest extent."

Smith wasn't the only AmEx executive to suspect Safra of dirty dealing. Freeman did, too. He believed Safra's people were planting stories in the European press suggesting that AmEx would never be able to compete in private banking. And he finally persuaded Robinson to allow him to look into the matter. "We kept reading how dumb and stupid we were," Freeman said.

Freeman's investigation began slowly. There were few leads. Then, in November, 1986, *The New York Times* published a story that alleged that Republic National Bank's corporate plane had been used by former White House Chief of Staff Robert McFarlane during the Iran-Contra affair. The article, citing European press reports, suggested the Republic jet ferried McFarlane to Teheran to meet with Iranian officials as part of the arms-for-hostages deal.

The report was more than just damaging to Safra. Freeman believed he had finally discovered Safra's weakness. If Safra indeed was a participant in Iran-Contra, the resulting congressional investigations, bad publicity, even possible criminal indictments would put Safra out of business. "We have crossed the Rubicon," Freeman triumphantly declared to Robinson.

Robinson was also delighted by this unexpected "opportunity." He had needed hard evidence of Safra's involvement. Safra had already applied for a new banking license with Swiss authorities, and Robinson knew he would be quickly turned down if there was reasonable suspicion that the Lebanese banker was a figure in Iran-Contra. "Find the evidence," he instructed Freeman.

By February, 1987, Freeman turned to Susan Cantor. A former associate producer for ABC News, Cantor held a master's degree in international relations from Yale. As a member of ABC's investigative unit, she had expertise in Latin American affairs. Cantor was said to be especially knowledgeable about Iran-Contra and the prolonged civil war in Nicaragua between the Sandinistas and the Contras. In fact, it was said that she was close to Contra leaders.

Freeman decided to enlist Cantor in his Safra project. "Here's the *New York Times* article. How do you check it out?" Freeman asked her.

Within weeks, Cantor was off to Europe checking leads. She checked the arrival and departure records at airports in Zurich, Geneva and Paris to track Safra's corporate plane. Cantor even searched for evidence of dummy corporations Safra might have set up to ship arms and money.

Before long, Cantor complained to Freeman that she needed help. An experienced investigator with some knowledge of financial matters would help, she said. Freeman agreed, and quickly called upon Paul Knight to help. Knight was the head of AmEx security for Europe and the Middle East. It was his job to battle card fraud and traveler's check counterfeiting. He was well-suited for his job. Knight was a former agent for the

Federal Bureau of Narcotics, the forerunner of the Drug Enforcement Agency, and he had extensive contacts with Interpol and other law enforcement agencies around the globe. Freeman recalled that when he sought Knight's advice about an investigator, AmEx's security expert didn't hesitate. "I have absolutely the right guy for you," he said. His name was Antonio Greco.

Greco had helped Knight in a big card fraud investigation a few years earlier and had worked for him periodically afterward. What Knight didn't mention, according to Freeman, was Greco's criminal record, which included several convictions in Italy on charges of theft and the handling of stolen goods. He had also been arrested several times in the U.S. for a variety of offenses, from carrying an unlicensed gun to smuggling. All the U.S. charges had been dropped.

"Do you want to meet him?" Knight asked Freeman.

"If you've already checked him out, I don't have to," Freeman responded.

In early 1987, American Express filed a criminal complaint against Safra's organization in Geneva, alleging unfair competition. AmEx lawyers filed similar charges in May with the Swiss banking authorities. Curiously, Safra's name was never mentioned in the filings because AmEx could not link the Lebanese banker himself to any underhanded practices. Desperate for evidence, AmEx's attorneys included the *New York Times* article that mentioned Safra's plane.

In later years, these attempts to undermine Safra's credibility would be considered mild. American Express's campaign against Edmond Safra was just beginning.

TEN

Power, Politics and Peter Cohen

Robinson was deeply concerned about the Safra situation. But he was *obsessed* with his own career aspirations. By 1987, having served ten years as CEO, he began looking for other challenges. Rather than casting an envious eye at other corporate empires, Robinson focused squarely on Washington.

Robinson launched a quiet campaign to be named Secretary of Commerce or Treasury in the next administration, even though he *publicly* denied any interest in a Washington job. George Bush, then Ronald Reagan's vice president, was the Republican front-runner. And Robinson worked feverishly to put his own name in play.

"Jim very much wanted a cabinet seat," recalled one congressman who dealt frequently with Robinson. "Everyone in Washington was aware of that."

Hardly a fanatical Republican, Robinson was nevertheless appealing to the Republican Party. On paper, his résumé of accomplishments rivaled those of Donald Regan, the combative CEO of Merrill Lynch who went on to serve as Reagan's Treasury Secretary and then his chief of staff. American Express was big, profitable and prestigious. Just as important, Robinson had been a major contributor to the Republican Party. He was a member of Team 100, a group of individuals who had raised at least $100,000 in donations for the Republican National Committee. In New York, Robinson had even positioned himself as George Bush's chief fund-raiser.

Then there were Robinson's connections. In the 1960s, these had helped launch Robinson's business career. A cadre of new friends and acquaintances would help do the same for his political career in the 1980s. Over the years, Robinson had recruited Republican notables Drew Lewis, Henry Kissinger and Gerald Ford for AmEx's board. Each proved valuable in broadening Robinson's political contacts.

In turn, they had found their relationship with American Express similarly rewarding. As head of Warner-AmEx, Lewis received a total of $12.6 million in salary, stock options and bonuses during his three-year tenure. Kissinger received not only his $36,000 fee as a board member but was paid another $420,000 as a consultant and lecturer for AmEx and Shearson. Ford, an advisor to Shearson, took home $200,000.

By the end of 1987, Robinson would be found at least once a week in Washington. AmEx even added a helicopter to its air force to enable the boss to commute from the Wall Street heliport. Often, he could be found on Capitol Hill. Ostensibly, Robinson would talk to key congressmen on trade and finance issues. But the exposure was invaluable.

"Robinson's *modus operandi* was to be a constant presence in Washington without ever lobbying personally," recalled Ron Walker, the former personnel chief for the Reagan White House. "He was very effective."

Robinson had also increased his public visibility. In 1988, he would succeed David Rockefeller as chairman of the influential New York City Partnership, a corporate group founded to promote economic development and education in New York City. Press interviews had become common, too. When *Business Week* writer Tony Bianco approached Robinson in the summer of 1987 about an in-depth personal profile, AmEx's CEO readily agreed. He granted Bianco unprecedented access, totaling some forty hours over four months. The cooperation was uncharacteristic. But it would result in a glowing cover story in January 1988 titled "Do You Know Me?"

It was widely believed around American Express that Linda Robinson was behind Jim's push for a public profile. To Robinson, the marriage had been a turning point. Far from settling down, Robinson's life became even more high-profile. Together, Jim and Linda became one of the hottest couples in New York society. They were fixtures on the black-tie circuit. Their circle of friends included Barbara Walters, Tom Brokaw, Frank Sinatra and Norman Pearlstine, managing editor of the *The Wall Street Journal.*

If the Robinsons couldn't be found at the Four Seasons, Le Cirque, or Robinson's favorite haunt, the 21 Club, chances were they were entertaining at their eight-room duplex at the exclusive Museum Tower, one door down from the Museum of Modern Art on West 53rd Street. Weekends would find them at their thirty-six-acre country estate in Litchfield County, Connecticut, which would be featured in an eight-page spread in *Architectural Digest.* Or they might slip away to their third home at the Palm Beach Polo and Country Club in Wellington, Florida.

And the Robinsons frequently popped up in gossip columns. In 1985, the *New York Post*'s "Suzy Says" chronicled Robinson's surprise fiftieth birthday party. Linda had booked the Mark Hellinger Theater so Jim and 200 guests could see a performance of the hit play *Tango Argentino.* For the occasion, the billboard read: "Tonight Only. Starring James D. Robinson III in *Tango Argentino.*"

Linda was also a powerful business ally. In 1986, she had founded her own PR firm with Jim Lake, her former boss in the Reagan campaign, and Kenneth Lerer, the orchestrator of Bess Myerson's run for the Senate in 1980. Around American Express, Robinson would insist that Linda's firm should not be shown any favoritism. But it was well-known that AmEx's CEO wanted his wife to succeed. In late 1987, Linda hired away Walter Montgomery, the thoughtful, bearded spokesman for American Express for the past four years. Robinson didn't interfere.

Thanks to her husband's influence and Linda's close ties to the media, Robinson, Lake, Lerer & Montgomery became one of the most powerful firms in New York. Linda herself became a key player on Wall Street as merger fever took hold and the stars of the takeover game sought her PR advice. Many also wanted to get closer to Robinson. Linda's clients included such corporate celebrities as junk bond king Michael Milken, Texaco CEO James Kinnear, and Ross Johnson, RJR Nabisco's chief. Her main client, if unofficial, remained Jim Robinson.

Linda was a major help to Robinson, but a far bigger part of his success in the late 1980s had to do with Peter Cohen. In typical Robinson style, AmEx's CEO had stood aside, allowing Cohen free reign at Shearson. And to Robinson, Cohen's management was paying off handsomely. The continuing riches of the bull market kept feeding Shearson's trading desk. What's more, the deal mania of the eighties provided a growing income. In 1986, Shearson's profits hit a record $346 million, up 100% from the previous year.

Within American Express, Shearson enjoyed a new exalted status. The frenzied growth of the card business was beginning to flatten out in the latter half of the eighties. TRS was still a money machine. In 1986, it earned $650 million. But Visa, MasterCard, even Sears, Roebuck and Co. and its Discover Card were attracting legions of consumers.

By 1986, Gerstner was sounding the same old warnings that Robinson had heard in the late seventies. *The business is maturing,* Gerstner would say. *If we want to grow, we'll have to go overseas.* To help pay for the push abroad, Robinson and Gerstner looked to Shearson. Cohen's ascendancy within American Express seemed assured.

He was a member of Robinson's inner circle, a close advisor on every topic from the economy to global expansion. Cohen would dine with Robinson frequently. He and his wife, Karen, also socialized frequently with Jim and Linda.

Cohen relished the attention. After years of hard work and self-doubt, he was finally at the top. Ever since Sandy Weill was exiled to Fireman's Fund, Cohen's paramount position at Shearson was unchallenged. Quick, tough, and often abrasive, Cohen believed he had finally received the recognition that he had long deserved. But his ambition was as fierce as ever. Cohen had grander plans for himself and Shearson. He was determined to transform Shearson into a global giant, just as Robinson had done with American Express. And he, too, had embarked on a buying binge that was supposed to project Shearson's might far beyond the confines of Wall Street.

Cohen's expansion strategy had begun three years earlier with Shearson's acquisition of the old-line investment banking firm Lehman Brothers, Kuhn Loeb. Cohen had always been eager to jump into the mergers and acquisitions—M&A—business. Although a giant on Wall Street, Shearson was considered a wirehouse, a firm that transacted trades for individuals by wire. Cohen cringed at the description as though it was a put-down. The 1980s marked the era of deals, from takeovers to leveraged buyouts. Cohen yearned to get into the fray.

Buying Lehman, the oldest partnership on Wall Street, went a long way toward satisfying his ambition. Lehman's investment bankers were the closest thing to aristocracy in the M&A world. Its client list was dominated by *Fortune* 500 types, and its team of bankers was the closest thing to first-string. It was said that Lehman associates would walk on hot coals to become a full partner.

Cohen looked seriously at Lehman after a March article in *Fortune* magazine suggested that Lehman was about to be sold. The firm had been torn apart by the fatal rivalry of its co-CEO's. Pete Peterson, the former chairman of Bell & Howell and Commerce Secretary under Richard Nixon, was handsome and patrician. His counterpart, Lewis Glucksman, was a trader by training who had spent years in the trenches on Wall Street. Their management styles were like oil and water. And as Lehman's managers fell into factional warfare, the firm's business eroded.

"If someone buys this firm it should be us," Cohen told Robinson. "It would put us far ahead of our five-year plan."

Robinson endorsed Cohen's idea. Shearson's expansion only furthered his own policies of acquisition. What's more, Lehman was tony and upscale. It had the kind of well-heeled image that would meld neatly with American Express. Likewise, Robinson hoped that Lehman's polish would rub off on Shearson.

Although Shearson had been part of the AmEx empire for three years, it still had a distinct earthy culture. Once, to celebrate Howard Clark Jr.'s fortieth birthday in 1984, Shearson executives had hired a stripper from Strip-O-Gram and brought her to a tax-planning session disguised as an accountant. No sooner had Clark convened the meeting than she whipped out a cassette player and began peeling off her clothes in rhythm to an exotic tune. Whistling and applauding, the crew from Shearson almost doubled over with laughter. AmEx executives were stone-faced. Lou Gerstner was horrified. Clark smiled nervously.

Lehman's refined style might also smooth Cohen's hard edges. As an AmEx board member and one of Robinson's top lieutenants, Cohen had been under pressure to spruce up his own image. At Robinson's urging, Cohen had embarked on an image-improvement kick. He took private Berlitz lessons in French and Italian. Cohen, who used to enjoy an evening of softball and beer, eventually began playing golf with AmEx board members. His taste in clothes grew even more selective. Italian suits had always been a must. Indeed, Shearson's chief even had a favorite tailor in Milan.

Despite Robinson's support, the purchase of Lehman was far from a cinch. Sandy Weill, then AmEx's president, was less than keen about the deal. Shearson's frugal founder was appalled at Lehman's reputation for excessiveness. Lehman's wine cellar was stocked with vintage Haut-Brion and its offices bristled with Impressionist paintings and other objets d'art. Even Lehman's resident chef debated whether a marriage between Lehman and the plebeian Shearson could work.

"Shearson taking over Lehman is like McDonald's taking over 21," commented William Proops, who was trained at the École Hôtellerie in Lausanne, Switzerland, and at the Cordon Bleu in Paris.

Cohen stood firm. By then he resented Weill's meddling. He brought his case directly to the board. He argued that Lehman had the potential to be involved in every big deal that would be coming down the pike. Cohen also warned that Merrill Lynch, his longtime adversary, would pounce on Lehman if Shearson didn't act.

"Maybe you think we can't afford to do this deal," he lectured the board. "But considering the franchise we are acquiring, I maintain that we can't afford *not* to do this deal. And do it now."

The board agreed. Shearson bought Lehman for $360 million.

Surprisingly, the merger produced the kind of image changes that Robinson had hoped for. Once Cohen himself studied Lehman up close, he began worrying about Shearson's reputation. A truly world-class operation couldn't afford such a Spartan, rough-hewn image. Before long, he was eager to spread Lehman's elegant style throughout his organization. He amassed an art collection valued as high as $22 million for Shearson's executive offices. Cohen, with Robinson's blessings, also built a $23 million corporate retreat at Vail, Colorado. The twenty-three-acre center, known as Beaver Creek, had an Olympic-size swimming pool, fourteen luxury bungalows and a conference center. By 1987, Shearson had acquired its own Gulfstream.

"Before Lehman we'd do business over lunch in Chinatown. Afterwards, it was the Four Seasons," said one Shearson executive.

Lehman wasn't the end of Cohen's expansion policy. Overseas, Shearson's presence was also spreading. When the London market was deregulated in October, 1986, Shearson was among the first wave of foreign firms that invaded the City. In Japan, Cohen spent $5 million for a seat on the Tokyo Stock Exchange. Indeed, Shearson became one of the biggest U.S. firms in Tokyo.

As the frenetic chief of his growing empire, Cohen personally went everywhere to drive his people. He was quick to reward those who delivered. Meetings in the Bahamas and million-dollar bonuses were just some of the perks. Cohen paid for some gifts out of his own pocket. Peter and his wife, Karen, once gave Cohen's secretary, Ellen Donnelly, a $6,000 black llama coat, which was more than Robinson's staff ever received. Gossip had it that AmEx's chief always put his gifts on the corporate expense account.

Shearson's success also further enhanced Cohen's position within AmEx, and he loved playing the role of golden boy. At board meetings, he sounded tough and arrogant. He would often dismiss directors with a quick "You don't understand the business." Even AmEx's CEO wasn't immune to Cohen's haughty behavior. Cohen would often duck Robinson's calls. "I'm busy right now," Cohen would tell his secretary. "Tell him I'll get back to him." Around Shearson, they called Cohen "The Cowboy" because of his cocky attitude.

Robinson was both appalled and fascinated by Cohen. He admired his brazen manner. He respected his work ethic. Shearson's chief was a harsher form of Weill, a daredevil like Sandy Lewis. Cohen was the swashbuckler Robinson wasn't. Unlike Jim, who dreaded confrontations, Peter unabashedly spoke his mind. Though some found this side of Cohen deeply distasteful, Robinson was not put off by it.

Still, even if he wanted to control Cohen, Robinson didn't have the means to do it. Confrontation was out of the question. Instead, Robinson would make subtle suggestions or quietly implore Cohen's aides to do something. "Tell Peter to be nicer to people," he would tell Jeffrey Lane, Shearson's president. Lane had first met Cohen when they both attended Columbia Business School. Cohen was the smartass, Lane the brown-nose, they would joke to each other. They both grew up under the tutelage of Sandy Weill.

As Shearson's success piled up, Cohen's private life went through a similar transformation. Peter and Karen enjoyed a status in the New York social scene similar to that of John and

Susan Gutfreund or Kohlberg Kravis Roberts & Co. boss Henry Kravis and his wife Carolyn Roehm. Their names frequently appeared in society columns. They often entertained at their East Hampton home. And their circle of friends widened to include a number of celebrities. The actor Michael Douglas, who portrayed the takeover artist Gordon Gckko in the film *Wall Street*, became an occasional visitor to the Cohen home.

Karen herself became an active social climber. A native of Cincinnati, Karen had met Cohen while both were students at Ohio State University. An interior decorator, she once headed the interior design center at B. Altman's. But she gave up her professional life in 1973 to raise a family. As Cohen's stature grew, Karen enjoyed the perks of being the boss's wife. Some people felt that Peter would have been happy staying in more, but that Karen pushed hard for visibility and status.

At Shearson, she enlisted the aid of two secretaries to help coordinate her social calendar with her husband's busy schedule. Shopping was another passion. Karen would make frequent excursions to Gucci's and Yves St. Laurent on Madison Avenue.

To friends, the pressures of society and a socially minded wife further fueled Peter's need for success. In the eighties, simply being a good CEO was just not enough. And Cohen knew that so well.

By the summer of 1987, Wall Street was undergoing a profound change. The Japanese had invaded in full force. After conquering the auto market, Japan's biggest brokerages and insurance companies launched a full-scale assault on the financial industry. Giants such as Nomura Securities and Nikko had established U.S. beachheads and were hiring away top talent from Wall Street firms. Other Japanese financial companies, fattened by Japan's prolonged economic boom, were scooping up pieces of existing U.S. investment houses. And they were paying top dollar. The previous year, Sumitomo had shelled out a hefty $600 million for a 12.5% stake in the august firm of Goldman, Sachs & Company.

And before long, there was similar interest in Shearson. In June, Nippon Life Insurance Company purchased a 13% stake in Shearson for a hefty $530 million. Henry Kissinger, Robinson's friend and fellow AmEx board member, handled the initial contacts. "This could be what you're looking for," Kissinger told Robinson.

Indeed, Robinson had been seeking an alliance with a Japanese company to help push the card. Even more pressing was the need for cash. The campaign to establish the card overseas was proving long and expensive. Foreigners didn't take to plastic like Americans. In Germany and Japan, the concept of credit was sneered at. If he was to succeed, Gerstner would need capital.

Another reason the Japanese offer looked so good to Robinson was his growing desire to lessen his stake in Shearson. He was increasingly anxious over Wall Street's spreading insider-trading scandal. The investigation into illicit stock market dealings had even come close to implicating Robinson himself.

Robinson ran up against the U.S. Attorney's office in the spring of 1987, when prosecutors began investigating Sandy Lewis for stock manipulation. Lewis's name cropped up during the government's investigation of Los Angeles trader Boyd Jefferies. The inquiry turned up evidence that Lewis had artificially propped up the price of Fireman's Fund by having Jefferies buy shares just before AmEx unloaded its remaining 41% stake in the company. According to the government, the purchase increased Fireman's Fund's share price to $38 from $37⅞.

Although the government's investigation focused on Lewis, U.S. Attorney Rudolph Giuliani and his staff also closely examined American Express for other culprits. Indeed, their investigation uncovered five phone calls between an AmEx executive and Lewis on the day that the manipulation allegedly occurred. Panic gripped AmEx's executive suite.

"Jim, the important thing is not to talk to anyone inside the company or outside about this," cautioned Kenneth Bialkin, AmEx's outside counsel. Bialkin, Sandy Weill's old friend, was an attorney with Skadden Arps and an advisor to Robinson. "Whatever you say could come back to hurt you. Be extremely careful."

Robinson heeded Bialkin's advice. He never even spoke to Lewis again. In April, 1987, Lewis was indicted for stock manipulation. He pleaded guilty in 1989 and was sentenced to three years' probation. To Robinson, however, the affair didn't end with Lewis's conviction. As late as 1990, AmEx executives believed the investigation was still open. The U.S. Attorney's office declined to comment.

The Lewis episode aside, not everyone on AmEx's board was happy with the Nippon transaction. Some were nervous about linking the American Express name with a Japanese company at a time when Washington and Tokyo were at loggerheads over trade. Japan-bashing was just coming into its own. Others thought the deal made little sense. "Shearson is going gangbusters," Alleghany CEO Fred Kirby argued at one board meeting. "Why the hell do we want to sell any of it?"

Cohen himself supported the deal. Not only did the sale to Nippon strengthen Shearson's efforts in Japan, but it also allowed Cohen more autonomy. Several months later, Cohen again was a chief proponent when AmEx decided to sell another 18% share in Shearson to the public. His attitude was, "We're on our own again."

As it turned out, the Shearson sale just squeaked by. By the end of the summer, the "For Sale" sign on Wall Street was down. The confidence that had reigned in the financial community was waning.

To an industry whose historical perspective was measured in days, things had been going too well too long. The economic expansion that had begun in 1981 had entered its sixth straight year. The bull market had raged for almost five years. The Dow Jones Industrial Average had climbed more than 1,000 points. Something had to give.

Economists were spinning out forecasts on the volatility of the dollar, the direction of interest rates and the ever-widening trade deficit. The era of prosperity was coming to a close. Many were sounding alarms of a recession.

Companies began trimming their spending plans, putting off projects. Investors, too, became nervous. Just the whiff of bad news and the market would stumble by 50 or 75 points.

By the fall, the angst was palpable. Everyone was expecting a market setback. Analysts were talking of a "correction." What the Street ended up with was a crash. October 19 would go down in the books as Bloody Monday.

Spooked by the possibility of higher interest rates and a slower economy and nervous over the 108-point plunge the previous Friday, investors began selling shares at a frenzied pace. And as the Dow fell further, the panic spread wider. By the end of the day, the Dow had plunged 508 points in the heaviest trading ever seen on the New York Stock Exchange. The collapse even surpassed the 1929 crash. And the damage was worldwide. In London, Paris, Frankfurt and Tokyo, share markets went into a dive. Authorities in Hong Kong closed the market.

On Wall Street, rumors were rampant. One false report had it that Goldman had lost $500 million and was about to fold. Other brokerages were reportedly in jeopardy.

Shearson was a madhouse. Pandemonium reigned in the

trading room. Pink sell slips were stacked everywhere. And Shearson's celebrated trading team, normally composed in the thick of battle, was becoming unglued. One trader incorrectly purchased a futures contract for the Standard & Poor's stock index when he was supposed to be selling. Shearson ended up losing $15 million.

The brokerage's margin accounts, Shearson's retail backbone, were also being pummeled. As stock prices went into a free-fall, Shearson's brokers called on their clients to ante up more money. But little was forthcoming. Many didn't have the cash on hand. By the time the market closed at 4:00 P.M., Shearson's estimated losses ran as high as $60 million.

Shearson's top executives were even more alarmed as they watched their own personal fortunes dissolve. Lane tried to combat the sinking morale by offering overnight loans to those with the biggest losses. "Focus on the business at hand," Lane would tell his staff.

Making matters worse was Cohen's absence. When the market crashed, Shearson's leader was on the other side of the world. For the previous couple of weeks, Cohen had been touring Asia, playing the role of global statesman. He had made stops in Tokyo, Hong Kong and Manila. When the market began its meltdown, Cohen was ending a reception for Chinese dignitaries at the Winter Palace in Beijing.

The trip to China was to have been the high point of Cohen's twelve-day tour. That day alone Cohen had lunch with the mayor of Beijing, cocktails with officials from the Bank of China and a lengthy meeting with engineers of the China State Construction Co. At the time, Shearson was in a joint venture with Tishman-Speyer to build a 250-unit residential complex in Beijing for foreign workers. "American Express Center" was the tentative name.

It had been Cohen's brainchild. And Robinson was ecstatic. It was the era of economic reform. Capitalist chutzpah was in great demand. Joint venture agreements with Western companies were being signed every week. AmEx's CEO wanted a visible presence. "That will get us in good with the Chinese," Robinson had once said in praise of Cohen's project. "Let's not spare any expense."

When Cohen entered the main hall of the Winter Palace, most of his guests had already arrived. With canapés and wine-glasses in hand, they quickly surrounded Shearson's CEO as he entered. After the New York market's plunge on Friday, Asian markets were already in a tailspin. They barraged him with questions. *Will New York's market crash? What's happening in Europe? Will your government do anything?*

Cohen reassured his guests. He was the consummate stockbroker, a lot of hype with just a pinch of truth thrown in for realism. A correction, he would describe it. He told them he didn't know how to interpret the notoriously panicky Tokyo and Hong Kong markets.

Cohen was jittery, however. He didn't foresee a collapse. Few did. But he was stuck on the other side of the world. He couldn't wait until he got home.

By the time he arrived back in New York on October 20, it was late afternoon. Wall Street's panic showed little sign of abating. People were talking about the frightening parallels to 1929. Fear was universal. Everyone spent their day gawking at Quotron terminals, which were as ubiquitous on Wall Street as yellow ties and red suspenders. Restaurants were empty at lunchtime; the bars filled after work.

No one was leaping out windows, but the shadow of the Great Depression loomed large on the Street. It couldn't hap-pen again, experts would say confidently. But nobody ruled out a deep recession. The Crash had wiped out $500 billion in stock value. Virtually overnight, millions of Americans felt less well-off. The era of prosperity was teetering. Economists warned that consumers would go into a shell, and as the buying slowed, so would the economy. Even Shearson's own chief economist, Allen Sinai, sounded gloomy. "I thought a recession was likely in 1989; now the concern is over 1988," he told an interviewer.

At AmEx, Robinson and his aides feared the worst. AmEx shares had skidded to $22 from $30 on October 19. But the biggest worry was about the weeks and months ahead. The card was in jeopardy. A recession would snap the spending spree that had propelled the company's earnings through the 1980s. "This could kill us," Gerstner moaned.

The outlook was even bleaker for Shearson. The Dow managed a 102-point gain the day after the Crash. But it was only a temporary reprieve. There was no more confidence, no more talk of record heights. Investors wanted out. Fidelity Investments Company, one of the biggest mutual fund managers, reported 200,000 phone calls on Bloody Monday from customers wanting to get their money out of stock funds.

At Shearson, Cohen ignored the stack of messages awaiting him. He had already phoned his wife from the airport. By this time, he had been awake for forty hours and was in no mood for schmoozing clients. Instead, he called a crisis meeting of his kitchen cabinet: Lane, George Sheinberg, who headed finance, Herb Freiman, the head of capital markets, and Dick Fuld, Shearson's trading chief.

By 5 P.M. Robinson phoned. He asked Cohen what shape Shearson was in and when he thought the market would stabilize. Then he turned quickly to the subject of image. The Crash was a black eye for the entire financial community, Robinson said. If Shearson looked damaged, the public perception of American Express would be harmed. Robinson didn't have to paint Cohen a picture.

Robinson urged Cohen to take a "proactive" approach. It

was typical Robinson jargon. He wanted Cohen to be highly visible, lots of television and radio. He also wanted Cohen to volunteer his services to the U.S. Treasury and the SEC. Both agencies were making rumblings about studying the causes of the Crash.

"We have to get involved," Robinson told Cohen.

Over the next couple of weeks the market calmed, but the angst prevailed on Wall Street. There was talk of government investigations and market reforms. Still, investors stayed away from the market in droves. Wall Street's final quarter would be a disaster.

Despite the Crash and the ensuing concerns about the economy, Cohen was unfazed. At Shearson it was business as usual. The Crash had done little to dampen Cohen's desire for expansion. Indeed, two months after the Crash, he had his eye on a new target: E. F. Hutton.

Ever since it pleaded guilty to 2,000 felony counts in 1985, Hutton had been on a downward spiral. Prosecutors had charged Hutton with check-kiting, writing checks before the funds were available. Its upscale client list, chock-full of Park Avenue surgeons and Arab sheikhs, was shrinking under the weight of bad publicity.

Even a management shake-up failed to help. In 1986, Hutton's board had hired Robert Rittereiser, the number three man at Merrill, to stem client defections. He was hard-nosed and squeaky-clean. But the customer erosion had continued. And the Crash didn't help matters. By November, Rittereiser and Hutton's board decided it was time to sell.

Rittereiser first approached William Schreyer, Merrill's easygoing and affable chairman. Initially, Schreyer was very receptive. Combining his sales force with Hutton's would create an army of 22,000 brokers nationwide.

But Schreyer soon changed his mind after taking a look at Hutton's books. Over the years, Hutton had developed a lucrative trade in limited partnerships. These were similar to shares in various ventures and were sold mainly to individuals. But Hutton had sold almost $1 billion worth of partnerships in speculative oil- and gas-drilling ventures. Most would fail, Schreyer figured, leaving Hutton's new owner with a mountain of lawsuits and millions in liabilities.

Within days, Rittereiser was negotiating with the next name on his short list of possible buyers: Peter Cohen. Shearson may have been his second choice, but Rittereiser reckoned if anyone was interested it would be Cohen.

For years, Shearson's CEO had been obsessed with running the biggest firm on the street. Indeed, the previous year, Cohen had offered $1.5 billion for Hutton. The offer, unexpected and low, was ultimately rejected by Hutton's board. But everyone knew Cohen was still hungry for Hutton's blue-blood franchise.

It was the Monday before Thanksgiving, a little after 8:00 A.M., when Rittereiser phoned Cohen. The call was hardly a surprise. He had been expecting something to break at Hutton after October 19, Bloody Monday.

Rittereiser sounded glum and tired. He kept the conversation short.

"We're seeking a buyer," Hutton's CEO said. "Are you interested?"

"Maybe," responded Cohen. He was trying to sound as disinterested as possible. "Who else are you talking to?"

Rittereiser said he had received several queries. But he declined to name any firms.

Merrill, PaineWebber and Dean Witter immediately sprung to Cohen's mind. Later, Cohen learned that his old boss, Sandy Weill, had even made a bid. That made the quest for

Hutton especially alluring to Cohen. Ego demanded that he outshine his old boss. As it turned out, Weill offered only $18 a share or $600 million, and was promptly turned down.

In truth, Cohen was the hottest prospect.

"We knew Cohen was eager," a former Hutton executive would later recall. "We wanted him to think he had hot competition. We set the rope out for Cohen and he hung himself."

Cohen was jubilant. Snaring Hutton would make Shearson the biggest retail firm on the Street, bigger than Merrill. He remained subdued on the phone.

"Sounds interesting," Cohen told Rittereiser. "I'll have to get back to you."

No sooner had Cohen hung up than he yelled to his secretary to get Robinson on the phone. Just a year before, Robinson and Gerstner had handed down an edict that American Express be among the top players in all its business endeavors.

Cohen gave AmEx's CEO a quick synopsis of his conversation with Rittereiser. The pair discussed if the timing was right so soon after the Crash. But Cohen warned Robinson about the competition.

"We could lose this," he cautioned.

AmEx's CEO agreed they would have to act swiftly.

"Let's start moving," Robinson told Cohen. Soon after, Cohen called an emergency meeting of Shearson's board.

It was shortly after 4:00 P.M. when Shearson's board gathered at Cohen's nineteenth-floor office at the American Express Tower of the World Financial Center. Cohen's office rivaled the splendor of Robinson's. The entrance was framed by a pair of hand-crafted oak doors. The interior was spacious and elegant, dominated by a massive oak desk.

Robinson and Gerstner were first to arrive, followed by Lane, Fuld, and Howard Clark Jr. Olivetti chairman Carlo De

Benedetti, Nobuyuki Adachi, a Nippon executive V.P., and a dozen other Shearson directors were patched in by phone.

Cohen was clearly on a high. Earlier in the day he had pitched the Hutton deal to AmEx's full board. He was given the green light to negotiate. It was up to the Shearson board to come up with a game plan.

"Their net worth is lousy," acknowledged Cohen as he began the session. The previous day, Shearson accountants had uncovered the same shaky limited partnerships that had frightened Merrill away.

But Cohen would not be deterred. There were many other firms circling Hutton, Cohen again warned. And with good reason. Hutton handled some $75 billion worth of stocks and bonds for its clients. Another $25 billion was locked up in Hutton's mutual funds. Once the market settled down, Shearson would have the largest and strongest sales force on the Street.

"We'll pick up 8,000 brokers. Just think of it," Cohen enthused.

"It's tempting," agreed Gerstner, turning toward Robinson as if to convince his boss.

Ever since he was informed of the Hutton deal, Gerstner had been hounding Cohen not to let it slip by. His concern had little to do with expanding Cohen's turf. Gerstner wasn't particularly a fan of Cohen's fiery style. A lightweight as a strategist, Gerstner thought to himself, a seat-of-the-pants manager. But he needed Shearson to help TRS, especially if the economy began sliding in response to the crash.

Price was Cohen's major concern. He felt $850 million, or $27 a share, was fair. Anything higher and he would come back to the board for permission.

"We can't pay too much in this kind of climate," Cohen said. He sounded uncharacteristically cautious.

"No!" thundered Gerstner, as he rose and slammed his fist on Cohen's desk.

"Don't lose this deal over a dollar or two a share," he continued, sneering at Cohen. "We have to do this!"

Robinson nodded. Although he was suspicious about Hutton's balance sheet, AmEx's chief was reluctant to overrule both Cohen and Gerstner. By then, Robinson was far more interested in international issues, such as trade and Third World debt. Those were the kinds of global policy matters that would attract major attention to Robinson.

What's more, the prospect of a fresh deal excited him. It would be an amazing sign of strength at a time when the rest of the financial community was still licking its wounds from Bloody Monday.

"Go get it, Peter," he said.

With the board in agreement, the discussion turned to the ticklish problem of paying for Hutton. American Express had traditionally paid for companies with stock. But the Crash had sorely affected Shearson's shares. A swap would have diluted the stock even more.

"The Japanese won't stand for a stock deal," Robinson howled. "Put it out of your mind."

That meant borrowing the cash, a risky maneuver given the uncertainties surrounding the economy.

Cohen voiced concern. "We're really stretching our resources," he said.

De Benedetti was more blunt. "What a strain!" he groaned.

But Robinson wouldn't budge. The relationship with the Japanese was just too valuable.

"We'll deal with this later," said Robinson as he headed for the door.

Although most of the bidders had dropped out by the end of November, Cohen remained convinced that everyone from Merrill to Sandy Weill was still after Hutton. He was more determined than ever to clinch the deal. After Gerstner's strong comments, he felt he couldn't back down. Robinson added to the pressure. "We can't afford to blow this," he would tell Cohen.

By chance, Lee Kimmell, a managing partner at Salomon Brothers and Hutton's lead investment banker, phoned that day. Still recovering from the Crash, Salomon at the time was trying to bolster its investment banking muscle. It hoped that fat M&A fees would compensate for the anemic returns from the trading desk. Kimmell wanted to know where Shearson stood. They arranged to meet the next day.

Not surprisingly, Kimmell was very receptive to talking about a deal with Cohen. Kimmell was more than smart, he was wise. Other Salomon bankers dressed alike and talked alike. They even tended to walk in a row as if they were linked. Indeed, on the Street, they were derisively known as the "sausages."

Kimmell, however, was no cookie-cutter version of the average Salomon banker. Tough and outspoken, he routinely unsettled his superiors by his brash remarks. Salomon president Thomas Strauss feared Kimmell, but not because of his abrasive style. Kimmell was rumored to be on the way up. Salomon's chief, John Gutfreund, prized Kimmell's feisty independence, and he often sought Kimmell's counsel.

The next day, Cohen, Lane and Jack Nusbaum, one of Shearson's outside attorneys, were in Hutton's boardroom. By 8:00 P.M. they had a deal. Shearson would pay $925 million, or $29.25 a share, for Hutton. At the time of the agreement, Hutton's book value was only $7.63 a share.

Still, Cohen was delighted. Shearson now rivaled Merrill as the biggest firm on the Street. Robinson also exulted in being number one. Little did he know it would be the last good news for some time.

ELEVEN

The End
of the
Eighties

Robinson was now entering one of the most treacherous periods of his career, thanks to two of the major figures in his life: his old nemesis Edmond Safra and the increasingly nettlesome Peter Cohen.

The first to irk Robinson was Cohen. The Shearson CEO's push to build an empire in the wake of the Crash was proving disastrous. Within months of the Hutton takeover, much of the firm's top talent bolted. Many felt Cohen was unpredictable. Others scoffed at the notion of being associated with Shearson's miserly image. Worse, Cohen never made a serious attempt to convince Hutton's brokers to remain. To them, he was aloof and indifferent. Upwards of 1,500, or 19%, of Hutton's army of brokers left for other firms, such as Merrill Lynch or Dean Witter.

Those who remained were having a tough time drumming up business. Burned by the Crash, investors remained on the sidelines. They wanted no part of the stock market. That left Cohen with a burdensome payroll and falling revenues. Worse, the acquisition saddled Shearson with an additional $1.1 billion in "good will," that is, the difference between Hutton's book value and the premium paid by Cohen. This "good will" would have to be written off over the next forty years. Shearson was no longer the lean money machine that Sandy Weill had built. It was bloated and in the red.

Robinson grew steadily anxious. He urged Cohen to pare his costs. *Things have to change. You have to focus on the problems.* But again he declined to interfere. Cohen remained firmly entrenched at Shearson. He continued to ignore Robinson. *Jim, I know what I'm doing.*

Despite Cohen's assurances, Robinson remained jumpy. Not only had the board begun rumbling about Shearson's increasing difficulties, but Robinson was also upset that any further reckless moves by Cohen would affect his professional record, as well as his post-AmEx aspirations.

He had reason to be concerned. Robinson's silent campaign stumbled badly in March, 1988, when he floated his own policy initiative to solve the Third World debt problems. Robinson's solution, which he outlined at an economic forum in Washington, was called the Institute for International Debt and Development, I2D2 for short. The agency would write off 40% of the existing $250 billion in developing-country debt.

Bankers howled. Most thought it was reckless and possibly ruinous to the banking system. At a meeting of financial figures at Citicorp headquarters, chairman John Reed pulled Freeman into his office. "You guys are crazy," Reed shouted. "You're going to destroy the banking system."

Worse, Robinson's idea had infuriated Bush's campaign staff. James Baker, who had resigned as Reagan's Treasury Secretary to head the Bush campaign, was especially roiled. He had personally warned Robinson that Bush aides were working on their own plan.

"Who do you think you are?" Baker yelled over the phone at Robinson after AmEx's CEO went public with his proposal.

Robinson's political plans were of no concern to Cohen, however. Cohen was on a roll. He felt unstoppable. With much of the Street still flat on its face from the Crash, Cohen continued to push hard for new conquests, especially in investment banking. He saw himself as Shearson's senior merger strategist, and he longed to go head to head with such M&A dynamos as Henry Kravis and Bruce Wasserstein. He let his staff know he wanted a deal, a big one.

Steve Waters and J. Tomilson Hill III, the co-heads of Shearson's M&A squad, were the frequent targets of Cohen's demands. In February, acting on a request of the British firm Beazer PLC for an aggregates company, Hill outlined a tempting takeover plan. The target he suggested was Koppers Company, a sleepy maker of chemicals and "aggregates," a rock used in construction materials. Hill figured Koppers would merely roll over. Its CEO, Charles Pullin, was close to retirement and the company had just gone through some lean years. The previous year it earned $11 million, less than Shearson's own bonus pool.

Hill figured Koppers could disappear overnight and no one would miss it. He didn't have to worry about white knights and other would-be rescuers. Even better, the company was tucked away in Pittsburgh, far away from the glare of the media.

Beazer PLC specialized in construction material and it had a string of acquisitions under its belt. Beazer had made the acquaintance of senior Shearson officials during a 1986 acquisition of a Texas building materials firm.

Shearson's own participation was a sign of its new role. No longer a go-between, Shearson itself was a full-fledged predator. Shearson agreed to kick in $50 million to do the deal, as well as provide $200 million in the form of a bridge loan. Shearson had no intention of keeping its stake. Instead, it hoped to sell it off for a big profit when the deal was done.

It was bold and brash and Cohen loved it. In March, Beazer and Shearson opened fire. Koppers received a formal offer of $1.27 billion, or $45 a share. Hill and Cohen predicted a quick capitulation.

Pullin had a different idea. Simple and austere, Pullin drove an Oldsmobile to work and typed his own letters. The only noticeable adornment in Pullin's office at Koppers was an oil painting of a quarry. But he was far from the bumpkin that Hill had assumed.

When the offer first surfaced, Pullin was furious. By coincidence, just the week before, a local Shearson executive had tried to persuade Pullin to hire Shearson to defend Koppers against the possibility of a hostile offer.

"They wanted me to buy burglary insurance from the burglar himself," Pullin yelped.

Worse, Koppers had been a long and faithful customer of American Express. Pullin's sales staff and executives all carried AmEx corporate cards.

Koppers's chief took the offensive. He and his staff knew AmEx would be very sensitive to any bad publicity, so they decided to arouse the public ire. First came a letter-writing campaign to the Business Roundtable. Pullin knew Robinson was a leading member of the exclusive CEO club.

"Was this the way an investment bank should behave?" Pullin wrote. He accused Shearson and American Express of unethical business practices. Not only was Shearson helping a foreign concern topple an American company, but it had also taken on the role of a raider.

Leading politicians in Pennsylvania joined the chorus of

critics. Republican Senator John Heinz threatened to introduce legislation in Congress that would bar the takeover. Governor Robert P. Casey banned Shearson from consideration as a financial advisor for a pending $150 million state bond issue. Pennsylvania Treasurer C. Davis Greene sent a letter to Cohen notifying him that the state was suspending all business activity with Shearson.

Next came a very public campaign to capture the media's attention. On March 23, Koppers held a rally outside its downtown headquarters. Several hundred employees as well as local officials crowded onto the street. Many were wearing AmEx-buster T-shirts with a bright red line blazoned across the American Express card.

Roger Beidler, Koppers's public relations manager, exhorted the crowd to cut up their AmEx cards and send them back to American Express. His staff even handed out scissors. Koppers chemists unveiled a special acid, "The Card Killer," that dissolved the plastic cards on contact.

The Koppers counterattack was stinging and visible. The protest not only made the Pittsburgh press, but was dutifully chronicled nationwide. It even made network news. Shearson's Pittsburgh and Harrisburg offices were deluged with angry phone calls. Companies and individuals began pulling their accounts.

"Christ, we're getting hate mail," one branch manager complained to Lane.

In New York, Robinson was raging. He urgently called Cohen on his direct line.

"Did you see it? Did you see it on TV?" he fumed at Cohen. "These people were cutting up their cards!"

"Jim," responded Cohen, "it will all work out."

His tone was confident, almost as if he were reassuring a

child. But Robinson wouldn't listen this time. It was clear that Cohen and his people had underestimated the potential backlash.

"Bullshit, Peter!" Robinson shot back. "You guys didn't do your homework. This is damaging. I want us out, now!"

Cohen went on the defensive. He warned Robinson that Shearson's M&A reputation was on the line. If he dropped the bid for Koppers, Shearson and American Express would look weak and indecisive.

"We'd look like idiots," Cohen cautioned.

"Idiots!" Robinson shouted. "That's how we look now."

Robinson fretted that the Koppers affair and grass-roots backlash would do only more damage.

Over the next few days, Robinson continued to hound Cohen. *Is there any way we can get out? No? Why?* Cohen played for time. Each time he would arrogantly brush Robinson aside.

"There'll be a happy ending," he would tell Robinson.

To his staff, Cohen would privately complain, "Robinson is driving me fucking crazy."

The following week, at Robinson's insistence, Cohen, Jeffrey Lane and Hill journeyed to Pittsburgh to do some quick public relations. They met with the mayor, local civic groups and even the CEOs of leading Pittsburgh corporations, such as Alcoa and Westinghouse. No layoffs, no disruptions, Cohen promised.

By April, the deal was done. Koppers fell to Beazer. True to Cohen's words, Beazer proved to be a model citizen. But Robinson's anger at Cohen hadn't subsided. Shearson and its leader were now a liability, a threat to the AmEx image, a threat to Robinson's future. Shearson was in a tailspin and Cohen was out of control. It was time to unload both.

Within weeks, American Express disclosed its intention to sell off much of its remaining stake in Shearson. The strategy was to "deconsolidate" Shearson, that is, reduce AmEx's ownership to less than 50%. That would, in effect, remove Shearson from its quarterly results.

From that point on, the bad blood between Robinson and Cohen would only worsen. Their mutual distrust peaked six months later when Shearson failed to pull off a leveraged buyout of RJR Nabisco.

Despite his misgivings about Cohen, Robinson had been keen on doing the RJR deal from the start. Ross Johnson, RJR's brash CEO, first outlined his plan for an $18 billion LBO to Robinson in late August, 1988. It was supposed to breathe some life into RJR's languid stock price. And he was eager to have Shearson handle the deal. As an AmEx board member and Robinson's pal, Johnson could keep close tabs on Shearson's progress. He also hoped to influence the firm's strategy.

Robinson was intrigued and eager to have Shearson broker the deal. Not only was he eager to please Johnson, a board ally, but the sheer magnitude of the deal was awe-inspiring. It was to be the biggest LBO in history, the kind of deal that would help resurrect Shearson's reputation and lend a little polish to his own.

Even the possibility that other board members would frown on such a high-profile deal didn't dissuade Robinson. By late 1988, LBOs were not as politically palatable as they used to be. There were open protests about the logic of buyouts. Taking a company private, then dismembering it and selling it off in pieces to pay for the deal didn't play well on Main Street after the Crash. Congress was also nosing about.

"If things go forward, this deal will be so big and so visible," Robinson told Cohen. "You'll have to run the deal and I'll be there with you."

Cohen needed little persuasion. He was positively ebullient. RJR would pay off handsomely in terms of fees and ego. If he could pull it off, Shearson would be catapulted into the top ranks of investment banks. It would be the hottest firm on the Street. Cohen would be the king of LBOs, the only title that had so far eluded him.

From the start, there were problems. Robinson demanded an RJR briefing every morning from Cohen or his assistant, Andrea Farace. And it was during those sessions that Robinson and Cohen often differed over strategy. The first conflict emerged over Johnson's management agreement if the deal was successful. He and his partners wanted terms that could have netted them $2.5 billion. Cohen objected strenuously.

"It won't pass the smell test," he told Robinson at one of their strategy sessions. "It could be our Achilles heel."

Robinson also objected. But he didn't want Cohen to back down. Robinson wasn't about to tell Ross Johnson to change his terms. AmEx's chief was adamant that the deal had to get done the way Johnson wanted.

"Do I have to get involved in this personally?" Robinson asked angrily. "Get this done now."

And then there was Linda. Johnson hired Linda Robinson's PR firm, Robinson, Lake, Lerer & Montgomery, to cement his relationship with AmEx's chief. At first, Cohen didn't mind, even though other Shearson executives were concerned about her participation.

To some of Cohen's subordinates, Linda was also meddlesome. In the spring of 1985, Cohen had been eager to help Ted Turner, the Atlanta cable TV king, in his proposed hostile takeover of CBS. Shearson had spent months mapping out a strategy. In fact, Cohen and Turner had become friends. Turner had taken the ultimate liberty—calling Cohen "Pete." Cohen would cringe, but say nothing. Shearson stood to pocket some $100 million in banking fees.

Robinson had also been enthusiastic, until Linda interfered. She staunchly opposed Shearson's involvement. "CBS is the Establishment! It's Black Rock! A deal like this could go over very badly and make you look bad," she said to her husband. Before long, Robinson ordered Shearson to back out of the deal, infuriating some Shearson executives.

As the RJR deal progressed, Linda was less of a PR maven than an active deal-maker herself. She served as one of Johnson's chief advisors, while committing, in the opinion of some, major publicity blunders. Against Cohen's wishes, Linda encouraged Johnson to grant a wide-ranging interview to *Time* magazine in November in the midst of the battle for RJR. An even more egregious mistake, in Cohen's mind, was Linda's absence during the interview in Atlanta. There was no one around to control what Johnson said. What followed was a distinctly critical cover story titled "A Game of Greed." Later, it was widely believed that the article convinced many RJR board members to turn against Johnson.

During the height of the battle for control of the company, when competing bids emerged, Linda even arranged a meeting between Johnson and Henry Kravis to hammer out a peace treaty. Kravis, the Street's reigning LBO monarch, joined the bidding for RJR shortly after Cohen had become involved. Amazingly, Cohen was never told of the meeting.

"I can't believe it! Your wife made me look stupid," Cohen would tell Robinson months later. "Why the hell didn't you tell me about the meeting? Why not, Jim?"

Robinson said mildly, "I thought you knew, Peter."

In the end, Kravis won the battle. The final price for RJR was $25 billion. The deal was a serious blow to Cohen's reputation. A "thuggish dummy" is the way a *Vanity Fair* article described Cohen's RJR role months later.

Worse, it was yet another failure for Robinson. In public,

he had deftly distanced himself from the RJR deal, allowing Cohen to shoulder all the blame at the end. But even with all the fingers pointing at Cohen, Robinson was profoundly disappointed. First there was Hutton, then Koppers, now RJR. American Express was no longer racking up the points as it had in the early eighties. Now it seemed that AmEx was stumbling from one setback to the next.

The saga of Peter Cohen and Shearson wasn't the only crisis that Robinson dealt with in 1988. Edmond Safra suddenly reemerged.

In January, 1988, Swiss banking authorities awarded Safra a new banking license. AmEx's complaints had been dismissed. Within days of Edmond Safra's court victory over American Express, he announced his intent to open a new bank in March. "Jim, Safra is going to kill us in Europe," Freeman told AmEx's chief. "This is a very dangerous situation. Very dangerous."

Robinson knew all too well of the consequences. For months, he had been thinking of ways to avoid a head-on competition with Safra. At one point, he even considered selling the bank when Smith and two top lieutenants, Robert Savage and Robert Budenbender, expressed interest in a leveraged buyout. Smith had figured Robinson was about to dump the bank. Although deposit levels had grown, TDB's Third World debt load was hurting. In 1987, the AmEx Bank had to add $900 million to its bad loan reserves.

Over breakfast in late December, Smith, Savage and Budenbender told Robinson they could take the bank private through an LBO, possibly merge with another private bank and then take it public again. Smith had carefully crafted the plan and the meeting to make it look as if Robinson would get credit for the idea. "Don't make Jim feel threatened," Smith counseled his partners. "Make him think it's his idea." Despite Robinson's initial excitement, the talks soon ended when neither side could agree on a price.

At American Express headquarters in New York, Bob Smith was desperate to minimize the impact of Safra's return. He consulted Freeman, who suggested that an effective public relations campaign would help make the bank look better. It was a crucial assignment.

Overlooking the PR powerhouses that had European experience, Smith selected Linda's firm. By giving Robinson Lake a $90,000 retainer, Smith was scoring points with his boss. Although there was talk that this could be a conflict of interest, Robinson didn't object. Still, the matter was put before the board to avoid any appearance of impropriety. The board saw no conflict and approved hiring the chairman's wife. But, in the opinion of some, Robinson Lake's strategy proved ineffectual. Linda and her partner Walter Montgomery had mapped out a campaign to bolster Smith's reputation. They hoped to convince reporters to write favorable stories about the bank. Another plan was to prepare pieces for the Op-Ed page of *The New York Times*. Hopefully, this would give both Smith and the bank increased prominence and credibility. But the *Times* had no interest in Smith's pieces, even his favorite one on the Third World debt. "It was rewritten again and again before the *Times* finally rejected it," recalled an employee familiar with the project. "It was a bad idea to begin with."

No matter. American Express had other options. Despite Safra's court victory, Freeman's intelligence-gathering campaign never stopped. Even after Susan Cantor asked Freeman for a "line job" and was transferred to AmEx's banking unit in mid-1988, she continued her Safra project. Bob Smith was the only one at the bank who knew that Cantor was investigating

Safra. He was told the findings would be passed on to Swiss authorities. "I didn't interfere. She worked for Freeman," Smith said.

Fellow staffers at the bank soon suspected that Cantor wasn't a typical employee. She did all her dictation behind closed doors. She never met with her supervisors. And Cantor treated Smith more like an equal than a boss. "The scuttlebutt was that she was Robinson's spy," recalled a former AmEx bank executive.

Smith's only role was approving Cantor's expenses. By 1988, the Safra project had become extremely expensive. From 1987 to 1988, Greco alone received $937,000 in salary and expenses from American Express, Freeman said. Lou Gerstner was especially upset one month in early 1988 when Freeman ran over his Corporate Affairs budget by $40,000. Freeman had an annual budget of $12 million.

"Jesus, Freeman. What's going on?" Gerstner asked. "When is this Safra thing going to end?"

"Lou, I want it to end tomorrow," Freeman answered.

Gerstner backed down, however, when Freeman told him that Robinson had authorized the project.

Despite Freeman's enthusiasm and heavy spending, Cantor was still unable to uncover any hard evidence that pointed to Safra's involvement in Iran-Contra or any other dirty business. Yet, Freeman was convinced that Safra was merely adept at hiding his dealings. Safra was "definitely involved" in Iran-Contra, Freeman believed. But he had not been investigated or exposed, thought Freeman, because of his close ties to the CIA, Israel's Mossad, and French intelligence.

Once, Freeman pulled aside Kenneth Bialkin and told him of his suspicions. "I've told my lawyer that if anything happens to me, it's because of violence by the Safra people," Freeman said solemnly.

Meanwhile, in Europe, Safra was hardly resting easy himself. Shortly after he reopened his bank, Safra was alarmed by a bizarre story that had appeared in *La Depeche du Midi,* a French magazine based in Toulouse. The story linked him and his business with money laundering, drug trafficking, the CIA, even Iran-Contra.

As 1988 wore on, similar reports appeared. In July, *Hoy,* a newspaper in Lima, Peru, made similar allegations. Then a paper in Mexico City, *Uno Mas Uno,* reprinted the allegations from the story in *Hoy.* In neither case had the publications offered up any concrete evidence. Still, that had been little comfort to Safra.

Finally, in August, *Minute,* a Paris-based paper, published a story supposedly outlining Safra's money-laundering career. That article and four subsequent *Minute* stories suggested that Safra was under investigation by the U.S. Senate. It even alleged that Safra had laundered substantial sums for the Medellín cartel and Panama strongman Manuel Noriega. The *Minute* article was especially painful to Safra because the publication, considered by many to be right-wing and anti-Semitic, was widely read.

What's more, Safra was busily planning to sell shares in his new company, Safra Republic Holdings S.A. The fall sale promised to be one of the largest initial public offerings in European history. The persistent talk that Safra was involved in sordid dealings could scuttle the capital-raising plan.

"Edmond is extremely concerned," Jeff Keil told Cohen. "We can't put our finger on it, but there seems to be a pattern to it."

Cohen also had reason to be nervous. Against the wishes of many American Express board members, he had successfully lobbied to have Shearson function as the lead public underwriter of the Safra Holding shares.

"What the hell are we doing this for?" one AmEx board member challenged Cohen. "We battle this guy while he works here. We take him to court to block his ability to do business. And now we're going to help him make money in a stock sale. This sounds crazy, absolutely crazy."

Cohen held the line.

"First of all, if we don't do it, somebody else will," Cohen said, echoing his winning arguments when he advocated the purchase of Lehman Brothers in 1984 and Hutton in 1987.

He had surprisingly strong support from Robinson, who believed Shearson's involvement in such a large-scale deal would help establish the firm in Europe.

"This is a golden opportunity for Shearson," Robinson said. "This is a deal that Shearson must do."

By the end of summer, Safra and his lieutenants suspected an organized effort was behind the articles. Several Safra aides believed that American Express was responsible. The company not only had the necessary global clout, but AmEx's sentiments against Safra were well-known after the prolonged battle to block the financier's new banking license.

Proof of any AmEx involvement wouldn't emerge until months later. By then, Safra had sued *Minute* for libel. In its defense, *Minute* produced a faxed copy of a 1967 *Life* magazine story on the Mafia. Safra's lawyers dismissed it at first. Safra wasn't even mentioned. But then one of them noticed a fax code number at the top of the sheet. It read: FEB 25 '88 21:26 AMEX CORP COMM NYC. A fax machine at AmEx's corporate communications department had sent the article.

Over the next few months, with damaging articles beginning to crop up in U.S. publications, Safra unleashed his own army of private investigators. He even hired New York attorney Stanley Arkin to help stop the stories. Arkin was tough and combative. He had vigorously defended several of the accused in Wall Street's insider trading scandals. By spring, Safra's investigators came up with the names Greco and Cantor.

At first, Safra thought of suing Robinson and American Express, but he wanted to avoid the publicity. Instead, in March, 1989, he flew to New York for a face-to-face meeting with Robinson. According to those close to both sides, Safra flat out accused Robinson's people of the smear campaign.

Robinson was astonished. He said he would check into the matter. Less than two weeks later, Robinson phoned Safra and denied any AmEx involvement. "You're wrong about us, Edmond," he said. "We're not pissing on you around the world."

Safra was fuming. To him, the evidence was irrefutable. Robinson was either lying or he had lost control of his organization. Still, Safra was reluctant to endure the publicity of a lawsuit. He asked his staff for alternatives and by May Arkin suggested one. In his regular column for the *New York Law Journal,* Arkin wrote about a hypothetical firm with a publicity-conscious CEO who was involved in a smear.

"Spreading of malicious rumor or flat-out lies . . . may well amount to a criminal fraud," Arkin wrote.

AmEx's legal department was stunned. AmEx's chief counsel, Gary Beller, called Bialkin, who was on business in Jerusalem. "Can you believe that?" Beller asked Bialkin.

"Stanley is really playing hardball," Bialkin replied. "But we have to avoid any suits."

Within weeks, Safra's lawyers presented their evidence to AmEx. Robinson agreed it was time to negotiate. After speaking to Freeman, both Beller and Bialkin had advised AmEx's CEO to seek a settlement. Despite Freeman's denials, the attorneys suspected that indeed a smear campaign had been underway.

"No matter how you look at it, Jim, it's a potentially serious blow," Bialkin told Robinson. "Jim, you have to apologize to him. It's clear that people acting on behalf of American Express were passing information about Safra."

Robinson agreed. But he insisted that the apology be kept quiet, away from the media.

In the meantime, Beller hired three outside law firms to supervise an internal investigation. One of the lawyers was John Martin Jr., a former U.S. Attorney, who began to focus his attention on Freeman, whose Safra project was well-known in the corporate suite. Smith, the only other possible mastermind, had resigned in February, 1989, after AmEx attorneys began questioning some of his financial transactions. One involved paying for an antique auto with a check from AmEx's bank.

Suspicion also fell on Cantor and Greco. Executives within American Express believed their intelligence-gathering efforts had degenerated into a smear campaign. Cantor continued to work at AmEx, though many of her colleagues avoided her.

Still, Freeman was the chief target of AmEx's in-house inquiry. Although he had an extensive file of newspaper clippings on Safra, he denied he was involved in any smear campaign. But Martin kept pressing. Soon, Freeman believed he was being set up. Robinson had barred Freeman from participating in any meetings about Safra.

"Am I going to have to resign?" Freeman asked Robinson.

"Don't worry," Robinson assured him. "You haven't done anything wrong."

By the start of July, attorneys for AmEx and Safra were hard at work negotiating a settlement. Safra's representatives agreed at first that the apology could remain secret. But they also wanted Robinson to make a huge donation to Safra's favorite charities. Safra wanted to inflict as much embarrassment on Robinson as possible.

Again, Robinson agreed. At a dinner at his apartment on

July 27 with Freeman, AmEx's legal staff and his wife Linda, Robinson expressed confidence that the matter would soon be over. He would offer a token $500,000 settlement to Safra's representatives that night. Robinson felt sure they would accept.

But when he returned later that evening after his meeting with Safra, Robinson was shaken. Safra had demanded $25 million, according to Freeman. Robinson agreed to $8 million over two years.

"At least it's a secret agreement," Robinson said.

Freeman shook his head.

"A secret?" he asked, incredulously. "Why would they want to keep it a secret? The whole idea of the apology is to make it public somehow."

Two days later, Smith sounded a similar warning when he visited Robinson at his apartment. Now a consultant to AmEx, Smith suggested that Robinson veto the settlement.

"I think you're out of your mind to settle this thing! Safra would be afraid to sue you! This thing will be all over the newspapers, Jim."

"Well, Bob, I think it's the best way out. We'll all sign releases. The letter won't be made public, Bob."

"Yeah, Jim. Yeah, sure. For about thirty seconds it won't be made public."

In a private letter to Safra dated July 24, 1989, Robinson apologized and admitted that "certain persons acting on behalf of American Express began an unauthorized and shameful effort to use the media to malign you." Robinson himself denied any knowledge of the smear campaign.

The next day, according to Freeman, Beller was told by Safra's attorneys that they had to make the letter public to comply with British securities regulations. Robinson's public humiliation was now complete.

Quickly labeled the "Safra Affair" by the press, the epi-

sode was a massive blow to American Express's reputation.
Several shareholder suits followed. Questions about Robinson's
involvement abounded all over the financial community. *How
could he not know? Who's in control?*

The next day, with board members and shareholders out
for vengeance, Robinson phoned Freeman at home in the evening. Freeman recalled the conversation as follows:

"I think you're going to have to take a couple of months'
leave of absence. There will be more investigations," Robinson
said.

AmEx's CEO sounded surprisingly emotional over the
phone. He was almost weeping. Then he began crying. Seeing
that he was unable to continue, Linda took the phone.

"Maybe you should come over here," Linda implored.
"This is a disastrous night. Jim is completely broken about this.
Maybe you could help?"

Freeman could barely suppress his anger. It was clear that
he was being axed, but it was Robinson who needed sympathy.
He declined.

"I have some calls to make," said Freeman, who then
spoke to his wife in Washington and then his lawyer. Their
advice was identical. *They're setting you up. Get out.*

The next day Freeman told Robinson he would retire by
the end of the year. In November, a month before his departure, Freeman was notified that the board had decided against
awarding him the $300,000 bonus he had expected in 1989.
Robinson said the board was still angry about the Safra Affair.

"I argued strenuously that they're doing a bad thing to a
good guy," Robinson explained.

Freeman was hardly sympathetic. "I'm turning out to be
more and more of the fall guy."

A couple of weeks later, Robinson came up with an alternative. He found a way to exercise Freeman's stock option and

award him 7,000 shares in AmEx stock. Robinson also agreed to give Freeman a contract when he moved back to Washington and established his own consulting firm.

Preoccupied with Safra from late 1988 through the summer of 1989, Robinson had not been paying close attention to Cohen and Shearson. But that was about to change. Robinson still blamed Cohen for mishandling the RJR deal. And then there was Cohen's warm relationship with Safra, AmEx's archenemy. Once, Robinson felt the friendship was an asset; now it was a liability.

Around Shearson, staffers questioned whether their boss would be around much longer. The same words of advice could be heard in the corridors and the men's room. *Peter better watch his ass.*

Cohen was no longer the resident *wunderkind.* After a record year in 1986, Shearson was trapped in a downward slide. Profits were running 88% lower than they were at the peak. Shearson's public shares were plunging. The company was trading at roughly half the $34 high it had reached in April, 1987.

Shearson was desperate for fresh capital. Cohen pleaded with Robinson to begin buying back the shares AmEx had previously sold. It would be a strong display of confidence and allow Cohen to raise some cash. Robinson refused. With little likelihood of Wall Street staging a comeback, Shearson had a dim future.

Much of the talent within Shearson also began abandoning ship. Peter Solomon, the top merchant banker, formed his own firm. So did Dan Good, who had solicited much of Shearson's corporate raider business.

In the press, it was open season on Cohen. The negative reviews first appeared shortly after the end of the RJR episode. But rather than subside, the criticisms only grew in intensity.

In a story entitled "The Peter Principle," *Forbes* writer Joe Queenan implied that Cohen couldn't fill Weill's shoes. Others raised similar questions. Before long, Cohen came to believe there was an organized effort to make him look bad in the press. Cohen eventually began to suspect Linda Robinson.

Robinson, too, turned cool. AmEx's chief, the master of subtlety, was moving quickly to distance himself from Cohen. They were no longer seen together socially. This time, it was Robinson who didn't return Cohen's phone calls. It was Robinson who didn't have time to meet. Often, AmEx's chief voiced his concern to other top executives. *Peter's under a lot of strain. Doesn't Peter look tired? I'm worried about Peter's health.*

For a while, there had been talk that Robinson was going to replace Cohen. Cohen even offered to resign in the spring of 1989, when he sensed Robinson's growing displeasure with his performance. Cohen felt burned out and deeply dejected. But AmEx's chief wouldn't hear of it. "I need you here," Robinson said. Then the Safra ordeal was in full swing and Robinson needed Cohen to smooth things over with his old friend, Edmond.

Cohen's survival was further ensured by a shift in Gerstner's fate. Up until late 1988, Gerstner had been repeatedly assured by Robinson and the board that he would assume the helm at American Express by 1991, at the latest. Robinson was reasonably sanguine about snagging a cabinet post after Bush was elected. Gerstner was the perfect successor. But Robinson's appointment never came. Baker remained furious with Robinson for his foray into policy matters the previous year. Bush decided to keep Nicholas Brady on as Treasury Secretary. The job at Commerce went to Robert Mosbacher, a Texas oil tycoon and a close friend of Bush.

Gerstner was quietly informed that Robinson was staying on. He was furious. And by late 1988, he had already begun looking for another job. At various times he was a serious contender for the top spots at United Air Lines and Pillsbury. Ironically, Gerstner finally accepted an offer from Henry Kravis to run RJR Nabisco. His compensation was rumored to be as high as $28 million over five years.

Robinson was in Washington on Friday, March 10, 1989, when he received the word. Gerstner told him matter-of-factly by phone that he was resigning. It was effective immediately. There would be no notice, no delays, Gerstner said.

Though he had suspected Gerstner would leave, Robinson was dumbfounded by the abruptness of the departure. Gerstner had been the guiding light behind TRS, the one most responsible for the success of the card. Now he was out. Even Safra had given Robinson two months' warning.

Robinson was nervous. He didn't like surprises, and he hadn't had any time for damage control. What about the market? What about the board? What about a successor? Late Friday, rumors of Gerstner's departure began to leak out. By late afternoon, Freeman was receiving calls from RJR's press people in Atlanta. Reporters were already calling.

Over the weekend, the AmEx brass hastily put together a press release announcing Gerstner's resignation. Aldo Papone would replace him as head of TRS. The following year, Papone would retire because of heart problems and be replaced by two AmEx veterans, Edwin M. Cooperman and G. Richard Thoman. Robinson declined to name a new president. Indeed, the job wouldn't be filled until September, 1991.

For a brief time after Gerstner's resignation, according to colleagues, Cohen thought he had a shot at the president's job. He seemed eager again. But he would dismiss staffers with a "We'll see. We'll see," when they told him he was a logical choice. The offer never came. And Cohen's despondency grew worse.

In mid-March, Cohen and his wife, Karen, took a spring vacation with his friend Tom Strauss, then president of Salomon Brothers, and his wife, Bonnie. The four had often vacationed together. This time they went on safari in Kenya.

When he returned in late March, Cohen was in worse shape. Sporting a full beard, his first since college, Cohen seemed distracted. At work, he would often close the big double doors to his office. Up until then Cohen had always kept the doors wide open. It had been good for morale to see the boss working.

Never much of a drinker, even socially, Cohen would occasionally retire to his office at the end of the day with a Styrofoam cup filled halfway with Scotch. Though he was never intoxicated, it was nonetheless startling for his team to observe him doing this. "Peter," asked one of them, "what is that?" Cohen replied wearily, "It helps me relax."

Cohen, according to various colleagues, also began seeing a psychiatrist for counseling and was given a prescription for a medicine to reduce anxiety.

By April, Cohen was exhausted and tired of fighting—fighting Robinson, the AmEx board, his subordinates. As Shearson continued to deteriorate, he began blaming his staff. "We have to cut costs," he would yell at weekly strategy meetings. "We need a fucking plan to turn this around."

No one was spared Cohen's rage, not even his friend Lane. Cohen had thought Lane was one of the most talented people at Shearson. He especially admired the way Lane kept current on Wall Street developments, no matter how slight. In fact, Cohen and his wife once gave Lane an antique vacuum cleaner for a birthday present in recognition of his ability to sweep up all the hot gossip.

Now, Cohen was growing increasingly disenchanted with

Lane's talents. A particularly disconcerting episode to both Cohen and Robinson occurred in December 1988 when an internal probe turned up evidence of "accounting errors" at The Boston Company, Shearson's prized money management unit. In a bid to curry favor from the home office, The Boston Company's president, James von Germeten, had overstated the subsidiary's 1988 pretax earnings by $30 million. He was promptly fired. Two other executives subsequently resigned.

"Jeffrey is letting me down," Cohen would complain to his peers on Wall Street.

In November, Cohen demoted Lane from Shearson's president to manager of the firm's money management division. Lane would resign before the end of the year.

Around Shearson, there was gossip that Cohen's secretary, Ellen Donnelly, was spying for Robinson. Six months later the suspicions about Donnelly's activities would intensify when she resigned and received a $200,000 severance package.

By the fall, Shearson had instituted layoffs and budget cuts. But nothing would stop the hemorrhaging.

Cohen's home life was just as pressured. The relentless barrage of bad press had even begun to affect his wife. Following a particularly unflattering article in the little-known *Quest* magazine, Karen phoned writer Hope Lampert and demanded a meeting. "I want to know why nobody likes my husband," she asked Lampert. When Cohen got wind of this, he forced Karen to cancel the meeting.

Shortly afterward, Cohen's seventeen-year-old daughter, Lauren, wrote an emotional letter to Lampert, asking many of the same questions her mother had wanted to address. The negative articles have become "destructive to my life," Lauren wrote.

Cohen felt increasingly alone and isolated. During previous crises, Cohen had often sought his father's advice. Sidney

Cohen had been part friend and part confessor to his son throughout his Wall Street career. He had passed away in 1987. Though he had grieved openly at the time, only now was Cohen appreciating the depth of his loss.

Toward the end of 1989, it was clear that Shearson was heading toward catastrophe. Profits were shrinking; the firm's capital looked thin. Wall Street's highly influential bond-rating agencies began raising questions. In letters, phone calls and closed-door meetings, representatives of Moody's Investors Services warned that Shearson's credit worthiness would be downgraded unless its financial position was shored up—possibly by a huge investment from its parent company. Finally, Moody's placed Shearson on its "watch" list of companies whose credit ratings would be reviewed for a possible downgrade.

The financial hemorrhaging was even raising serious questions about American Express's financial footing. Almost daily, *The Wall Street Journal* was chronicling the brokerage's worsening woes, and the intense public scrutiny was undermining AmEx's stock. The price was approaching the neighborhood where it had traded fully five years before. Shareholders were in revolt. Robinson was even beginning to feel the heat from his usually compliant board of directors. They demanded a solution.

Cohen had been working on his own capital plan for months—Project Spring, he called it optimistically. He wanted to issue more stock to the public to buttress Shearson's capital. He never quite finished the proposal. But Robinson couldn't wait any longer.

AmEx's chief was effectively blocked from selling his company's remaining shares in Shearson. If AmEx's stake in the brokerage fell below 40%, Nippon had the right to sell its

Shearson shares back to American Express—at the original price of $34. At the time, Shearson's shares were below $20.

Robinson was desperate for a partner. At one point, he had even pushed for a deal with First Executive Corporation. It made no matter that the Los Angeles insurance company had upwards of $3 billion worth of junk bonds on its books. The AmEx board balked at that proposal.

"You mean that piece of shit?" snarled board member Richard M. Furland, the president of Bristol-Myers Squibb, when Robinson presented the proposal.

Next, Robinson turned to Ronald O. Perelman. A canny corporate raider, Perelman had installed himself as chief executive at Revlon several years earlier, after masterminding the leveraged buyout of the giant cosmetics firm. But he was still eager to win a spot on Wall Street. Just two years before, he had staged an unsuccessful run at Salomon Brothers Inc.

A close friend of Robinson and his wife, Linda, who sat on Revlon's board, Perelman offered to invest $250 million in Shearson. Throughout November, they talked. The Robinsons even spent two consecutive weekends at Perelman's East Hampton estate, hammering out the details. A deal looked easy and Robinson felt as if he would soon be off the hook.

But Shearson's investment bankers were horrified. Teaming up with a known predator such as Perelman would spook their corporate clients, they argued. Many threatened to resign.

Cohen, however, was surprisingly passive. He, too, thought a deal with Perelman would destroy Shearson's credibility. But he feared that a showdown with Robinson at that point would cost him his job.

"We should talk about it," Cohen told Robinson.

As it turned out, there wouldn't be enough time. Robinson had hoped to keep the negotiations quiet to avert mass defections at Shearson and to avoid a backlash from other Shearson shareholders. Within days, *The New York Times* got wind of the story.

When a reporter phoned Robinson for a comment, AmEx's CEO was furious. He believed Cohen had purposely leaked the story to skew the deal. No sooner had he finished with the *Times* reporter than he phoned Cohen at home.

"Jim, it wasn't me," Cohen said.

"Goddamn it, Peter, I know it was you," Robinson yelled. "This screws up everything!"

The *Times* article appeared on December 7. Sure enough, the talks with Perelman ended that day.

Within days, Cohen suggested an alternative plan to save Shearson. A secondary offering of Shearson common stock at $14 a share could raise the $250 million that Perelman had offered, he insisted.

The plan was farfetched. The public had no evident appetite for more Shearson shares. The relentless descent of its stock had continued throughout 1989. By the start of 1990, the shares had plunged to as low as $10, almost a third of what it was after the Crash.

Still, Robinson agreed to the Cohen plan. The offering was announced on December 14. Publicly, Robinson even played cheerleader as Cohen left on a three-week journey to visit institutional investors throughout the U.S. and Europe. In the back of his mind, however, AmEx's CEO must have been chuckling. At last, Cohen would be out of his hair. This was his chance to do something about Shearson.

TWELVE

Primerica
and the
Price of Vanity

With Cohen away, Robinson went to work. Aside from Perelman, AmEx's chief knew he would have trouble finding a buyer who would be interested enough to take on Shearson's problems. Most of Wall Street was in the midst of downsizing. Everyone wanted to be leaner and meaner. Shearson was neither. Still, thought Robinson, there was one potential buyer, an old acquaintance who had a weakness when it came to talking deals: Sandy Weill.

As it happened, Weill had phoned Robinson in mid-January 1990 to ask how things were going. The two often chatted about business because Weill found shop talk entertaining and useful.

In 1988, Weill had purchased Primerica, and was once again active on Wall Street. Primerica was a financial conglomerate that was highly profitable, but it still lacked any notable distinction. Roughly 95% of the company's profits came from mundane products such as auto loans and mobile home mortgages made by Commercial Credit, its subsidiary finance company. And Primerica's brokerage unit, Smith Barney, Harris

Upham & Co. Inc., was badly outgunned by industry giants, such as Merrill Lynch.

Robinson discussed Shearson's woes at length and Weill listened attentively. He was sympathetic as Robinson complained about the financial press's latest barbs, as well as the suspicious commentaries being churned out by securities analysts. He wondered aloud when the crisis would pass. Then Robinson stunned Weill.

"Maybe we should do something with you. Are you interested in talking?"

The phone fell silent. Weill wasn't sure whether Robinson was joking or serious. He had thought of the possibilities of a Shearson–Smith Barney combination from time to time. But he didn't think Robinson would do something that radical.

"Sounds good. Let's talk," Weill quickly responded.

Robinson moved fast. He alerted his right-hand man, Clark, to start scrutinizing Shearson's numbers, explaining that AmEx might be able to work something out with Weill. The talks with Weill had to be kept confidential. He didn't want to repeat the experience he had with Perelman.

By Super Bowl Weekend, January 27–28, American Express and Primerica were ready to talk seriously. It was a busy weekend at Shearson. Under pressure from Moody's and Standard & Poor's, Robert Druskin, Shearson's chief financial officer, was under orders somehow to find more capital on the firm's balance sheet to show that Shearson still had resources to call on. The credit rating agencies weren't sure if Shearson had enough cash on hand to meet its debt obligations. Shearson had almost $80 billion worth of assets on its books, but it was unclear how much of it was cash and other liquid assets that could be sold off. Druskin had been keeping an almost hourly log on Shearson's financial position and was sure he could come up with a few extra million somewhere. He had grown accustomed to this type of emergency. During the week, his once ten-hour days had stretched out to fifteen. Weekend labor was nothing new.

At forty-four, Druskin was an old hand at Shearson. He was one of the veterans who could trace his tenure back to Sandy Weill's days. With a thick brown mustache and a stern look, Druskin was considered about the best numbers man around. He was calm, focused and he wasn't much into corporate politics. That made him something of an oddball at Shearson, where backbiting and power jockeying became favorite pastimes under Cohen's tension-filled rule. It also gained him recognition at AmEx. Only a handful of AmEx executives knew about the discussions with Primerica. None was as well equipped as Druskin when it came to Shearson's finances. They needed at least one Shearson insider to help them put the deal together. Druskin was it.

It was late Saturday as the exhausted Druskin packed up his files and prepared to drive home to New Jersey when Clark pulled him aside.

"Bring in a suit tomorrow, Bob. You're going to be speaking at the board meeting," Clark said.

Nothing new, Druskin thought to himself. *Another grilling.* He had been through it a half-dozen times before. The board would quiz him on Shearson's numbers, express their concern and send him on his way.

As ordered, Druskin reported for work at Shearson Sunday morning, lugging a dark-blue suit over his shoulder. Clark and Druskin worked through the early afternoon. They had just about found the entire $400 million worth of assets they needed to show the bond ratings agencies. But then Clark suggested they take a break. They went downstairs for a couple of hamburgers at one of the sidewalk cafés outside the World Financial Center. That's when Clark said there would be a slight change of plans. Before the board meeting, Robinson wanted to talk briefly to Druskin about Shearson at Skadden Arps's uptown offices.

Heading back to the offices after lunch, Druskin changed into his suit. Grabbing a sheaf of confidential documents about Shearson's finances, he followed Clark downstairs and into a black company limousine.

As their car sailed through the empty Manhattan streets, Clark turned to Druskin and dropped a bomb.

"I didn't tell you the whole truth," Clark confided.

Druskin looked up, amazed. *The whole truth about what?* he wondered.

"You're the only guy who knows this," Clark said, staring right at Druskin, and stressed, "and you can't tell anyone, okay?"

Druskin nodded. "Okay, what is it?"

"We're talking with Sandy Weill about combining Shearson and Smith Barney," Clark said.

Druskin was silent. It was the first that anyone at Shearson knew about the deal.

By the time the pair reached their destination, Druskin was a little more animated. He gave Robinson a quick rundown on his weekend's labor. "Good work, Bob," Robinson said. But there was something else that he wanted Druskin to do. Robinson asked Druskin if Clark had told him what was happening. Druskin nodded.

"Then go to Primerica. Talk with Sandy," Robinson said.

AmEx's CEO wasn't comfortable discussing Shearson's problems with someone as knowledgeable and probing as Weill. He also knew Druskin and Weill had a great deal of mutual respect. That would only help to facilitate the deal.

A few minutes later, Druskin found himself at Primerica's offices. Weill greeted him with a bear hug. Weill had hired

Druskin to work for the old Shearson Hammill in the early 1970s and was thrilled to see his longtime friend. Druskin briefed Weill and answered a seemingly unending list of questions for the next three hours. Weill's intelligence on Shearson was good. His questions were direct. When they finished, Weill shook his hand warmly and beamed.

"Bob, I'm really looking forward to working with you again," Weill said.

Robinson was counting on exactly that kind of affection from Weill. Many of Weill's friends and colleagues believed that he regretted selling Shearson to American Express in the first place. Robinson was gambling that Weill's emotional attachments were still strong enough to help him pull off the deal.

Weill's fondness for Shearson was no secret. They called Primerica "Shearson North" because Weill had hired away so many Shearson executives. Both Weill's son and daughter worked in Shearson's asset management division, and even his eighty-three-year-old father Mac worked part-time in the brokerage's Miami office.

For Weill, the deal was seductive. At fifty-six, his reputation as one of the greats of Wall Street had come, gone, and was rising again. Getting control of Shearson would surely put him back on top again. Shearson was his invention, perhaps his biggest success in life. And now he was about to snatch it back before any more harm could be done by AmEx.

Ever since resigning from AmEx in 1985, Weill had wandered from one missed opportunity to another, never coming near his original success with Shearson. In one particularly painful and widely publicized incident in March, 1986, Weill had put together an elaborate financing plan to help the troubled Bank of America with a cash infusion of $1 billion. In return, he would take control of the giant San Francisco bank. But the bank's directors unanimously voted against Weill's proposed bailout. Instead they decided to raise the capital by themselves. The defeat stung Weill.

With the purchase of Primerica in 1988, Weill took his first big step back to Wall Street. It was proving a slow journey at best. While Smith Barney had developed a reputation as a shrewd bond trading house, it was still puny by Wall Street standards. When it came to retail brokering, Smith Barney trailed the pack.

And when it came to investment banking, Primerica's brokerage was a chronic also-ran. Goldman, Sachs & Co. and Morgan Stanley scooped up the choicest business. They were the darlings of the *Fortune* 500. What was left was pretty slim pickings. Supermarkets, discount stores and the occasional retail-chain mergers made up the bulk of the remaining business. And even then, Smith Barney had trouble competing. At the end of 1989, it wasn't even clear that Primerica qualified as an investment house.

Acquiring Shearson could put Weill back on top. Having acquired a string of troubled companies over the years, Weill had a knack for getting problem firms on track. By slashing expense accounts, trimming staff and wiping out the most insignificant of corporate perks, Weill had been able to squeeze profits from some of the worst pieces of wreckage that Wall Street had ever seen. Weill felt confident he could pull off a similar rescue with Shearson.

"We all debated this point very much," said one Primerica senior executive. "We wanted to be sure we weren't doing this for just selfish personal reasons."

The deal that Robinson was offering Weill was plain enough, what they call a "no-brainer" on the Street. AmEx would merge Shearson with Smith Barney, Harris Upham & Co. The firms would each hold 40% of the new company, with the remaining shares sold to Nippon Life Insurance Company.

The Tokyo insurance giant still had the 13% share in Shearson it had bought in 1987, and the Japanese had indicated that they wanted the relationship to continue.

The combination would create a financial giant. With 14,000 brokers and a legion of investment bankers, 3,000 strong, the Shearson–Smith Barney combination would dominate Wall Street. Better yet for Robinson, it would reduce AmEx's stake in Shearson from 61% to 40%, allowing Robinson to take Shearson off his books. From now on, it would be a minority investment that would no longer weigh heavily on AmEx's bottom line.

At first, a quick deal seemed likely over the Super Bowl Weekend. After Weill grilled Druskin, he and Robinson began talking. It was agreed that Robinson would put up Shearson, while Primerica kicked in Smith Barney. Weill would be the CEO of the new firm, with Frank Zarb, the head of Smith Barney, serving as president.

Then the talks turned to money. Robinson and Weill fell into bickering about Shearson's potential liabilities. Right there, the negotiations stumbled. Chief among Weill's concerns was a $500 million bridge loan that Shearson made to finance the takeover of Massachusetts-based Prime Computer Inc. the previous summer. Prime was supposed to pay the loan back after issuing junk bonds, but the junk market had collapsed. Shearson was stuck. And then there was Balcor. The Chicago-based real estate firm that Shearson had acquired in 1983 was listing badly. It had $114 million in bad commercial real estate loans and only $50 million in reserves.

"Your brokerage is awful," Weill told him bluntly. "Shearson is in terrible shape."

Weill wanted some assurances that American Express would stand ready with fresh capital if the new company got into trouble. They were talking about a contribution in excess of $1 billion. That proved too dear for Robinson. By Sunday evening, the early optimism had faded. The deal stalled. Still, it proved to be a valuable learning experience for Robinson, who was stunned by the extent of Shearson's problems. The next day, Robinson decided to confront Peter Cohen.

Rumors that Peter Cohen was about to be fired were all over Wall Street by the time Shearson's CEO returned from his capital-raising trip on Monday, January 29. Cohen himself had heard the talk of his imminent demise for a couple of weeks. Arthur Levitt, who had recently retired as chairman of the American Stock Exchange, told Cohen discreetly that Robinson was talking to him about the top position at Shearson. Levitt was flattered, but he told Cohen, "I don't need this."

Cohen was still unaware of the Shearson–Smith Barney deal. But he, too, felt his days were numbered. Ironically, at the same time that Robinson and Weill were talking, Cohen was meeting with his attorneys, Jack Nusbaum and Martin Lipton, to discuss what kind of severance package he should ask for.

"Don't wait. This is killing you," counseled Nusbaum, a longtime friend of Cohen's.

That Monday Robinson called a meeting in the AmEx boardroom. Frustrated by the dim prospects of the capital-raising plan Cohen had outlined earlier, Robinson declared it dead.

"Shearson's basic business is okay and the industry will turn around," Robinson said confidently. Then, turning to face Cohen, Robinson added: "Shearson's problem is management."

Cohen was humiliated. Still, Shearson's CEO had trouble grasping what Robinson was saying. Given the sheer magnitude of Shearson's problems, he felt it would be difficult for Robinson to find a worthy replacement. Back in his office, he phoned Robinson, determined to force the issue.

"I guess you want to see me," he said.

"Be here at four," Robinson answered brusquely.

When Cohen arrived at Robinson's office at the World Financial Center, he was confused, his thoughts a jumble of conflicting emotions. Intellectually, his fate was clear. Cohen almost welcomed the end. The constant bruising pressure on him and his family would be over. Still, after more than seven years at Shearson's helm, Cohen couldn't accept being cast aside. The scenario, according to Wall Street sources, went like this:

"Jim, why?" Cohen asked Robinson. He felt Robinson's earlier treatment at the boardroom was harsh and unnecessary. Robinson could have spoken with him privately.

Then, almost by reflex, he asked Robinson to give him a vote of confidence.

"I still have to know that you support me," Cohen said.

Robinson sat motionless behind his desk.

"Peter, my confidence in you has been broken. I want to make changes. I'm thinking about bringing in Howard as president and chief operating officer."

Cohen began to get angry. He had previously suggested that Howard Clark Jr., AmEx's CFO, be sent to Shearson, but Robinson had refused.

"Jim, I told you that six months ago," Cohen responded.

AmEx's chief ignored him.

"That's not all," Robinson continued in the same calm demeanor. "Maybe we need a new chairman."

"What do you mean a new chairman? What do you mean a new chairman?" Cohen shouted.

It was a response motivated more by emotion than reason. Cohen wasn't surprised by Robinson's words. *Hearing* them was another matter. Cohen tried one last time to convince AmEx's CEO to back down.

235

"Jim," Cohen argued. "If you do this, the press will go to town."

Robinson didn't care. Not even bad publicity mattered anymore. Cohen was out.

For appearance' sake, Cohen was allowed to serve as CEO until March 1. San Francisco investment banker F. Warren Hellman would take over. A former partner in Lehman Brothers, Hellman was also said to be a big investor in Shearson and had been advising Robinson over the years.

Over the next few months, AmEx and Cohen negotiated a complex severance package. The divorce was far from easy. Cohen chose Safra's attorney, Stanley Arkin, to represent him. AmEx brought in attorney Arthur Liman, the counsel to the special Senate committee that had investigated the Iran-Contra scandal.

By June, both sides came to an understanding. Cohen would remain on the Shearson payroll as a consultant until November, 1991, with an office and secretary paid for by American Express. Cohen's severance package, which included various stock options, was valued well in excess of $10 million. Even by Wall Street's standards, the agreement appeared generous. What's more, it included a provision that prohibited Cohen from suing any AmEx directors or officers and their families. Such liability protection isn't unique, but extending protection to family members is highly unusual. Within days of the agreement, there was speculation that the provisions were intended to protect Linda Robinson, Cohen's perceived nemesis since the days of RJR Nabisco.

By February, the deal with Weill and Primerica had lain dormant for weeks. Weill and his wife Joan took off for a vacation. Weill even managed to play in the Bing Crosby Pro-Am golf tournament in Pebble Beach, California.

Meanwhile, Robinson engaged in less sunny pursuits. With Cohen and his misguided stock plans behind him, Robinson began groping for yet another solution to the problems at Shearson.

Before long, Robinson had even more cause for concern. On February 13, Drexel Burnham Lambert, the house of junk, filed for bankruptcy. For the first time in modern history, a major Wall Street firm went belly-up. There was a spreading panic in the financial community.

Almost immediately, Robinson and Weill realized the implications for Shearson. Weill phoned Robinson three days after Drexel's bankruptcy. The conversation centered on the Drexel catastrophe. Although neither man was a friend of Drexel's junk king, Michael Milken, each had met him several times over the years. They debated how much he was responsible for Drexel's downfall. Neither one mentioned their own deal, though it wasn't far from their thoughts. Then Weill told Robinson that he and Joan would be in Palm Beach during the upcoming Washington's Birthday weekend. As it turned out, Jim and Linda Robinson would be spending the weekend at their vacation condominium at the Palm Beach Polo and Country Club.

"Great," said Robinson, always a gracious host. "Come on over for dinner. It'll be just the four of us."

It was supposed to be a purely social gathering. No talk of business. Wall Street was not a favorite subject around Weill's wife, Joan. Married for twenty-seven years, Joan Weill was smart. Her husband was said to listen carefully to Joan and heed her advice. She was also well-read and always had a best-seller at her bedside. She was even known to glance at *The Wall Street Journal*.

There were the usual hugs and cozy salutations as the four gathered for a seafood feast of lobster and shrimp at one of the club's four restaurants. At first, there was some strained conversation about the weather. But Drexel's sudden demise proved a rich topic of conversation. It was obvious to everyone at the table that the panic induced by Drexel could quickly overwhelm Shearson.

Seizing the opening, Weill suggested that they try again to work out a deal.

"It wouldn't be impossible," he said. "We came so close."

Robinson, recalling the first ill-fated attempt, especially the prohibitive billion-dollar-plus price tag, was hesitant. American Express's own investment bankers and lawyers advised him against such a deal, Robinson said. And that made the board's approval even more tenuous.

"I just can't do it. The lawyers are dead against it," Robinson said.

His tone suggested the deal was dead. Weill, however, suspected Robinson was trying to talk down the price. He felt Robinson needed just a little prodding.

"You don't know until you try," Weill argued.

When Robinson arrived at his office the following Tuesday morning, the mood on Wall Street was bleak. The atmosphere at Shearson was even darker. A week had passed since the Drexel debacle, and the financial community was anticipating additional victims. Not since the market crash of 1987 had the Street been so shaken. Waiting for the ripples to be felt was agonizing. Lunchtime crowds were visibly absent from the usual haunts. Only the bars were doing a brisk nighttime business. Secretaries and brokers gathered around the water coolers, speculating about office closings and layoffs. It seemed as if everyone was working on a résumé.

For Shearson, a crisis was looming. In the minds of most Wall Street executives, Shearson was the other shoe just waiting to drop. Trading desks all over the Street were speculating that the brokerage was on the brink of collapse. Many were having second thoughts about doing business with Shearson. Wall Street's omnipresent rumormongers began taking aim at Shearson. *What's the difference between Drexel and Shearson? About six months.*

The panic soon spread. Suddenly Robinson was being questioned by the Federal Reserve Board and the Securities and Exchange Commission about Shearson's abilities to meet its obligations. Even the New York Stock Exchange was pestering Robinson about Shearson's capital strength. Creditors were also jittery. Fidelity Investments Company, the giant mutual fund company, was worried about Shearson's commercial paper. Shearson's bankers were also alarmed. The world's largest banks customarily extended billions of dollars to Wall Street firms, allowing them to trade everything from bonds to currencies. But after the Drexel collapse, foreign banks were threatening to cut back their lines of credit to Shearson. American banks were also growing increasingly leery. Chase Manhattan and Manufacturers Hanover Trust were especially reluctant to extend any more credit to Shearson.

Not even Robinson's willingness to muster American Express's financial resources in support of Shearson could ease the snowballing alarm. Robinson, never a hands on manager, suddenly found himself almost totally absorbed by Shearson's worsening plight. A crisis had gripped AmEx's executive suite. And Robinson had converted his office into a War Room. Reams of computer printouts were spread across the carpeting of his fifty-first-floor office at the World Financial Center, and his usually well-ordered desk was awash in faxes and memos. Accustomed to chatting with Shearson's finance department once or twice a year, Robinson was now checking in several times a day.

"What are the credit markets doing? Can I call anyone and

assure them?" Robinson asked, his fear worsening with every response he received.

Finally, with his room to maneuver all but gone, Robinson made the one call that he hoped would make a difference. He phoned Weill. They agreed to meet the following Saturday. The deal was on again.

A chill wind had swept the streets clear of pedestrians as Robinson's limousine glided through the sparse Manhattan traffic. It was a wintry Saturday morning and AmEx's CEO sat bundled in the back seat wearing a thick black wool coat, a beige scarf wound tightly around his neck. Robinson looked somber, almost pained. Cradled in his lap was a stack of files and memorandums about yet another crisis at Shearson.

It was a short trip from Robinson's midtown duplex to the East Side law offices of Skadden Arps. The ride usually takes ten minutes. This time it took five. A good omen, Robinson thought. He hoped the rest of the day would pass as easily. That afternoon he had scheduled a two o'clock meeting with Weill at Primerica's offices. But first he wanted one last briefing by his advisors at Skadden Arps before heading for the showdown with Weill.

The reception area was deserted as Robinson got off the elevator at Skadden's twenty-eighth-floor offices. Following the din of voices, he swept by the line of empty secretarial desks and found his way to the corner office of Joseph Flom. There James Wolfensohn, the amiable Australian investment banker, was in a spirited debate about negotiating tactics with Howard Clark Jr. and Gary Beller, AmEx's chief counsel. Leaning back in the black leather chair behind his desk was Flom.

At sixty-five, with a shock of white hair, the crusty Flom was a senior partner at Skadden Arps and perhaps the firm's most ruthless takeover expert. Tough-looking, with a quick wit and withering tongue, Flom was one of the most skillful negotiators on Wall Street. For him, it was an art. A graduate of City College of New York and Harvard Law School, Flom had been an M&A pioneer in the 1950s. He could trace his association with AmEx's CEO all the way back to Robinson's ill-fated attempt to acquire McGraw-Hill. Flom had been by Robinson's side for a decade. Since Harry Freeman resigned, he had become Robinson's closest advisor.

After exchanging a few pleasantries, Flom began. He pulled no punches. He had doubts. As Flom well knew, Weill was perceived by critics on Wall Street as a vulture, always lurking about troubled companies that he could buy on the cheap. Shearson was just the latest victim. He warned Robinson that the upcoming talks would be treacherous. Weill was cunning, Flom said. And Primerica's chief still had a lot of friends at Shearson, so his intelligence was bound to be pretty accurate. *Be decisive,* Flom told Robinson. *Don't waver.*

By the time Robinson and his entourage arrived at Primerica in the early afternoon, Weill's people were already assembled in Primerica's thirty-sixth-floor boardroom.

With a twelve-foot-high ceiling and a panoramic view of the East River, with Queens just beyond, Primerica's boardroom wasn't much like the one at American Express. In contrast to the lush paneling and deep leather chairs in AmEx's boardroom, Primerica's looked almost trashy. There was not a single painting or flash of color. The walls of Primerica's boardroom were covered with a beige, burlap-like wallpaper that was curling at the edges. The twelve-foot-long conference table was shabby, scarred by cigar ash and crusted with coffee rings. It was just the way Weill wanted it. It was his workroom.

As soon as Robinson entered the room, Weill jumped up

to greet him. He pumped his hand and slapped him on the back. Robinson flinched. He never felt comfortable with such familiar physical contact.

"Sandy," Robinson said, smiling, "this completes the circle. We broke apart once. Now, we're together again."

Weill grinned. "I can't wait, Jim."

Despite outward calmness, there was a sense of urgency as the second meeting convened. The Drexel fiasco had altered the equation. Shearson looked like it was hurtling toward disaster. And that gave Weill the advantage. It didn't take long for tensions to surface.

Weill had a checklist of Shearson's problems. He read them off one by one. They were the same old complaints: Balcor, bridge loans, and The Boston Company. But this time Weill sounded more threatening.

"This stuff scares the hell out of me, Jim," said Weill, almost daring Robinson to defend himself.

Robinson glared. "You're just looking for the potholes. And you're overstating the size of the potholes, too."

By now Joe Flom was seething. Weill, the vulture, was up to his old tricks.

"Sandy, you're just trying to knock down the price," Flom shot back.

Weill wouldn't back down. "Joe," he said. "These are big worries. I need some protection."

"We won't be lowballed," Flom declared.

He then produced his own list of worries. Flom said Weill was contributing next to nothing. He hadn't offered any cash. And Smith Barney, though in better shape than Shearson, had a pretty skimpy business. Weill backed off.

Over the next nine hours, Robinson and Weill struck several compromises. Weill agreed to pump more assets into the new ventures, including Margareten, Primerica's mortgage finance unit. For his part, Robinson said he was willing to come up with fresh capital. He said AmEx would inject $750 million into Shearson on Monday. It wasn't the billion-dollar commitment Weill initially wanted. But it was enough to do the deal.

By eleven o'clock, both sides were satisfied. Everyone was dead tired and eager to go home. But as they drew away from the conference table, Robinson had one last question: what should the new firm be called? It seemed a rather small point, but to Robinson it was critical. Image was just as important as the deal itself. He still hoped to look like a winner.

"Shearson is the bigger of the two," Robinson pointed out. "Shearson–Smith Barney sounds pretty good."

No one responded. The Primerica team clearly felt it was not the moment to argue. Finally Frank Zarb broke the silence. "Let's get the hell out of here and go home. I can't keep my eyes open."

On Monday morning, Weill began his day as usual. Up at seven-thirty, he grabbed a quick breakfast and did a quick mental check of the day's itinerary, mostly routine documentation to take care of some loose ends for the accountants. Both sides had agreed that Zarb would smooth the deal with regulators. As the former Energy Secretary under Gerald Ford, Zarb was a skillful operator within the Beltway. The deal was done— or at least Weill thought so.

Weill left his Upper East Side apartment at eight-thirty and strolled to his office. At ten o'clock, he and Robinson would visit the bond ratings agencies to outline their plan.

It would be a short meeting. If Moody's and S&P didn't think the new firm was viable, the merger couldn't fly. Their approval was vital since not a single pension fund or bank would even consider investing in the new firm's commercial paper if the ratings agencies gave it a low rating.

Robinson arrived at Moody's first, accompanied by Clark

and AmEx Treasurer Joan Spero. Weill showed up five minutes later, with Jamie Dimon in tow. Dimon had been Weill's top aide ever since the pair worked together at AmEx. Then the entourage proceeded to a twelfth-floor conference room to meet with Moody's representatives.

The meeting was scheduled to last forty-five minutes. In keeping with protocol, Robinson, the head of the larger company, made the first statement, lasting about ten minutes. He outlined the merger between Shearson and Smith Barney and pointed out that American Express would contribute $750 million to the new company. Weill spoke next, emphasizing the potential of the new firm.

Then it was Moody's turn. After pelting their visitors with a series of questions about the financial ties between the new firm and the parent companies, Moody's vice president and top financial analyst, Christopher Mahoney, asked Robinson pointedly: "Tell me, what will your company's continuing role be in the new entity?"

Robinson paused. He was never good at impromptu sessions like this. In the thirteen years he had been AmEx's CEO, he had rarely visited the ratings agencies. All that was needed was an indication that AmEx would have some contingency plan in place to help out the company financially if problems crept up. A letter of credit, or even some profound expression of commitment from Robinson, would do it.

But Robinson was more interested in unloading Shearson than in maintaining close ties.

"The new company will stand alone," he responded. Then, after hesitating, he added tentatively: "We'll be there if needed."

Everyone looked astonished. It was hardly the kind of direct, confident statement of support that Moody's expected.

An hour later, Robinson gave a similarly tentative performance at S&P. *Oh God, this is trouble,* Weill thought to himself.

As the day dragged on, the prospects for a deal got worse. That afternoon, Tom Hill, the head of Shearson's investment bank, demanded a meeting with Robinson. Because Hill was Shearson's top merger maestro and its single biggest revenue producer, Robinson agreed.

Days before, Hill had been tipped about the deal with Primerica. But he remained silent, hoping that the talks would fall through. Now, when the deal seemed on the verge of closing, he knew he had to act immediately. Trim, intense and somewhat pompous, Hill had ambition enough to burn. No deal was too big, no job out of reach. For years, he had looked covetously at the top spot. It was his corporate destiny. With Cohen dethroned, he had hoped to take over. He had already begun campaigning for the new job. Flom and Linda Robinson were his strongest supporters. Now, all of sudden, Weill was in his way.

Hill told Robinson it was a foolhardy deal. It made Robinson look like a hapless victim being bailed out by the crafty Weill. Hill also warned that Shearson's investment bankers wouldn't stand for a takeover by Weill. There was already talk of mass resignations, even a leveraged buyout, to keep Shearson out of Weill's clutches.

Robinson was noticeably nervous. The last thing he needed was another major embarrassment. The thought of Shearson's top talent walking out the door would harm the firm's image even more.

Robinson was beginning to have second thoughts.

Two days later, that became very apparent to Weill. Rising early Wednesday morning, Weill switched on Cable News Network to find out what had happened overnight in the London and Tokyo financial markets. To his astonishment, Stuart Varney, the co-anchor of CNN's "Business Day," was quoting an article from the *Financial Times* of London, which said Primerica and American Express were negotiating a deal for Shearson. In an interview with two *FT* reporters the previous day, Robinson had acknowledged that the two sides were talking.

Up until then, Weill had prided himself and Robinson on how both were able to maintain a cloak of secrecy around the entire deal. There was barely a whisper on Wall Street. That was essential. He knew from experience that nothing can kill a deal faster than the public's prying eyes. Shareholders, board members, even employees get spooked. After all, mergers always mean a new balance of power. Executives are rotated; jobs are lost.

By the time Weill reached his desk at nine o'clock, the worst had already occurred. Employees at Smith Barney's ninety-six retail offices were in an uproar. After Weill had built up Smith Barney for three years, many of his brokers thought he was destroying the franchise by tying it up with the much bigger Shearson. Many suspected Weill was driven by pure ego and the satisfaction of running Shearson again. Minutes before the market opened at nine-thirty, Weill got on the company's internal squawk box to calm jittery staffers. It didn't help.

At ten o'clock, a furious Weill phoned Robinson.

"So what the hell is going on, Jim?" asked Weill.

Robinson said he had granted the *FT* interview on Tuesday, with the understanding that it would be embargoed until Thursday, when most of the loose ends of the deal would be settled. He had no idea that it would appear so soon.

"Sandy," he said apologetically, "I didn't mean for the story in the paper to come out that way. You've got to believe me."

They chatted for a few more minutes, but the warmth that was evident in their relationship had evaporated. By the time he hung up, Weill suspected that Robinson was trying to scuttle the deal. Still, he tried one more time.

Later that Wednesday, Weill, Robinson, Flom, and Zarb met at Weill's library at Primerica. To assuage the ratings agencies, it was decided that AmEx would have to weigh in with more financial muscle. Under the new terms, American Express would hold on to The Boston Company, as well as the bridge loan to Prime Computer. Those were pretty stiff terms, but even Robinson agreed it was the only way to ensure Moody's and S&P's approval. For the moment, everything appeared to be back on track.

Then Robinson shocked his Primerica hosts. Almost as an afterthought, Robinson told Weill he was considering a plan to buttress Shearson by purchasing the 39% of the firm that AmEx didn't already hold. As part of the plan, Robinson would have to pay as much as $1 billion. It was a radical solution, but Robinson said he owed it to the board to give them at least two options to consider.

Weill was dumbfounded. He quickly glanced at Zarb, who was shaking his head. Furious, Weill kept his anger in check.

"Whatever you think is best, Jim," said Weill, as he tried to read Robinson's motives. "But we still have a good deal. Don't walk away from it."

By the next day, any lingering hope that Weill was holding on to was snuffed out when he picked up *The New York Times*. Halfway through breakfast, Weill scanned the front page. To his horror, in the lower right-hand corner, there was a black and white photograph of himself staring back. With his coffee cup suspended in midair, he read the headline aloud: "Shearson Deal May Embrace the Man who Built the Firm." The story provided a glowing account of Weill's career and return to Wall

Street. Worse, it made it appear that he was about to rescue Robinson.

"The attitude at AmEx after *The New York Times* story was 'Those bastards at Primerica. They got a leg up on us,'" recalled one investment banker who participated in the negotiations.

Both sides denied leaking the story to the *Times*. But it didn't much matter by then. Weill realized that the deal was dead. He knew Robinson wouldn't tolerate any perception that he was being bailed out, especially by his former number two executive. Still, he didn't want to be upstaged by Robinson. If the deal was going to be killed, he was the one who would do it. Shortly before AmEx's board meeting on March 4, Weill faxed a letter to Robinson. Primerica was no longer interested in pursuing the deal.

That night, American Express announced that it would purchase the remaining shares in Shearson that it didn't already own. In addition, Robinson disclosed plans to pump $1 billion into Shearson, raising much of the money from a new offering of AmEx stock. It was a step that angered many of the company's biggest shareholders. But Robinson felt relieved. He wouldn't stand for any hint of a bailout by Weill. Within hours, AmEx's finely-tuned public relations machine began planting stories on how Robinson saved Shearson. AmEx's CEO named Howard Clark Jr. as Shearson's new chairman. AmEx spokesmen said that it was an issue of integrity. Jim believes in fixing AmEx's problems, was the gist of what they repeated over the next several days. On Wall Street, there was a different view: Robinson blew it. His ego had gotten in the way of a deal that would have rid him of a corporate blight. Despite the infusion of cash, Shearson still remained a big problem for Robinson. To make matters worse, there were already rumblings of deep trouble elsewhere at AmEx. The vaunted card business, the heart and soul of the corporation, would be the next source of major headlines and deep embarrassment.

THIRTEEN

Credit and Credibility

While Robinson's efforts to unload Shearson may have floundered, that didn't stop him from trying to discard other unwanted businesses at AmEx. Within days of backing out of the deal with Sandy Weill, Robinson rid himself of TDB, ending one of the more painful sagas of his career.

The company announced on March 4 that it had completed the sale of TDB to another Swiss private banker. The previous December, AmEx had negotiated a tentative deal with Geneva-based Compagnie de Banque et d' Investissement, but it had taken several months to complete the paperwork and obtain Swiss approvals.

Robinson denied that the success of Safra's new bank, which he started eight months after pulling out of AmEx, had anything to do with selling off TDB. American Express had boasted that it had doubled the size of TDB to $12 billion in assets under its management.

Still, few in the banking community were surprised by AmEx's decision to bail out of TDB. AmEx had never been considered a serious player in private banking. The "synergy"

that Robinson hoped would emerge between TDB and the rest
of AmEx never materialized. Just as Safra had warned, TDB's
secretive clients scoffed at AmEx's attempts to market charge
cards and investment products. What's more, AmEx was no
match for private banking titans such as Credit Suisse or Swiss
Bank Corporation. AmEx's publicity machine tried to obscure
its strategic defeat by pointing up the final sale price of $1
billion, nearly twice what AmEx paid for TDB.

Shearson's deepening problems, however, allowed Robinson little time for self-congratulation. In the first quarter of
1990, Shearson's red ink climbed to $915 million. The staggering
amount overwhelmed its parent. American Express posted a
$620 million loss, the largest quarterly loss in the company's
140-year history.

In response, Robinson asked the board to name him Chief
Quality Officer, an indication that AmEx's CEO remained committed to excellence. But it was too late for such publicity ploys.
AmEx's chief needed a solution. Huge doses of capital couldn't
stop the hemorrhaging, and there was little chance of finding
another buyer. There was virtually no interest in AmEx's
bloated and loss-ridden brokerage. Robinson decided it was
time to shrink the house that Cohen built.

Following Robinson's orders, Clark began a sweeping
reorganization. More than 4,000 brokers, about a third of
Shearson's total, left the firm for other Wall Street jobs.
Roughly 20% of the firm's investment bankers were let go.
Clark took some tentative steps to spruce up Shearson's tattered image. The name Hutton, which Cohen had so proudly
added to Shearson's corporate logo in 1987, was dropped. He
also split the firm in two, renaming the investment banking arm
Lehman Brothers in a vain attempt to recapture the old partnership's luster.

Clark also began shedding much of the once-treasured

assets that had been so eagerly amassed in the eighties. From its $1 billion junk bond portfolio to its European mortgage operations, Shearson would end up trimming some $25 billion in assets. Still, talk of selling off AmEx's brokerage never faded. "As soon as they find a buyer, it's gone," said one analyst.

At Shearson, morale slid. Ever since the talks with Primerica, few believed Robinson's avowed allegiance to rescuing Shearson. Indeed, after the talks broke down, Clark had straightforwardly told Shearson's brokers that AmEx had tried to acquire Smith Barney. The distrust only mounted.

By 1991, the card also ran up against the sobering realities of the new decade. Analysts predicted a comeback for AmEx as the economy recovered. Over the long term, the outlook was gloomy. Experts had been warning that the number of AmEx's cards in circulation would peak in the U.S. by the year 2000. And the hoped-for growth overseas had proven tough to come by. In Europe, Visa was better known and more widely accepted.

Consumers were no longer buying AmEx's message. Prestige, the byword of the 1980s, was ill-suited to the more austere nineties. The Baby Boomers had babies of their own. College tuition and retirement were uppermost in their minds. Weekend getaways to exotic locales, once depicted in AmEx's ad campaign, were no longer relevant. Conspicuous spending was out, saving was in.

The product that former AmEx CEO Ralph Reed proclaimed would "liberate the American wallet from its multiplicity of credit cards" failed in its mission. At $55 a year, AmEx's mighty green card was more an indulgence than a necessity. Most banks were charging $20 or less for Visa and MasterCard. More than 4 million of AT&T's card customers hadn't paid anything. The telecommunications giant had waived its fee to lure new customers.

Worse, the competition was getting fiercer. Ameritech, one of the Baby Bells created by the breakup of AT&T, announced plans to offer MasterCard. And Sears was suing Visa for the right to issue a bank card in addition to its Discover Card. There were rumblings that the finance division of General Motors was also thinking of getting into the card business. Consumers were awash in cards. Fewer and fewer noticed any distinction. Image alone was no longer an incentive to use the card. Plastic was plastic. Membership had fewer privileges.

For AmEx, many analysts and competitors were forecasting further merchant and even membership fee reductions. It would become a smaller company in the years ahead, perhaps focusing solely on its travel and entertainment clientele. American Express still dominated the world of corporate expense accounts. In December, 1991, AmEx announced that it would acquire Lifeco Travel Services, the nation's fifth-largest travel agency and a specialist in business travel. "A lot of people are saying there is no need for an American Express card," said one analyst. "That means the golden age of American Express has probably passed." Another analyst was more blunt: "This company was never preeminent in anything—except image."

The gloom at TRS worsened steadily as 1991 dragged on. AmEx selectively began waiving its annual fee to retain cardmembers, but abruptly stopped when *The Wall Street Journal* reported it. Then came the merchant revolts. After the showdown in Boston, AmEx had reduced its restaurant discount fees around the nation, a move that would cost the company up to $30 million in revenues. By June, Ed Cooperman turned his attention to Optima, AmEx's credit card. Trapped in a stubborn recession, Optima users had trouble meeting their bills. Delinquencies were rising.

Optima had been AmEx's brightest hope. Unlike AmEx's green, gold and platinum cards, Optima wasn't a charge card which had to be paid off in full every month. It was a classic credit card, allowing users to pay off their bills over time in exchange for a finance charge. To guard against deadbeats and late payers, AmEx issued the card only to existing charge card holders who had solid track records when it came to paying their bills.

Optima was supposed to beat back the bank cards, especially the gold variety. The premium card offered by banks conveyed the same prestige as AmEx's plastic; it had lured away legions of consumers who preferred the convenience of a revolving credit line. At first glance, Optima looked promising. Its annual fee was just $15 and its finance charge, initially 13%, then 16.5%, was far lower than the lofty 19.8% charged by big banks.

Few questioned the strategy. American Express officials encouraged the view that Optima was well-received and growing quickly. In 1989, analyst Michael Goldstein of Sanford C. Bernstein & Co. predicted that Optima would account for almost 20% of TRS's profits, or $400 million, by 1993.

By 1991, there were over 3 million Optima cards in circulation, with outstanding charges, or receivables, amounting to $7 billion. There was even talk of a nationwide launch to go head-to-head with the bank cards. Up until then, Robinson had astutely steered clear of any suggestion that Optima would be offered to the general public to avoid a confrontation with the banks, which issued the bulk of AmEx's traveler's checks. But with Optima earnings expected to surpass traveler's check profits by three to one in a couple of years, such caution was no longer necessary. In late 1990 and early 1991, competitors suspected that AmEx mailed millions of Optima solicitations.

Most were sent to households in the Midwest, where the regional economy remained relatively stable.

In June, Cooperman dispatched a team of auditors and lawyers to gauge the depth of the problems at Optima's Jacksonville, Florida, center. Over the summer, they found evidence that write-offs were being purposely delayed. When credit card bills are past due for 180 days, the accounts are automatically written off and turned over to bill collectors. "It was not illegal," said a senior AmEx official. "They thought if they could delay reporting the problems, they would go away when the recession ended."

Still, Wall Street analysts and much of the public were stunned on October 2, when they picked up their newspapers to read that AmEx was taking a $265 million hit to third-quarter earnings at its TRS division. Roughly 8% of Optima's outstanding receivables would be charged off. "Optima Backfires on American Express," howled the headline in *The Wall Street Journal*. Optima was derisively renamed Pessima in the financial community.

Embarrassed AmEx officials explained how they would have to set aside money to cover defaults on AmEx's Optima credit card and to pay for a reorganization of its charge card business. Roughly 1,700 TRS staffers, 3% of the division's work force, would be laid off. The write-off would result in a loss of $88 million in the third quarter, the first quarterly loss in TRS history. AmEx as a whole would report a 93% earnings drop. Ironically, Shearson posted a 23% profit gain in the quarter, to $63 million.

Despite AmEx's insistence that the problems were confined to Optima, there were few believers on Wall Street. Almost immediately, concern focused on the green, gold and platinum cards. Since only existing AmEx cardmembers qualified for Optima, the disbelief was understandable. And Robinson only added to the confusion. When asked by *The Wall Street Journal* why AmEx customers would pay off their charge cards, but not Optima, Robinson answered: "I don't know."

Wall Street was alarmed by signs of Robinson's inattention to the core business, as well as the company's astounding announcement. AmEx's stock slid to 21, a six-year low. Moody's soon downgraded the rating on about $7 billion of the company's long-term debt. This unprecedented action was again the result of the problems at TRS.

At first, competitors blamed AmEx's poor credit controls for all the problems. Indeed, bank card default rates were roughly half of Optima's charge-off. Competitors were quick to point out that many of AmEx's charge cards were used by businessmen for corporate expenses. Most paid their charge card bills in a timely fashion because they were reimbursed through their expense accounts. By contrast, Optima was a consumer product, designed to be used for leisure and household expenditures.

Two days later, AmEx acknowledged that some of its staffers may not have written off bad debts quickly enough. The company asked Skadden Arps, AmEx's outside counsel, to investigate the card defaults at Optima. Bank regulators at the Federal Deposit Insurance Corporation also began looking into the matter. Because Optima's revolving credit was essentially a loan, it was issued by AmEx's Centurion Bank. Eventually, several AmEx executives would lose their jobs.

The Optima affair only heightened suspicions that American Express would become a much smaller company in the years ahead. During a telephone conference with analysts following the disclosure of Optima, AmEx officials indicated that other parts of the corporation could be sold off. Indeed, as part of the reorganization, AmEx disclosed that it was sharply scaling back its merchandising efforts. The company had once been the fifth-largest mail order merchandiser in the country, selling everything from computers to cashmere sweaters to cardholders. AmEx also tried to sell its publishing division to a group led by Henry Kravis; the deal fell through.

"The only thing that's sacrosanct is TRS," said Harvey Golub. The former CEO of IDS, AmEx's financial services firm based in Minneapolis, had been appointed AmEx's president on July 21. Golub had also taken over responsibility for TRS. Cooperman would later resign and go to work for Sandy Weill at Primerica.

"Even IDS?" asked one analyst.

"I just made my statement," Golub retorted.

By the fall of 1991, AmEx was in a state of siege. Robinson was no longer a corporate celebrity. Wall Street analysts sniped at his abilities, while the press questioned his strategies. The corporate machine that he had assembled through the 1980s by accident and design was slowing. Revenues were down. Profits were lagging. Many of AmEx's competitors, who felt Robinson had escaped criticism despite his poor management, were delighted. "All of a sudden, you see Mr. Smiling Atlanta's Teflon wearing thin," said the CEO of a rival Wall Street firm.

Linda faced a troubled adjustment to the new era as well. After some people questioned her handling of Ross Johnson's PR during the LBO battle for RJR Nabisco, she was no longer perceived as the witty and trendy spokesperson for Wall Street's takeover crowd. With the acquisition business in a slump, her firm was no longer as visible, her counsel less sought after.

Her past associations continued to dog her. In April, 1990, Michael Milken, Robinson Lake's biggest-paying customer during the 1980s, had pleaded guilty to securities fraud. Milken was sentenced to ten years in prison. Yet, the government's investigation was far from over. The FDIC filed a civil suit against Milken in connection with the marketing of junk bonds to savings and loans. By September, Cravath, Swaine & Moore, the renowned New York law firm and the FDIC's legal counsel, began pestering Robinson Lake for documents on Milken. Cravath attorneys became increasingly frustrated by what they considered the firm's lack of cooperation.

Away from the office, the Robinsons pursued a less visible lifestyle. With their professional lives under pressure, both shunned the publicity they had once sought. They were infrequent guests at formal affairs. Their names rarely surfaced in the gossip columns.

The Optima episode also renewed speculation about Robinson's future. Nineteen ninety-two marked his fifteenth anniversary as CEO of American Express. It had been an unusually long tenure, and many analysts believed that American Express needed fresh management.

Not since Sandy Weill had resigned in 1985 had there been any serious talk about a successor to Robinson. Even the Safra Affair, while a blow to AmEx's integrity, was not considered serious enough to persuade Robinson's loyal board members to dislodge their benefactor.

The bottom line was another matter. With the company facing steep hurdles in the years ahead, there was open discussion on Wall Street about Robinson's successor. "If I were Jim Robinson, I would want to do the best for the company," said one Street analyst. "I would retire tomorrow. The general impression is that he has mismanaged American Express."

The board, too, was growing increasingly impatient, according to AmEx insiders. Although the board was still loaded with Robinson loyalists and friends, such as Drew Lewis, Henry Kissinger, and former opera singer Beverly Sills, AmEx's directors were no longer as forgiving.

After the Safra Affair, the board had cautioned Robinson. *We can't have any more missteps.* But the deterioration in AmEx's core business raised new alarms. The merchant revolt in Boston was especially worrisome. Perhaps Robinson's toughest critic on the board was Roger S. Penske. The president of Penske Corp. was also very vocal about AmEx's growing problems. He carefully questioned Robinson at a June board meeting. *What's happening to our franchise? Why didn't anybody handle the problem in Boston sooner? Will there be any more surprises?*

At the same meeting, the board also discussed Robinson's possible successors. Most of the talk focused on Golub. At fifty-two, he was widely considered to be the most effective manager AmEx had. As the head of IDS, Golub had transformed AmEx's subsidiary into one of the mainstays of the corporation. Unlike Robinson, Golub was tough and hands-on, a cross between Weill and Gerstner. Indeed, Golub was Brooklyn-born like his former mentor Weill. He was also an alumnus of McKinsey, as was Gerstner. Though a promising candidate, the board believed that "Harvey needed more seasoning," said a source close to the board. If so, executives at AmEx speculated that Penske might step in as an interim chairman until Golub was ready.

Robinson denied that he had any plans to step down. Indeed, it was widely rumored within American Express that he reluctantly promoted Golub only after he was pressured to do so by the board. Still, Robinson's room to maneuver may have been sharply curtailed. On August 1, Warren Buffett, a partner in Weill's scheme to buy Fireman's Fund, had invested $300 million of much-needed capital into American Express. Buffett's preferred shares could eventually be exchanged for a 2½% stake in AmEx and a bigger voice in its management. Many on Wall Street believed that Buffett would take a more active role in AmEx after sorting out the problems at Salomon Brothers. Buffett, whose Berkshire Hathaway owns a 14% interest in Salomon, replaced Gutfreund in August when the government disclosed Salomon's irregularities in trading Treasury bonds.

Few on Wall Street expected Robinson to be shoved aside soon. For the sake of image, Robinson would have to find another job before he could move on. And that wouldn't be easy. AmEx's chief had dim prospects for a position in Washington. Jim Baker was hardly a friend. Worse, the Safra Affair had tainted Robinson's reputation. And there was little likelihood of taking over the helm at another company given his mixed track record at American Express. Many on Wall Street believed Robinson would end up as an ambassador or the head of a major university. Both possibilities would be face-saving, while allowing Robinson a public forum.

In the meantime, Robinson's empire was shrinking. And for the first time since he took over as CEO in 1977, AmEx's core business was in serious jeopardy. Despite the daunting problems that faced him, Robinson appeared increasingly isolated in his fifty-first-floor office at American Express Tower. He was surrounded by a group of faceless subordinates, who had yet to finish business school when Robinson embarked on his empire building.

The characters that had guided Robinson and helped shape AmEx in the eighties had long since moved on. Sandy Weill was steadily enlarging Primerica's profits. Peter Cohen had gone into business on his own. Lou Gerstner reigned as CEO of RJR Nabisco. Harry Freeman had opened up shop as a Washington consultant. In Geneva, Edmond Safra's banking empire was growing. These men, too, shared the blame for AmEx's worsening problems. Each had his own agenda.

Each had pursued his singular goals. Each expanded his kingdom. Weighing the benefits for American Express and its shareholders was more an afterthought than a prime consideration.

Still, Robinson couldn't be excused. His vanity and preoccupation with image worked in the booming 1980s, a period of unprecedented excess. But the years ahead will be decidedly more frugal. Without a clearly defined strategy and the strength to forge a single management team from the disparate players that passed through AmEx's doors, Robinson's vision for American Express was more illusory than real. In the end, AmEx was a collection of purchases and personalities, not a cohesive corporation.

As AmEx neared the end of 1991, the company had lost its way. Earlier in the year, AmEx had purchased $2 million worth of commercial airtime for the telecast of the World Series. But two weeks before the October 23 opener, the company had yet to put together an acceptable ad campaign to fill the time. The company that had created "Do You Know Me?", "Don't Leave Home Without It" and "Membership Has Its Privileges" appeared momentarily tongue-tied, its direction confused. Even a new advertising agency, Chiat/Day/Mojo, could not do much to make a dent.

In many ways, marketing was almost an afterthought. The challenges facing American Express could not be overcome by snappy sloganeering. Robinson needed more than just words. He needed an entirely new strategy to prosper in the 1990s. His first step would be to figure out how he could undo the damage he had inflicted on American Express in the 1980s.

Robinson's latest woes made the bitter scene of the spring before seem almost incidental. The image of "The Card" being impaled on a butcher's knife was nothing compared with a new embarrassment. AmEx's faltering earnings, lousy credit picture and tarnished reputation had now inspired a nasty little question on Wall Street: If American Express were a person, and not this giant, floundering corporation, would it be eligible for one of its own precious green cards?

Index